Auntie T.S

Thank you for your
support and encouragema
and when you read this
dont say I didnt warn you
:)

Love
Samantha
2019

PRODIGAL

SAMANTHA SANCHEZ

"AND NOT MANY DAYS AFTER THE YOUNGER SON GATHERED ALL TOGETHER AND TOOK HIS JOURNEY INTO A FAR COUNTRY AND THERE WASTED HIS SUBSTANCE WITH RIOTOUS LIVING" -LUKE 15:13

"BUT THE FRUIT OF THE SPIRIT IS LOVE, JOY, PEACE, LONGSUFFERING, KINDNESS, GOODNESS, FAITHFULNESS, GENTLENESS, SELF CONTROL," -GALATIANS 5:22

Introduction

You ever wonder why God didn't just erase Satan when he and his followers rebelled against Him in heaven? Or, since He's all seeing, all knowing, why create him at all? He knew what was going to happen. He knew what would happen when He put the Tree of Knowledge in the Garden with Adam and Eve. So if He didn't want us to eat from the tree, then why was it there? He knew we would be manipulated by Satan.

These are questions I had never asked myself before. I never even thought to ask them before the things that happened, happened. I was taught never to question God's actions. That they weren't for us to know or He'd have told us. But when I did start asking questions and thinking about things, it seemed like God wanted us to fail. So what was the point of it all? What were we supposed to learn?

ONE

It's bad enough to go through horrible, humiliating and heartbreaking things in private, imagine going through your struggles on Reality TV, in front of the entire world, with everyone and their mama judging you. From tweeted criticisms and cruel jokes, to gossiping on the blogs about your life (and getting it wrong most of the time), it was frustrating. True, there were a lot of people who were sympathetic, who sided with me and defended me, but the bad somehow always stuck out more than the good.

The show was called "The Breakfast Club", A reality show adaptation of the 1985 John Hughes Movie. It was essentially the same premise: a group of individuals with drastically different personalities learning to get along. Only instead of high school, we were at San Diego College and instead of being trapped in detention, we were forced to live together every semester. Another major difference were the archetypes and the cultural backgrounds. For one, we were all minorities and second we didn't stick to the labels of "The Criminal", "The Princess", "The Basket Case", "The Brain", and "The Athlete". We were labeled "The Clown", "The Wanna Be", "The Preacher's Kid", "The Free Spirit", "The Chameleon", "The Musician" and later "The Dreamer". I honestly didn't know what I was getting into. I didn't realize how big the show would turn out to be, or the opportunities it would lead me to. All I cared about was getting away from my mundane everyday life. I felt invisible to most of my family, I had very few actual friends, I worked retail at Target and I went to church with my mom every Sunday, sang in the choir and was a part of the youth ministry. Majority of my free time growing up was church related. I wasn't allowed to go anywhere except for church or church related activities. By the time I was 21, I was so sick of my life that "wildin' out" was the next natural step. So I auditioned for the show with my friend Kyanna. When I say "friend" I use the term loosely. We were similar in that neither of us were part of the "it crowd" we were in the choir together, we hung out together at church events because we didn't fit in with the group, she and her sister spent the night at my house for my 18th birthday a few years before but outside of church we didn't really see each other. We had hoped we'd get cast together, that maybe the show would help us bond since we'd be living together. It was supposed to be me and her against the rest of the cast. We both had aspirations for musical theater, broadway and Hollywood, though she had more experience than me in that department. Kyanna had been in numerous productions in the community since high school. My mom wouldn't allow me to participate in community productions because she didn't believe it was safe. As it turned out the producers for The Breakfast Club only wanted one of us and they chose me.

Everything happened so fast after that. I auditioned in the beginning of June, got cast at the end and got the contract in the beginning of July. I was offered ten thousand an episode for thirteen episodes and if the show was picked up for a second season we would get the same. We would have our classes and materials paid for as well but as far as daily living expenses (food, gas, cell phone bills, personal shopping) we would have to work. It was set up so that we could work at a restaurant close to campus as servers or bussers or hosts or cooks (it would depend on the owners to decide). I got an advance on my first episode when I signed and the rest we'd get after the season ended. I used the money I had to pay the back rent that my mom was struggling with. We were a month away from being evicted and homeless because my hours at Target weren't enough to even pay half the rent and it had just increased. One of the first things I would do when I got the rest of the money was find us a house to live in. As much as my mother got on my nerves and as much as I desperately needed separation from her, that was the woman who gave me life and love of course I'm gonna take care of her first.

I walked into the house that first day excited, yet nervous. We were moving in a week before the semester actually started and I didn't know what to expect. Who were my roommates? Would they like me? I didn't usually get along with females so that part scared me. I wasn't checking for guys. I had a boyfriend. He was in the Navy and stationed in the Pacific Islands, he was supposed to be home for Christmas and I couldn't wait. He thought going on TV was dumb, he wasn't into pop culture or anything as superficial as that but he supported me going back to school and if this was a way for me to be able to do that then he was all for it.

The house the producers chose for us to live and film in was gorgeous. It was close to campus and not too far from the gaslamp downtown. There were restaurants and taco shops and shopping centers on the main street. The trolley even had a station on campus. The house itself wasn't on the main road, but around the corner and a few blocks down. It was two stories with a high wooden gated driveway, adjacent to a small gate. Behind the gate was a winding stone pathway leading to the front door. The front yard was a beautiful garden with lush green plants and hibiscus flowers on each side of the door and small palm trees lining the way up the stone path. I felt like I was walking through a story book. I didn't have my license yet but I had a bus and trolley pass. The producers sent a car to pick me up and take me to the house the first day. I was relieved because I didn't want my mom to drop me off. She'd have insisted on coming in and meeting everyone and that was not the first impression I wanted to make. She and the rest of my family were completely against me doing the show. My mom because she worried about me all the time and my cousins were worried about how it would make the family look. My grandfather was a well known Bishop in San Diego and I was supposed to present myself in a manner befitting a preacher's daughter. They were hypocrites anyway, as if they were squeaky clean shining examples of Christ-Like behavior. I was doing it anyway, it was time to come out of their shadows, and if the rest of them didn't like it they could suck it.

I was the last roommate to arrive at the house. There was a total of six of us. Two females and four guys.

"Hey!" A tall light skinned guy, who greatly resembled Ludacris greeted me. He was grabbing a bottle of water out of the refrigerator when I walked in. Everyone else was gathered around the pool.

"I'm DeVon, what's your name?"

"I'm Lyric." I smiled shaking his hand. It wasn't my real name. I was bored with my real name and I wanted to be someone different for the show. I wasn't going to allow myself to be invisible. My future on the show depended on me making myself memorable. I'd heard the name "Lyric" at a bus stop once. It belonged to the cutest little girl. I thought it was pretty and different and since I didn't plan on having children anytime soon, I decided to adopt it for myself.

"Hey that's a cool name like a song Lyric."

"Yea." I laughed. DeVon was really friendly. Not in a flirty type of way, but in an energetic happy kind of way. It made me feel comfortable to match his energy but I was still nervous around new people.

"Yea, well welcome home, Lyric. Come on let me introduce you to the rest of the house." He led me outside and immediately ahead of me floating around in the pool was a short, skinny dark skinned boy wearing domo swim trunks.

"That's Monroe."

"Hey." Monroe greeted bobbing his head up. He pointed to the short light skinned girl with blue braids, in a yellow bikini top and dark blue basketball shorts, kicking her feet in the water, "That's Athena"

"Hello." she waved smiling. I liked her already. She was friendly she didn't just stare at me looking me up and down in disgust like I was somehow beneath her in some way. That's usually the response I get from females. Athena didn't seem like that and I was grateful for it.

"This nigga over here is Christopher." DeVon continued. Sitting in one of the seats at the patio table was a tall brown beanstalk of a guy. He was the tallest one in the house but seemed to be the least groomed. His hair looked like he hadn't combed it in days, as it lay matted and halfway hidden underneath a tight grey and black striped zip up hoodie over a solid blue faded t-shirt.

"And next to him is Anthony." he said lastly. Anthony was preoccupied with his phone when I came in, trying very hard to look cool, he threw up a half hearted sideways peace sign as a greeting. Anthony was taller than DeVon but shorter than Christopher and he was built like a football player. He wasn't muscular, but he had big broad shoulders and he had a bit of a belly on him. He wasn't fat but he was burly like a bear. He had bushy eyebrows and he must have needed to wear glasses because he was squinting a lot reading his text messages.

"Ya'll this is Lyric."

"Nice to meet you." Athena greeted "I think we're sharing a room."

"Hey Ant why don't you help her with her stuff and give her a tour of the house." DeVon suggested.

"Why?" He asked disinterested. I found that to be kind of rude. "Because…"

"Why don't you do it?"

"You know, that's okay just point me to my room and I'll show myself around." I said. I wouldn't inflict myself on someone who didn't want to be around me.

"No, Anthony's gonna help you." DeVon said "Nigga, get up!"

"I'll just find it myself." I insisted. Anthony couldn't be bothered and it was clear that DeVon was trying to push me on him for some reason.

"I'll show you." Christopher said ending the argument. He stood up and took my carry on bag and my suitcase and led me back inside the house.

"Don't mind Anthony," he said. "He's a dumbass". Christopher's voice had a bit of a lilt to it. I wasn't sure if he was gay or just super metro sexual. He sounded a little like Jack from Will and Grace but slightly less flamboyant

"No I'm not." Anthony defended.

"Yes you are. Shut up." Christopher said. It wasn't in a mean way but in a dismissive way.

Christopher walked me to the bedroom to the left of the back patio, but if you were coming in the front door it would be to the right. There were cameras everywhere. Not just the guys with cameras following us around.

There were cameras mounted above the doorways of every room. There were 4 bedrooms in the two story house; two downstairs and two upstairs and we were paired two to a room. The one to the left of the front door had a bathroom and shower attached to it. The one I was in didn't. We had to use the one in the hallway. The upstairs bedroom had a balcony attached to it that looked over the backyard. The 2nd upstairs bedroom was the only bedroom with a door and a lock. Officially, It was The Guest Room but as our time there progressed it would be renamed The Boom Boom Room, the room we would bring a certain kind of overnight guest to. We had an alcove upstairs with a window that looked over the front yard. From the view it was positioned above the garage. There was another alcove underneath the stairs and the garage would be where we would do our own recorded confessionals aside from the green screen narratives we'd do periodically once an episode was put together.

After my tour of this awesome house I'd be living in for the next four months, I changed into something I could wear in the pool. I was heavy and I couldn't pull off a bikini with as many rolls as I had, I wouldn't subject myself to that kind of criticism from the world. I knew I was bigger than your average female. I wasn't one of the Klumps but I wasn't a Victoria's Secret model either. At a size 15, 190 pounds, I was uncomfortable in a bathing suit. I may have been uncomfortable with my weight, but I had a pretty face, I was light brown skinned, and since I was mixed with both black and Mexican I had hair that I didn't have to buy, glue or sew in. I was also a 36 DD and that was enough to make up for having an unattractive belly most of the time. So instead of a bathing suit, I wore a tank top that hung low over my boobs but hung loose over my stomach and I wore a pair of my cousin James' basketball shorts that I stole from him. I let my hair stay down to accentuate my face. I wasn't trying to impress anyone specific but I couldn't look unattractive on camera.

The first week was cool. Everyone was getting to know each other. Athena, "The Free Spirit", was 20 going on 21, a Marine Biology major from Orange County. Her parents were from South Africa and emigrated here. Athena was the first generation to be born in America. She liked horror movies, gruesome zombies and vampires, an interest she and I both shared. She wasn't a girly girl either, she hated superficiality. She thought about things like sex and relationships the way a guy would, Athena was the most emotionally mature of us all.

DeVon, "The Clown", had just turned 21, and was a business major from Detroit with an interest in music. He moved to San Diego with his mom when he was 12. He was a Marvel Comic obsessive, more specifically

Spider-Man. He had dubbed himself the black Peter Parker. He was everyone's little brother when it came to maturity. Everyone except for Anthony that is.

Anthony, "The Wanna Be", was 21 going on 22, same age as me, and a music major. He aspired to be a rapper under the moniker "Two Ton Guns" a reference to the biceps and the force behind his fist when he hits you. Although, the more I got to know Anthony, the more I believed that if he ever actually got into a fight, depending on who he was fighting, he'd get beat down rather than beat someone down. He was from New York but he claimed Skyline Piru. Which itself was laughable because Anthony seemed as soft as a pillow. I'd hung around a lot of thugs around that time, legitimate hood niggas and the air around them was different, than the air around Anthony. When Anthony said "blood" it didn't sound natural or believable, it sounded like he was trying and failing to give the impression of being hard. I was tougher than he was and I was the nicest girl you'd ever met.

Monroe, "The Chameleon," was also 20 going on 21, a dance major from St. Louis. He was a mix of a street smart dude from the hood, who could also blend in with white suburban skater boys at the same time. He wasn't a thug, he didn't bang, but he could be just as intimidating. It was believable when he said he'd beat someone down. The threats were usually made toward Anthony, whenever he did or said something stupid, which was often. Monroe was goofy and liked anime characters and white girls and wasn't really into relationships. He had a piercing in the corner of his mouth and in his tongue. He was similar to Christopher in their taste in music. Alternative and indie rock. He was well versed in current hip hop trends as well and he and Christopher were the ones we would go to when we needed new music on our mp3 players.

Christopher, "The Musician" who was 23 was the oldest one in the house. He said he wasn't gay that he had a fiance named Lanay in Los Angeles but nobody knew if he was lying or telling the truth. He never really seemed enthusiastic about anything. He could take it or leave it whatever it was. He was an undeclared major who judging by the looks of him could have been homeless. His hair stayed in the same matted birds nest in back of his head. It looked as if he hadn't combed it in months. He also wore the same sweater every day, a thin grey hoodie with black stripes. It looked old and worn out. He swore he came from money but he certainly didn't seem like it.

Then there was me, Lyric, "The Preacher's Kid." (As well as great grandkid, grandkid and niece.) I was 21 going on 22 a theater major, Born and raised in San Diego, California. My mother was the latest in a long line of family preachers, I was expected to be the next. My father was a construction worker, the only one in his family full of teachers and store managers and professionals, that took after my grandfather and worked hard labor. He encouraged me to just get a good job and keep it. Maybe go to nursing school and just be a nurse. He told me I was too old to be chasing dreams. I should have done it right after high school. I knew he just wanted me to be able to take care of myself in life, but I didn't want to be a preacher and I didn't want to be a nurse. I didn't know what I wanted out of life other than to act and be on stage, so there I was. At least I had a shot, and I had money to support myself in the process.

My castmates and I all seemed to become best friends and family right away. Some people grew closer with one more than they did the other. Athena and DeVon paired up by the third day, and he was immediately joined to her hip and wherever Athena went DeVon was sure to go. It reminded me of the nursery rhyme about Mary and her little lamb. It was an unlikely pairing with their personalities being so different but I guess opposites attract. Monroe and Christopher were brothers in music arguing over which band they liked. Anthony and I were sort of the odd ones out. We weren't a couple, and we weren't friends either.

I don't know what it was but, Anthony wouldn't really even interact with me that first. I'd catch him staring at my boobs sometimes or my face but for some reason he didn't like to be left alone with me. I don't know if he thought that I was into him and chose to walk away because he wasn't interested or if it was something else, but it was weird. At times, he even seemed scared of me. I would attempt to be friendly and speak to him and he wouldn't even look at me or he'd answer "Why?" to every question I asked him, looking at me cautiously out the side of his eye while leaning away from me.

Anthony was always on his phone. So much so, that DeVon snatched it from him and threw it in the bushes in an attempt to get him to pay attention to me. It didn't work though he was more concerned with finding his phone than talking to me. Anthony was so eager to escape my presence that he practically became DeVon's shadow. Even if DeVon was going somewhere with Athena, Anthony would rather tag along as a third wheel than be anywhere near me. I admit that it did make me feel a bit insecure. Was there something wrong with me? Was I ugly? Did I do or say something that bothered him? I wasn't trying to do anything with him, if that's what he was worried about. I thought he was sort of cute, I mean he wasn't completely unattractive but I wasn't trying to push up on him.

Athena and I got along perfectly. We were the same in that our interests

SAMANTHA SANCHEZ

weren't the common, stereotypical "black" girl interests. We didn't care too much about makeup and being girly and froo froo. We both always got along better with guys than we did girls. Although I was a bit more girly than she was. I couldn't exactly relate to Monroe and Christopher yet but they were nice so we hung out. Christopher was obsessed with the size of my boobs. Not in a sexual way, in a "Hey, your boobs are big. Can I touch them just to be a weirdo?" kind of way. Monroe asked me if I'd had any cute friends that I could hook him up with and then begged me not to have sex with Anthony. They insisted his behavior was due to the fact that he was attracted to me and was just being a dumbass about it. Trying to play cool like he wasn't. I told them that I had no intention of having sex with Anthony. I had a boyfriend and even though we were long distance, I had every intention of staying faithful to him.

Things changed that first Friday night we were in the house. I hadn't actually heard from my boyfriend all week. He'd been on the ship and phone calls were limited. But as I was getting ready that night, It was Monroe and Athena's 21st birthday and we were all going to On Broadway to celebrate. I had just finished my makeup when I finally got the phone call I was waiting for.

"Hi." I greeted happily.

"How's it going?" he asked. He didn't sound too happy. He sounded tired. "It's alright getting ready to head out to the club with roommates."

"Oh cool. Hey, I have a question for you."

"What's up?"

"Why do you love me? You spend one night with me and you're ready to spend the rest of your life with me?"

"Whoa, I don't remember saying anything about the rest of my life, it's a bit too soon for that don't you think?"

"See, that's my point. Honestly, I don't see this relationship going anywhere." My heart just collapsed in on itself and all the air that was in me had gone.

"You don't?" I asked trying to keep the pain out of my voice.

"No. I'm sorry, I don't." He said sorry but he didn't even sound sympathetic. This is the dude that told me all he wanted was for someone to love him. To hold his head at night and tell him that it was all going to be alright. He's had so much happen to him in his life that he didn't even want to tell me about it was so traumatizing. And I did love him even though he thought no one did or would. I was willing to hold him down no matter what and now suddenly he didn't see this relationship going anywhere?

"I'm confused. A week ago you couldn't wait to see me and now you don't see this relationship going anywhere?" I wanted to cry but I held it in. I didn't want to give him the satisfaction of knowing that my heart was breaking.

"When did I say that?"

"Last friday, on messenger."

"That wasn't me. I let my friend use my computer, he must have been talking to you as me. I'm sorry about that. I should probably stop letting him do that."

"Wow."

I couldn't think of anything else to say and I could feel my voice was about to break. I couldn't let that happen. I would never, if I could help it, give a man the satisfaction of knowing how much he hurt me. I'd never let them see or hear me cry over them.

"Well, whatever then. I said I was here for as long as you wanted me and I guess now...I don't know whatever, I got to go." I hung up without so much as a goodbye. All I could think about was getting drunk and not feeling the fist clutched around my heart trying to rip it from my body. He had been my first. It was only supposed to be a drunken hook up. I was supposed to wait until I was married but that night I realized that if I waited for marriage, I'd be waiting a very long time. I would perhaps have even died a virgin the way my love life had been going by that point. I wasn't naive enough to think that the first guy I ever had sex with would be the one I would spend the rest of my life with. Hell, I didn't even expect to see or talk to him again after our one night stand. Then he looked me in my eyes and told me I was his dreamgirl that I was perfect. I laughed it off at first, dismissed it as the ramblings of a drunk man. Then a few weeks later during one of our many phone calls he told me that he meant it, he wasn't just drunk and that it wasn't just sex to him. The more we talked, texted and emailed, the more I fell for him and then he told me he loved me and he wanted me to be his girl. That he could see himself married to me one day. I thought it was my own twisted, kinky, kind of fairy tale. Now out of nowhere, he doesn't love me anymore? He doesn't see a future with me now? Well, fine, I wouldn't worry about him anymore either.

"You ok?" Athena asked, she'd overheard the conversation

"Yep." I said. Trying to convince myself more than her. I dug into my suitcase for the red leather corset I packed for the nights that I felt insecure

"Can you tie this for me?"

"Ooh! I love corsets. Put it on! Hurry up!" I kept the same black heels on that I originally had on and luckily the smokey eye make up I had on worked for the change. Athena pulled my corset tight until I could barely breathe and my boobs were as high as my neck. I was going to get some attention tonight and I hoped that he'd see this one day and realize what he gave up.

In retrospect, I was stupid to believe that it could ever work, to believe that love could transcend all things. I did though. I honestly believed our differences didn't matter. So what if he wanted marriage and the thought of marriage petrified me? I'd get over it. Who cares if I wanted kids one day and he didn't think he'd be a suitable father? He'd get past it. And ok, so yea, I believed in Jesus and he worshiped some Egyptian god, it's not that big of a deal. We could have found a way to respect each other's beliefs without compromising our own. If we loved each other we could have found a way right?

Two

God lets us feel pain so we can learn to work through it and learn from it, but I didn't want to work through it. I didn't want it to exist within me at all. I was embarrassed and angry, sad. Then I began to realize, well hope, actually, that he was just trippin' out. He told me before that he wasn't sure if he would be able to make it home for Christmas, and wasn't sure when, if ever, he would be able to come home at all and he probably didn't know what that meant for us. Maybe he thought he was doing what was best for me. Then again maybe not.

During one of my trips to the bar, I was standing with Monroe when Christy walked up. Christy was mixed with Black and Japanese and hated the Black side of her. She hated Black men, preferring White or Asian men. I used to count Christy as a friend until she became so negative about my relationship. According to Christy, he could never love anyone else except his ex fiance/ high school sweetheart. That all she would have to do is snap her fingers and he would come running. I found that statement to be disrespectful and insensitive to my feelings for him, and to the relationship I was hoping to build with him. Which is what, I believed, was her intention. So I stopped talking to her.

"So I didn't know you guys had broken up." She said.

"Why would you?" I asked careful not to reveal any information that she could spread back around.

"Did you know he got engaged?" "What? To who?" I asked.

"I don't know some white girl."

"Wow." I said trying to recover my composure.

"Yea, apparently they've been talking for a while, that boy has always been in a rush to get married." She shook her head.

"How do you know?"

"His brother's wife told me."

"When?"

"Like a couple days ago."

"Wow." I said. I could feel the heat rising in my face and the tears starting to gloss over my eyes.

Not only had he been cheating on me for who knows how long, but he got engaged a couple days ago? He just broke up with me tonight!
I said on green screen

"How do you feel about that?"

The cameras are rolling, the cameras are rolling. A little voice reminded me. The cameras are rolling and you don't want to cry in front of her, she'll go back and tell everyone we know and then he will know just how much he hurt you The music changed in that moment and Monroe intervened before I could reveal how I really felt.

Ric looked like she was about to break down and this 'homegirl' of hers was waitin' for it. Monroe said in his green screen replay

"C'mon Lyric let's dance." Monroe said handing me my drink ushering me away into the crowd. "You ok?" He asked me when we got to the edge of the dance floor. Next to where Athena and DeVon were grinding on each other. I looked off into space my face cracking and fixing itself uncontrollably as I fought to maintain a straight face.

"What happened?" Athena asked walking over. DeVon holding her around her waist.

"She just found out the nigga that just broke up with her is engaged already." "Oh wow, what a d--k!" Athena gasped.

"Wow that sucks." DeVon said "But hey don't trip off it Lyric, that just means he's not the one for you."

"I need a drink,." I exhaled finally. I walked over to the VIP table where Anthony was talking to a girl. I told him to scoot over. I poured myself a glass of vodka cran, easy on the cran and chugged it down. The rest of the night was a blur. I didn't cry. I smiled and flirted, reveling in the attention my boobs were getting me throughout the night. Every time I started to feel something other than blissful indifference, I would have another drink or take another shot. My heart hurt less when I was drunk.

When I woke up the next morning, I was still kind of drunk and apparently not alone. Anthony was next to me still asleep, and neither of us had clothes on. I didn't remember anything about the night before and at the moment I didn't care. Even though I was still a little tipsy, it wasn't enough to keep the pain away.

There's a song by John Mayer that goes "When you're dreaming with a broken heart, the waking up is the hardest part. You roll out of bed and down on your knees and for a moment you can hardly breathe" I wished this was all some kind of bad dream.

I felt the wave of sorrow threatening to crash over me and I went into the bathroom where no one could see me, where the cameras couldn't follow. I turned on the shower and stepped in and let it out. Crying hurt my stomach muscles just as much as crunches did, only I couldn't stop no matter how much I wanted to. Eventually all the tears had been expelled and I just felt numb and tired. I couldn't find my clothes, probably because I wasn't in my own room so slid into one of Anthony's T-shirts so I wouldn't have to walk across the living room naked, in front of all the cameras. Athena and DeVon were still having sex in her bed and didn't seem to notice that I had walked in. I didn't care what they were doing, I climbed into my bed, I plugged in my headphones, faced the wall and turned the volume up on my Queen of the Damned soundtrack playlist and went back to sleep. When I wake up I'll put on a smile and act like I'm alright until I am. Because I would be.

I truly had no real memory of the night. There were flashes here and there and stories of what happened. The funniest, it seemed, was when I bit Anthony and he screamed. I faintly remember him asking for head and I remember saying no and warning him that if he put something in my mouth that I didn't want there that I would bite it. Apparently he didn't believe me and he got himself bit. DeVon told me Anthony freaked out and ran into the living room naked covering himself whining about how I bit him. I came out the room, also naked, covering nothing at all, calling him a b--h and saying I didn't even bite him that hard and to stop crying. It was quite the entertainment for the evening. Anthony kept telling DeVon that he couldn't have sex with me, that he didn't want to and DeVon told him to just go lay down with me.

Apparently laying down wasn't all that happened and apparently Anthony wasn't exactly a responsible sex partner either. Ever since that night everyone in the house had been stuck on the idea that I was pregnant because Anthony failed to do the one thing that was a requisite for contact. Not once, Not twice but...

"SIX TIMES!!" DeVon cackled

"Shut up already." I snapped "You're irritating me."

"Yea you don't want to stress the pregnant lady out, that would be bad for the baby." Christopher joked.

"I'm not pregnant." I argued for the hundredth time "I took the morning after pill."

"Two days later and you forgot to take the second one on time." Athena chimed in.

"I'm NOT pregnant." I grumbled pouring myself a vodka orange juice.

"Don't drink, baby mama." Anthony laughed trying to reach for my cup I moved it out of his reach and glared at him hatefully, wishing that I could inflict pain with a single concentrated stare.

"Don't. Call. Me. That." I warned through gritted teeth and stormed outside to the back patio taking the bottle of vodka with me so they couldn't pour it out like they did my last one.

I'm glad Anthony can laugh about it and treat it like some big joke. I said sarcastically in the confessional.

I couldn't see or feel the humor. I couldn't feel anything except an excruciatingly empty hollowness. I continued to have sex with him a couple of times after that night. Just to see. He was there and I still needed to feel some kind of affection, I was searching for someone to fill the hole that has just been punched in my spirit. I thought that Anthony could be that person. I only had my recently exed boyfriend to compare it to and since I was losing my virginity with him it was painful, but I at least felt some pleasure through the pain and it lasted what seemed like hours. With Anthony, it was fast, and I mostly just felt the pressure of his body on mine. Was that what sex really was? After the pain of losing her virginity, a female has that to look forward to? If so, I could have waited another five months before doing that again. Maybe it's just sex with Anthony that lacked excitement. He was fond of the jack rabbit style of sex. It was all about getting his and nothing about making sure I enjoyed myself as well or maybe he thought it was just as pleasurable for me as it was for him. I wouldn't experience "good sex" until later.

When Anthony told me that he hadn't used a condom at all that night, I should have beat him into the cement. He blamed it on me. He said that I wouldn't let him that I wouldn't get off of him. He said he didn't even want to have sex with me in the first place that DeVon made him.

"How did DeVon make you have sex with someone?" Monroe asked him. "Did he hold a gun to your head? Get the f--k outta hear with that! You wanted it, you liked it or it wouldn't have happened six times in one night."

"I was just trying to put her to sleep, she wouldn't leave me alone."

"Why would you try and put a drunk girl to bed? That's just dumb cuz then you don't know if it's you or the alcohol that was knocking her out."

"I didn't care which one it was." He laughed "I just wanted her to leave me alone."

If I'd known Anthony was going to turn into such a jerk after having sex, I never would have gone there with him. It's possible to have sex with someone and be cool with them after. It's possible to not talk about them like they were some parasite you were trying to get rid of. I didn't want Anthony to be my man, the idea never crossed my mind. He was the one who suggested a friends with benefits. Now he says he does it because he just wanted me to "leave him alone." Was I so gross to him that he didn't want to touch me or something? Was that how he felt the few times we'd had sex after that night? And he said it like the idea was so ridiculous. To hear him say that someone else made him do it was offensive and humiliating. Hearing him say he "took one for the team", that he kept me occupied so that DeVon could get it in with Athena, made me hate him. I may not have been supermodel gorgeous but was I really so unattractive to him that he felt the need to run the other way? What the hell? This wasn't making any sense to me.

I'd be lying if I said I wasn't worried about being pregnant but I thought that if I didn't take a test If I waited it out, If I prayed for my period to come it wouldn't happen. So since sex wasn't filling my emotional void, I used alcohol to drown myself. If I wasn't at work or in class, I'd sleep. I'd snack throughout the day but I wouldn't actually eat a meal. There were days where I even skipped class because I just couldn't make myself get up out of bed and function.

SAMANTHA SANCHEZ

THREE

I was in denial but, The BFC, as DeVon had now dubbed the roommates, since our show was called The Breakfast Club and we were the club members, were absolutely convinced that I was pregnant. They tried to keep me away from alcohol, going so far as to empty my suitcases to see if I had brought more. I hadn't but they wanted to make sure. They could keep me away from alcohol at the clubhouse but in a crowded club, It was a whole different scheme. Four different dance floors on 2 levels with bars and bar carts on each one. Anthony's inattention didn't bother me when I was surrounded by so many, more appealing, men. There were guys here who would have gladly and without complaint tried make me feel better and gorgeous and beautiful and sexy. I wasn't going to take any of them home though. Every time I thought about it though, that little voice in the back of my head started telling me how tacky it would be to have sex with a dude while possibly being pregnant with another man's baby. I would wait, until after my period just to be sure. The falter in my resolve not to be trashy, came in the form of a light skinned golden god of a man with a smile as bright as the sun, and dimples as deep as the ocean. Trey was the answer to a lonely hearts prayer.

DeVon, Athena and I were at the mall in Mission Valley. It was still a month away but I was looking to put together a Halloween Costume. I had gotten a fluffy black punk rock skirt from Hot Topic and some red fishnets and wings to match. All I needed was a black corset and some black boots to complete the outfit. I hadn't celebrated Halloween since I was 10 years old. My mom had gotten saved after that and wouldn't allow it. "It's the devil's day" she said. So on Halloween nights we'd go to some bogus harvest festival at church.

They finally convinced me to get a home pregnancy test from target while we were there but I was waiting til I got back to the house to take it. Something about a public bathroom just didn't feel right. As we were getting ready to leave DeVon had decided that he was going to kill himself. He had been moody and sarcastic all day. He never said what it was and I guess he decided he'd had enough and was going to go get hit by a trolley. I honestly to this day believe he was just acting like that for attention. Athena had told me that DeVon was having a hard time because he was starting to feel like maybe she was better off without him, that he was messing up her life. Sure they had gotten in their fair share of disagreements. He gets pissed off because Athena was so friendly. He accused her of flirting with guys all the time. He was jealous of her ex boyfriend, Roman, with whom she was still friends. He was also jealous because he believed one of her best friends Xavier had a crush on her. He'd been weird all day and we had no idea why he was so pissed. Usually he was all lovey dovey and attached to her booty.

"Here, take my phone, take my backpack." he said dropping his things by my feet. "Bye Athena, I'm gonna go throw myself in front of the trolley." Athena just stood there silently staring at him in a defiant glare. "Take care of her Ric, I hope you name your baby after me, if it's a boy." He started walking away. His steps and his posture reminded me of a velociraptor in Jurassic Park.

"D, Stop playin!" I called after him. Suicide wasn't anything to joke about. Not even for the sake of good television.

"I'm not playin'!" He said quickly walking back toward us. "She's better off without me."

"Obviously not if she wants you around." Athena stayed silent I wasn't sure if she was choosing not to engage in this ridiculousness or if she was just at a loss for words.

"Whatever, I'm going to go jump in front of a trolley." He said backing away from us

"Bye, Athena."

This was really irritating. All three of us knew he wasn't going to go throw himself in front of a trolley. He just wanted some attention. Idiot! I was ready to cuss him out when a familiar face came into view. Dressed in black, with a black hat to match, this tall, skinny, yet muscular man took all my irritation, all my hurt, all my sorrow away just at the sight of him. I think I smiled for the first time in a month.

"Freakboy!" I called to him. He was walking by himself and veered in my direction when I called him. I threw my arms around his neck and caught on as he walked into my hug walking me backwards in the process. Freakboy was my nickname for Trey, it had been ever since he sucked on my finger in front of the cross at our second meeting. I met him two years ago at church on Easter Sunday as a guest of Kyanna's brother. She introduced him to me as her brother, though they weren't actually related. I remember thinking how fine and sexy he was and thinking he would never love me. A man as fine as that had to have a girlfriend that he was going to marry soon. She was probably short and skinny with long hair. He hugged me so tight that all of my stress was gone. Time seemed to freeze during our embrace. I breathed in the scent of him and wished we weren't in public.

Being around him made me forget why I was hurting in the first place, who I was even hurting about. Every other man completely vanished from my mind when Trey was around. We'd been in occasional contact ever since we met but with changing phone numbers and the way life unfolds it was never able to be consistent. Earlier on that year, we ended up spending the day together. He had gotten put out of his sister's house again and was staying at Kyanna's house, since he was best friends with her brother. I just happened to be there that day hanging out with Kyanna. We managed to find ourselves alone together and I had started to lose my virginity to him but I was scared (and sober) and changed my mind. I changed it again a couple days later but by then he'd gotten arrested. I still didn't know what he did. A month later I met my recently exed boyfriend and that was it.

"Kyanna told me you got locked up a few months ago." I said when we pulled apart. We still held onto each other's fingertips, he let go of one hand to pull his pant leg up showing his ankle monitor.

"Not yet." He laughed, just as happy to see me as I was to see him.

"When do you go in?"

"December."

"For how long?"

"A couple years maybe."

Trey was a thug, no doubt about it but he wasn't a disrespectful one. At least not to me. He was a lover and a fighter but what a lot of thugs lacked was a pretty boy swag and Trey had an abundance of that.

"So what's going on with you?" he asked looking at the camera crew

"Just pretend they're not here." Athena chimed in. I had forgotten she was there for a minute.

"Trey, this is Athena." I introduced. He shook her hand politely

"Hi nice to meet you." She said

"You too," he said and then turned his eyes back on me.

I think this is the first time I've seen Lyric light up like this since we met. She is smiling ear to ear and I think I see a little blushing too. Who is this Freakboy that's got her so enthralled? Athena mused in her confessional

DeVon had made his way back to us again. The sight of Trey probably made him curious and perhaps a little irritated that we weren't paying him attention. He was acting like an idiot and here comes this new dude being introduced to his girlfriend.

"I thought you were going to get hit by a trolley." I said. "Trolley's late." he answered "Hey, man, I'm DeVon."

He held his hand up to slap Trey's. They did some weird guy handshake that involved fist bumping and left it at that.

"Hey, Athena, can I talk to you over here for a minute." DeVon asked

"Sure." she said walking away and leaving me and Trey to stare goofily into each other's faces. I pulled him into another hug this time wrapping my arms around his waist and resting my face on his chest.

"I missed you." I said

"I missed you too." He said resting his head on top of mine. "Baby you got a big?" He was asking for a cigarette. He often replaced his C's with B's. It was representative of what part of town he lived in. If someone lived in/ spent a lot of time in an area that was heavily populated by bloods then C's were replaced with B's. If someone lived in/spent a lot of time in an area that was heavily populated by crips then B's were replaced with C's.

"No they took my cigarettes away along with my liquor." I pouted

"Why?" he laughed. I hesitated. I didn't want to tell him.

"Because... there's a very strong possibility that I might be pregnant." I pouted into his chest. He pulled me away looking into my face.

"Whaaat?" he laughed,

"I haven't taken the test yet, it's in my purse" I said refusing to meet his eyes. "Who the daddy? Do I know him?"

"No. At least I hope not." I said "He's one of my roommates."

"One of em? How many roommates do you got? What I miss?" I took a deep breath and I gave him the abridged version of what was happening. "Dang boo, he trapped you." Trey laughed

"It's not funny," I pouted. "He keep saying how he was forced to do it, how he didn't want to and I could just get an abortion."

"First of all, any man that says he was forced to have sex with you, is probably a homo," he laughed. "And second of all, you better not get an abortion." He said raising my face up by the chin and staring into my eyes and he kissed me. "F--k that lame dude, he sound like a b---h. I'ma take care of you and the baby if you pregnant. "You ain't even gon have to deal with him. I got you."

"You gon be locked up. How you gon take care of anyone from prison?" I laughed.

"Yo, Ric, we out!" DeVon called "You comin?"

"Ric?" Trey asked.

"Lyric. I changed my name."

"Lyric huh?" he laughed "It's different I'm wit it."

He side nodded in the direction of DeVon and Athena, "Let's go." he said and wrapped his arm around me and walked toward them.

"Where we goin?"

"To the house. I want to know if I'm finna be a uncle."

"I wish you was the daddy." I said to myself.

Four

The BFC was tickled pink about Trey's reaction to Anthony. He walked into the clubhouse and immediately asked who the baby daddy was.

"Anthony, this is Trey. Ant, this is Ric's 'Freakboy'" Anthony looked confused and threatened. He was adamant that he didn't want anything to do with me and yet I could have sworn there was jealousy in his eyes when he registered Trey's arm around my neck and my fingers interlocked with his fingers as they hung over my shoulder. Trey burst out laughing.

"For real, babe?!" He chastised me playfully.

"In her defense, she was really really really drunk." Athena offered

"Baby if you thought blood was attractive when you were drunk, what would I have looked like?"

"Probably, a golden god." I said truthfully.

"Did he just call her baby? Is this her boyfriend or somethin?" Anthony asked.

"Or somethin." Trey answered "Why? You got an issue with that?" He slid me behind him with one arm. "You wanna handle it, blood?" He stretched both his arms out wide, welcoming and from the amused, excited look in his eye, hoping for, a physical confrontation. I'd only known Anthony for a month, but I already knew that he wasn't bold enough to present one. From the nervous expression on his face, he was scared to get hit.

*Anthony is a wanna be thug who brags about his affliations, Droppin'
Skyline, bangin blood left and right to make himself seem more
hardcore. I know twelve and thirteen year olds who could whup his
ass.* I said in my narrative

"Nah, I'm good." Anthony said trying and failing to keep the fear out of his eyes. "That's all you, blood." He said. I was the "that" that was all Trey's. He held out his hand in peace to slap Trey's.

"Man, there was never any doubt about what's mine." He wrapped his arm around my waist and pulled me to him. Ignoring Anthony's raised hand. I loved how possessive and aggressive my Freakboy was. He has always known, without knowing that he knows, how to make me feel more confident.

"C'mon, babe let's go find out if I'm gon be a daddy. Where the bathroom at?"

"If you gonna be a daddy?" Anthony asked

"Yea, you might be the one that got her pregnant but your baby finna be calling me daddy." Trey said trying to provoke him into a fight.

Monroe and DeVon's eyes bucked wide and they covered their mouths with their fist looking back and forth between Trey and Anthony to see what would happen next.

"What the f--k?"

"Damn." Christopher said.

"Ey, you need to check your boy." Anthony addressed to me.

"Why don't you check me?" Trey offered.

The boys waited with baited breath to see what would happen.

"How about we wait and see if she's really pregnant first?" Athena said

The Executive Producer wanted to get my immediate reaction to the news, whatever it may be. I allowed one camera and Trey in the bathroom with me, I peed on the stick and when the time was up I looked at it.

Positive. Positive? Positive?! Oh God! I knew everyone was outside waiting with baited breath and ready to laugh. When the test came out positive, I collapsed in tears and Trey caught me before I could hit the ground. He held me and comforted me. I kicked the camera operator out and stayed in the bathroom, cradled in Trey's arms.

"You gon be good, babe." Trey said "It's gon be ok."

"How?" I asked "You really think I'm going to get any support from that nigga out there?"

"F--k that b---h made ass nigga" He said.

"I feel like my life is over."

"It's not over, it's just going to be different now. Think of it as a new life long adventure. You like adventure."

I didn't reply I just sat there. Thinking. Abortion definitely wasn't an option. No offense and nothing against the women who have had abortions, but personally I didn't feel like abortion was a fix it solution for irresponsibility. I couldn't give it up for adoption, I couldn't bear having a child and then giving it away. My mom is going to be so embarrassed because it wasn't even that I got pregnant by my boyfriend, I got drunk and had irresponsible sex with a guy I barely knew. Not even a decent guy, A guy who thinks its funny to tell the world that he never wanted to have sex with me. Did he honestly believe that it would have happened if I wasn't drunk, desperate and heartbroken?

"Where's your head at?" He asked kissing my temple

"I don't want this to be happening. This isn't how it's supposed to happen."

"I know, babe but you got this. You tougher than you think you are. You can handle this and you ain't even gon have to handle it alone. You got me, you got your mom. Even if that soft ass nigga out there don't step up, you and the little nugget you got gonna be taken care of."

"Nugget?" I laughed for the first time in weeks. "Yea, that's what I'm gonna call it. A nugget."

"Ok." I laughed. Then a realization hit me. "God! this means I have to stop drinking."

"Yea, I'm gonna need you to cut that out. I can't have you drowning the nugget. Or having it come out retarded or some s--t." I laughed.

"No more crying ok?" he said wiping my face. "C'mon, time to get up." He stood up and extended his hand to me and pulled me up. We opened the door and faced everyone.

"Are you ok?" Monroe asked.

"She gon be fine" Trey answered for me.

"Anthony's waiting outside to talk to you." DeVon said.

I looked out at the patio and saw Anthony watching from table. I ignored him. "Go on." Trey encouraged "I gotta get home anyway."

"Why?" I asked not wanting to be left alone.

"Curfew. If I'm not back home by 7pm they add two years on my sentence."

I think he could sense my anxiety at the thought of him leaving. The last time we separated it was 6 months before I saw him again. In the span of an hour he'd become my biggest comfort and support. I only had a couple more months left before he was gone for a couple years and that was scary enough. I didn't want him to leave today. I wanted him to stay and hold me and make me forget. I walked him to the door and held it open for him.

"You got my number. Text me." He said "I can come back tomorrow."

"I get out of class at one." I informed him looking up at him with puppy dog eyes. "I'll be here at 1:15."

I held up my pinky to him "Promise?" He smiled and locked my pinky with his.

"Promise." He pulled me tight against him and kissed me goodbye. A couple of quick pecks and then a little longer and deeper. If he hadn't stopped when he did he would have been sentenced to an additional two years because no way was I going to let him walk out of this house.

"I will definitely be seeing you tomorrow." He smiled. He looked toward the roommates who were failing in their attempts not to be obviously nosey "Ya'll got her?"

SAMANTHA SANCHEZ

"We got her man." DeVon said. DeVon was highly amused by the situation. Trey chuckled, kissed me sweetly again before smacking my behind hard enough to make a sound. I didn't flinch from the sting I just smirked at him as he walked out. I closed the door behind him and walked back to the living room.

"Woooow." Monroe laughed imitating Flavor Flav.

"You in love, Lyric?" Christopher asked.

"Huh?" I asked still caught up in the clouds.

"I think that means yes." Athena laughed. I tried to act normal like it was no big deal but I couldn't hide my smile. I don't know what lingered the longest, his kiss, or the smack. I liked the smack almost as much as I liked the kiss. I could kiss him for days. I had almost forgotten what his lips felt like.

"Dang, Ant, you can't even keep your baby mama! Yo game must be hella weak!" Monroe teased, yelling so Anthony could hear him from outside.

"What?" Anthony asked sticking his head in from the back patio.

"Maybe not." Athena offered "Lyric's been predisposed to Trey anyway he's her 'Freakboy' so maybe Anthony's game isn't necessarily weak as much as Lyric is biased toward her Freakboy."

"What's that mean?" Anthony asked

"It's...never mind." Athena said.

"Still..." Christopher chimed in "Yo baby mama is choosing another nigga over you WHILE she's pregnant. I mean that's harsh. The hormones haven't even kicked in yet."

"What are you talking about? She's not choosing him over me. We're not even together."

"I'm gonna go take a shower and relax so I can study." I declared wanting no part of the discussion anymore.

"Aren't you gonna go talk to Ant?" DeVon asked.

"No. I don't want to talk about it right now." I said and walked away and let them continue to roast Anthony by speculating about the extent of my relationship with Trey.

I ignored them and walked into the bathroom turned on Beyonce's new Sasha Fierce album and stepped in the shower. I took my time and dried and flattened my hair. I needed to process this new information and what it meant without all eyes on me. Without everyone in the house putting their opinions and predictions on me.

I guess I feel scared. I said in my confessional *Obviously, this is unplanned and I don't feel ready for it. But it's happening. I'm going to be a mother.*

A few hours later, I was annoyed, but the rest of the evening went by smoothly. Nobody got cussed out. Christopher and Athena got some homework done, DeVon had obviously abandoned the suicide trip he was on earlier and was clowning around with Monroe,wondering aloud what kind of child my baby would be. Monroe agreed with Trey that he hoped the baby looked like me and not Anthony. I got a little offended when they said that the child would act as stupid as him. They said that Anthony always boasted he was the "freshest nigga alive" so my baby, if it was a boy, would boast that he was the "freshest lil nigga alive." I eventually separated myself from them. I was curled up in the alcove upstairs reading The Ramayana for my Mythology class. I was engrossed in this story of a Prince named Rama going through Hell and high water to rescue his wife Sita who had been tricked and kidnapped by the monster Ravana.

"Ay, we need to talk." Anthony asked coming up the stairs. That's how he addressed me. He never said my name I was always "Ay."

"I have nothing to say to you." I said picking up my cup of orange juice and taking a sip.

"You're still drinking?" he asked.

"It's just orange juice." I said turning back to my book. "Goodbye. I'm studying."

"We need to talk about this." He insisted sitting on the end of the bench by my feet "There's nothing to talk about." I argued "I'm pregnant. That's that. Bye now." I said gently kicking him to get off the bench and out of my space.

"Come on, please. We need to talk about this." I'd never seen him so serious in the entire month I'd lived here and he'd never said please.

"Talk about what?" I asked annoyed.

"Ok, look you're cool peeps, I like you and all…" he replied "and I can be there for you but I can't be with you. You know?"

I gave up trying to read I laid the book down and scooted upright. I had to hear this pile of delusional bull that was coming out of his mouth.

"What are you talking about?" I asked.

"I'm not trying to be in a relationship. Just because you're pregnant with my seed I don't want you to think that we finna be together."

"Don't nobody here want to be in a relationship with you."

"Alright then, well good cuz DeVon said that you might expect that."

"DeVon lied to you. I like you and all but I don't want you. If you want to be there for the baby then cool but I'm not going to force you."

I didn't have the energy or inclination to make a man handle his

SAMANTHA SANCHEZ

responsibilities. I'll let the courts do it for me when I file for child support.

"That guy you brought in here today was that your ex boyfriend."

"No."

"Oh DeVon said that he was your ex boyfriend."

"We never dated."

"Did you have sex with him?"

"None of your business."

"It kinda is my business, you said you having my baby and now this nigga sayin he's daddy."

"No what he said was, the baby would call him daddy instead of you. Not that it was his baby."

"What did he mean my baby finna call him daddy though? If that's my seed then why would it call another dude daddy?"

I rolled my eyes "He meant that he doesn't expect you to step up so he's going to."

"That's my child though."

"And?"

"And my kid isn't going to be callin' another nigga daddy, that's what's not going to happen."

"So you gonna step up then?"

He paused before he answered "Honestly, I'm not ready for a baby right now."

"So you don't want it then?"

"Do you?"

"I'm asking you. What do you want to do?"

It's up to you. I'm just sayin' I'm not ready, my life is too chaotic. I'm not ready for a baby.

"You think I'm ready for this?"

"I don't know, but I just got a lot going on in my life right now."

"And I don't?"

"Ok look, I'm wanted for murder back in Brooklyn."

"Murder?" I asked in disbelief, trying not to laugh. This dude ain't wanted for no murder.

I don't know him that well yet but I know that he's not bold enough to take a life. If he was that bold, is he really stupid enough to talk about it on camera?

"Yea, well what had happened was…."

That's how you know he's lying! I laughed. When a dude starts a story with "What had happened was…." Man shut the hell up. Your soft ass ain't foolin nobody.

"My cousin did it." He said "But I was in the car when he did it. So I'm wanted too. That's why I came out here." He finished. I felt the annoyance rising in me. I had no patience for him at all. "I don't care, that has nothing to do with what is going on with our situation. I need to know if I can count on you for support during this pregnancy or not."

"I mean...yea I can support you, I just don't want to be in a relationship right now. We can still be cuddy buddies though you do got some good p---y."

"Goodbye, Anthony." I said dismissively. I picked my book back up hoping he would take the hint and leave. He didn't.

"Hey are you gonna f--k that Freakboy, dude?" He asked after a minute

"That's none of your business."

"Well, you can't f--k nobody but me, you know that right?"

"Excuse me?" I asked daring him to repeat his command.

"That's mine." He said pointing to the lower half of my body.

"No, it's mine." I insisted "And I can give it to whomever I damn well choose."

"No you can't."

"You just said that you didn't want to be with me."

"I don't."

"You tryin to tell me who I can and can't have sex with, is some relationship type s--t."

"You got my seedling inside you." He said.

"And? That makes you my baby daddy not my man."

"I know, I'm just sayin...I don't want the DNA to get mixed up and then you not know who the father is. That'd be horrible."

I paused and looked at him in astonishment. Did he really just say that? Is he serious? Is he that slow? He gotta know that's not how it works.

"What?" he asked at my dumbfounded expression. I didn't even dignify it with a response. I grabbed my orange juice, and my book and I walked away. It was too outrageous. I was speechless.

"Wooooow!" Trey laughed the next day as he rubbed a fresh coat of sunblock on my shoulders. His hands were rough but they felt good on my skin. Athena, DeVon, Monroe and I had the day off from working at the restaurant and decided to take advantage of the sun and heat while we still had it and have a backyard BBQ with just us.

"He didn't want the DNA to get mixed up?"

"Yea, cuz that would be horrible." I mocked.

SAMANTHA SANCHEZ

"Did he not take any sex ed classes in school?" Athena asked.

"I don't even think he had sex before Lyric to be honest." Monroe said "He seem like he scared of p---y."

"Damn." Trey laughed.

"And I never told that dumbass that you expected a relationship from him." DeVon said "I told him that some females do, and some don't and that he needed to talk to you and find out where you stood cuz you the only one that knows."

"I can kinda see how he misunderstood though." Athena offered "It's Anthony."

"He also said he's wanted for murder." I informed them. Everyone froze and all at once busted out laughing.

"Who that nigga kill?" Monroe asked skeptically.

"He said that it was actually his cousin that did it, he was just there when it happened so he's wanted too."

"Blood is ugly and stupid." Trey said. "He really is." Monroe agreed "Bomedy."

"God it's going to be a long nine months." I sighed.

"Man, I really hope the nugget look like you." Trey said.

"Hella." Monroe agreed.

"C'mon ya'll go easy on the dude, he's funny." DeVon defended.

"Whatever." I said.

"Babe, c'mon let's go to 7-11 real quick." Trey said "I kinda want a slurpee."

We climbed out of the pool dried off and went into my room to change. We goofed around a bit exchanged a couple of quick kisses and then we headed out to the store. I thought about going up to The Guest Room but even though it was him, I didn't feel right about it. I was pregnant with someone else's child and it would be too weird. I'd feel gross about myself if I had sex with another man. The timing was so horrible it was almost laughable. Before I met my ex Trey was all I thought about, all I wanted. If he hadn't gotten arrested and if I hadn't thought that I'd never see him again, my ex wouldn't have even been a factor in my life. Neither would Anthony for that matter. Since the day that I met him, It's always been Trey and anyone else I've dated since then has been because Trey wasn't available and the timing wasn't right. I never expressed my feelings to him I was scared to because I wasn't sure how he felt and I couldn't handle the rejection from him too, of all people.

"So let me ask you somethin'." Trey said as we walked down the street hands clasped together. "What happened? Why this dude?"

"What do you mean? I told you what happened. I was drunk, I was sad, he was there."

"No I mean, six months ago you were too scared to let me take you, you wanted to wait...and now you pregnant."

"Ok, first of all..." I said getting defensive "You already know I didn't plan any of this. I don't even remember most of it."

"Calm down, I'm not attacking you, don't be so defensive."

"Second of all..." I said a little more calmly. "I wanted you to be the one to take me. Yea I was scared that day, but then I changed my mind and you disappeared. I called you, I texted you. Then Kyanna told me you were locked up and I didn't think I'd ever see you again. What did you expect me to do?"

"I mean you could have waited."

"You could have not done what you did to get arrested." I retorted "How was I supposed to know I'd see you again? I thought you were done with me because I said no."

"Nah, I could never be mad at a female for sayin' no, and I could never be done with you." He said wrapping his arms around me as we walked. "Only punks act like that. At least tell me you didn't let that ugly ass dude take you."

"He didn't take me." I laughed happy to be able to please him.

"The ex dude?"

"Yea." I said a sudden shame coming over me. I had forgotten about him so easily once Trey came back around. How much could I have loved him if I forget that he even exists when I'm with Trey?

"Was he ugly too?" He joked.

"Well nobody compares to you, boo." I said "I'm so glad you're here."

"Me too."

"The BFC is throwin' a Halloween party next month, you're coming right."

"I don't know I might be in jail by then."

"I thought you said you don't go in until December."

"That was the plan, but I got a call from my lawyer this morning and I have to go to court tomorrow."

"Meaning you might go to jail tomorrow?"

"Probably."

"Well there goes my happy buzz." I pouted "I just got you back and you're leaving again."

"You can write to me though."

"It's not the same thing."

"I know. I'm sorry." he buried his face in the gap between my neck and shoulder and nuzzled and kissed.

"How will I know where to write to you?"

"I'm gonna have my brother call you and give you the address as soon as I find out where I'm going to be."

"I'm sad now." I said.

"Don't be. If I get locked up I'll be back before you know it, and I'm coming straight to you as soon as I can."

"Promise?" I asked, holding up my pinky.

"Promise" He chuckled locking pinkies with me. "And don't trip off yo' baby daddy. I'll take care of you and the little nugget when he or she gets here." He said rubbing my stomach affectionately.

"How you gon take care of us, if you locked up?" I laughed.

"I'm gonna have my people lookin out for you." He said.

"Aww, nobody's ever had my back before." I laughed trying not to show how bummed out I really was. Life sucks and then you die.

After we got our slurpees, I waited at the bus stop with him. He held me as we waited, stroking my face with the backs of his fingertips like he was trying to memorize the curves of my cheeks and lips and chin. I stared into his deep brown eyes. I wished I could keep him forever. Nobody else's opinion of me would matter if he loved me and claimed me as his. When the bus came he kissed me goodbye, said he'd call me when he got home and I walked home alone and dejected but resolved to make the best of a bad situation. It wasn't the end of the world. Life goes on and I was certain that Trey's and my story wasn't over and as far as my pregnancy, just because I wasn't into church life right now doesn't mean that I didn't believe in God or in the fact that he has a plan for my life. Whether I agreed with his plan or not really didn't matter to Him. I knew without a doubt that there were no accidents with God. He doesn't make them. Whether I was ready for a child or not, he was giving me one and he wouldn't give me more than he knew I could handle. I would try not to look on this as a burden. I thought I'd make a pretty good mom. Speaking of Moms, I prayed and asked God for the courage to tell mine.

FIVE

To say the news went over well with my mother would be an over statement. However, it did go better than expected. She wasn't happy about how it happened but it was happening and she would be there to support me. I wish I could say things were that simple with Anthony.

I hadn't had a drink since I found out I was pregnant but being around Anthony really made me want to drown everything out. I was aware of my insecurities but Anthony didn't seem to be aware of his own. He had no sense of self. He seemed directionless like he was trying to be someone he wasn't because it's who he thought he should be. Anthony lived to imitate other guys whether they be celebrities or family members, even DeVon. Once a female told him he looked like Drake and he became insufferable. Anthony already boasted about being such a big ladies man, ninety five percent of the time it always sounded like a lie. For example: he told us a story about having sex with a married woman in the bathroom at Jack n The Box because she said her husband wasn't "hittin' it right". He said at first he didn't want to because she was married but then she accused him of being gay so he "beat it up" to prove that he wasn't. It was such an outrageous story that it couldn't possibly be true but he was adamant and insistent that it happened that way. The moment he realized that being on TV, especially if the show was a hit, could get him females just for being famous, he became even more insufferable. His regard for me was almost non-existent. I was just the baby mama. I didn't necessarily matter until he was horny. In his mind, as his baby mama, I was guaranteed sex.

Despite his previous claims of not being into me and not wanting to have sex with me, whenever we found ourselves alone, he'd made very clear to me that he'd be open to a friends with benefits situation. Even before Trey left, he knew that I was lonely. Now with Trey locked away and no word from his brother on where to write him, the hurt over my ex began to sink in again, And I couldn't numb them this time. It was clear that Anthony didn't want a relationship with me, and I certainly didn't want one with him but I needed that attention. Even if it was temporary, fake and empty. Trey was gone, I was sad, and I felt ugly. I was only going to get fatter and gross as this pregnancy continued and Anthony seemed to want me, at least sexually, and that was an ego booster but even though I would always say no when he tried I knew it was only a matter of time before I gave in. Just not yet and not so easy this time.

My mom took time off of work to go with me to my first Doctor's appointment when I was 8 weeks along. The entire BFC decided they wanted to go and support me. Even Christopher who took every opportunity he could to remind me how gross it was that I was pregnant by Anthony, and Monroe would chime in making predictions that my baby would inherit Anthony's stupidity. Athena was my only support system in the house. DeVon thought the entire situation was hilarious. He kept insisting that Anthony and I would be the ghetto version of "Knocked Up."

Hey now that The Freakboy guy is out the way, cuz he's in prison, Anthony has a clear path to pursue Lyric. I know he's into her and I think she could be into him to if she gave him chance. He said in his confessional

Both Anthony and I protested that idea. Anthony, because he was too cool to catch feelings for any female. He told us that he couldn't fall in love because his heart got broken years ago and since then he's never been able to really catch feelings for or love another female. I protested the idea because I just couldn't see myself ending up with Anthony. I couldn't think about Anthony as anything more than a co-parent.

When I got called into the office the nurse would only let my mom, Anthony and one camera operator in the room. If everyone went there'd be no room for the doctor. DeVon had to practically make Anthony get up and go with us. Having him not be there would have actually have been better than having them there. All he could do was make comments about how much more weight I would gain. He wasn't doing it to be mean. I think he didn't really grasp that he was being insensitive. I snapped at him and told him to shut up. My weight always was a sensitive subject for me it probably always would be. It seemed to be the thing in my family, to talk about how much weight we've lost while trying to lose weight and different methods on how to do it. Anthony also complained about how long the doctor was taking and that he or she needed to hurry up because he had some place he had to be. So finally my mom suggested he just go ahead and go if that was more important to him. It was a test that he failed by actually leaving. I found out later the place, that he had to be, was at the taco shop in City Heights to meet up with someone who wanted to buy bootleg DVDs off of him. Selling bootlegs was more important to him than checking on the health and development of his child. Great start to parenting right?

The appointment itself was invasive, like any woman's doctor appointment would be but seeing that I'd never had a woman's doctor appointment prior to now made it all the more awkward. The best part though was hearing the baby's heartbeat. It almost made me forget about the discomfort of the trasvaginal ultra sound. The heart was fluttering and it sounded so strong. I believe that was the first time it really hit me that there was a whole new life inside of me. No matter how that life got there, it was there and it my responsibility to take care of. I asked the doctor about my drinking in the early days of my pregnancy if that could have caused some kind of damage. They told me it was hard to say but as long as I stopped drinking immediately it probably wouldn't impact the health of the baby, but that they would run tests to find out as I progressed in my pregnancy. I was due in June and as long as I took care of myself from here on out and remained stress free, there was no reason I shouldn't have a healthy baby.

DeVon and Monroe had been planning The First Annual BFC Halloween Party almost since the day we moved in the house. There would be alcohol, weed, hoochies, and a house full of dudes trying to get at them. We lowered the privacy sheets on all the bedrooms and posted a "DO NOT ENTER" sign on all of them. It may be a party but nobody would be hooking up in our beds. I didn't like the way my dark fairy costume looked on me. It was a good idea in theory but the reality didn't match the idea I had in my head for what I wanted to look like. I needed to lose a few pounds before I could pull this off and that wouldn't be happening for a while. So earlier when Athena drove to Wal Mart to pick up some more supplies I picked up a simple witch costume. A black dress with black laced sleeves, cut into frills at the wrists and ankles. It hugged my hips and hid my stomach while at the same time showed ample cleavage.

Monroe, who was in charge of music, was a vampire. His costume consisted of simply dracula fangs... the rest were his street clothes. Athena did add a little make up to his face to make him look pale but other than that... Christopher had disappeared a week before. We had a day off from filming and he just never came back. His stuff was still in the house though so we were sure he would be coming back eventually. DeVon was some sort of skeleton monster with a skeleton hoodie and mask that only covered the top half of his face. Athena was a zombie cheerleader wearing a black and green uniform with her hair in pigtails. She had replaced the blue hair from the beginning of the semester with green.

Everyone invited friends and relatives to the party, all of whom were apparently excited to be on TV. My family was different. They weren't too supportive of me going on TV. They didn't understand my need to be noticed, to be seen as someone in my own right, as my own individual rather than just as their relative. That was my mom's side, my dad's side however were all for it, they were excited about it. They knew my aspirations and my dreams and they saw it as a platform into the entertainment industry. My cousin Hector and his girlfriend Laura, who was also pregnant, with their 3rd child, came, along with my cousin Monique and her new boyfriend, my cousin Talia and my cousin Joanna came together. Talia, Joanna and I called ourselves The Putas Primas. The three of us were stuck like glue, they were the best friends I'd ever had. They were only eighteen and technically weren't allowed to drink so we made it seem like they had sober cups that, when no one was looking, I spiked for them. They were the first ones I told that I was pregnant, and they were extremely supportive and excellent at keeping secrets.

Even though they didn't approve, cousins from my mom's side of the family were there too. My cousin James and his girlfriend Jaycee. He was the only one on that side of the family that I was close to in any kind of way. Sur,e there were moments when my other cousins and I connected, but not all consistently and not when we were all together. When we were all together, I was the odd one out. I honestly felt like my cousins could barely tolerate me. James was the only one I felt loved by and his girlfriend was the only one who seemed to care about my well being. James who was a six foot five inch football player, and next year's NFL hopeful, at San Diego State came dressed as Tyler Perry's Madea. He borrowed one of our grandmother's wigs and dresses to complete it, but he wore his own shoes and socks. Jaycee, who was not only beautiful but smart, also had the perfect body for her costume. She came dressed as a Victoria's Secret Angel. She was going to graduate, along with James from State next year with a degree in Sports Management. She planned on managing James' career and from what I knew of her, she'd be a formidable opponent during contract negotiations.

"MiMi!" James called over the music. "Why ain't you drinkin?"

"MiMi? Who's Mimi?" DeVon asked We were all gathered in a group. DeVon, Athena, James, Jaycee and I.

"I am." I admitted "MiMi is short for Naomi."

"Hold up! Your name's Naomi?"

I guess he wasn't paying attention when the nurse called my name at the Doctor's office.

"Where the hell did Lyric come from?" He asked.

"Who's Lyric?"James asked.

"Me also." I laughed "I changed my name, member I told you."

"Man, your mama named you Naomi Marie Reyes. Here, have a drink." He handed me his cup. I hadn't drank in almost 2 months. I longed for the dizzy numbness that it brought. I could smell the alcohol, I could see the smile it would put on my face and the elation I'd feel in my heart.

"Nope." Athena said taking the cup from me.

"Aww come on! Just a little bit won't hurt!" I pouted.

"No alcohol." Athena said.

"You're pregnant, it's not good for the baby." DeVon said.

"Woah, you're pregnant?" Jaycee asked.

"Thanks DeVon," I said sarcastically.

"You're pregnant?" James asked "Wait when did you start f---in? I didn't even know you had a boyfriend. Is he here? Where he at?" He scanned the crowd, looking for who he thought could be my boyfriend.

"He's outside by the pool right there. The one dressed like Soulja Boy and trying to talk to that girl. He's not my boyfriend though." I said before they could ask what he was doing trying to talk to another female.

"MiMi?! Him?! Really?! He looks like he's corny."

"He is." DeVon admitted.

"He's not THAT bad." Jaycee tried to defend.

"Yes he is!" James laughed.

"It's Halloween." she rationalized.

"Actually he dresses kinda off on most days." Athena mentioned. I shot her a look, a sarcastic thank you. I was already embarrassed about him I didn't need her help in furthering that.

"MiMi, really?" James asked in a laugh. "Who is this nigga?"

"I'm going to get some air." I said morosely walking out of the house. I was ashamed, I was embarrassed of myself. I didn't need James' laughing at me making it worse than it already was. Trey clowning Anthony was one thing, he did that to anyone who wasn't him. James brought home the feeling of just exactly how screwed I was for the next 18 years, at least. I flocked over to the Putas Primas who were looking around for me.

"There you are!" Talia said "Hey we're going to head out, my friend from school is having a party too so we're gonna swing by there."

"Oh OK, well thank you for coming." I said kind of sad to see them go cuz they were going to be my hiding place.

"You ok?" Joanna asked. "Why do you have that weird look on your face?"

"James just found out I'm pregnant and I had to point out who Anthony was. I'm just a little embarrassed by him is all."

"Don't be." Joanna said. "I mean maybe he'll surprise you and turn into a decent dad."

"Maybe."

SAMANTHA SANCHEZ

"You'll be ok, Puta." Talia said. Touching my cheek with hers as we hugged goodbye. "Call me later if you need to talk, yea?"

"Yea, but text me when you get to your friends house and when you get home, and let me know you got there safely. Both of you."

"You already sound like a mom." Joanna said giving me her hug.

"Be careful."

"OK OK." she laughed.

"Love you guys."

I flocked over to Hector, his girlfriend, and his sister and her boyfriend who were smoking by the trees.

"You guys havin fun?" I asked.

"Yea, it's a cool party good music." Hector said.

"What's up wit you ma?" a dude with a bushy beard and a dirty du rag said putting his arm around me. "I was wonderin' where you ran off to." Disgusted, I removed his arm and shoved him away. I'd been dodging this dude all night. Anthony called him his uncle but I really don't think they were related. I was polite the first two times hoping he'd catch the hint and back off but clearly I couldn't be nice anymore.

"Don't touch me." I said rudely.

"Woah, what's the issue, mamas? I'm just trying to talk to you."

"No thank you."

"Woah, like that? Alright. My bad." He walked away and I turned my attention back onto my cousins. Who were a little taken aback and disgusted by this dudes advances as well. I could tell by Hector's posture that if they guy hadn't left when he did, he was going to speak up and ask him to leave.

"Anyway, Talia and Joanna just left" I said.

"Cool, I think we're about to head out soon too. It's getting late. We gotta get back to the kids you know?" Monique said. She had a daughter of her own at home too.

"No, not you guys too." I pouted.

"Yea, but hey are you gonna be cool? I mean who was that guy?" Hector asked following him with his eyes.

"I don't know, my baby daddy's uncle I think."

"Wait what the f--k? Why is your baby daddy's uncle pushin up on you? Doesn't he know you're pregnant by his nephew?" Laura asked.

"I don't know what he knows, I've been kind of avoiding him all night."

"But are you going to be alright if we go?" Hector asked.

"I can handle myself." I said "There's security everywhere too."

I really didn't want them to go, but they had been with me all night and they had work and kids in the morning. I hugged and kissed them all goodbye and was making my way back into the house when Jaycee found me.

"Hey you ok?" She asked.

"Yea, I'm good." I said.

"Come here, let's talk." She pulled me aside onto the alcove under the stairs. "So what happened? What's going on with this dude?"

I took a deep breath and exhaled and went through the story again.

"So you don't remember anything that happened?"

"Not really, some flashes here and there."

"Ok, MiMi did you know that what happened could be considered rape?"

"Rape? What? No."

"You were drunk, he was sober, You weren't in the right mind to consent to sex let alone unprotected sex."

"No, I'm pretty sure it was my idea." I defended. "Whether I remember everything or not I knew what I was doing."

"Ok, but still..."

"I'm not mad that we had sex. I was drunk and I wanted to feel better, I made a stupid decision. I'm mad that i'm pregnant and I don't feel ready."

"Ok calm down." she said soothingly "It's going to be ok."

"It's all just happening so fast and I don't know what I should be doing. I'm working I'm going to school, I'm not prepared enough, this isn't how I wanted to have a baby."

"I know sweetie, but this is all happening for a reason. God has a plan for you you know that right? Philipians 4:13 right? 'I can do all things through Christ who strengthens me.'"

"Yea." I said unenthusiastically.

"Let me ask you something, you're choosing to keep the baby right?"

"Yea."

"Is it because you want to? Or because you feel like you have to?"

I opened my mouth to speak but I couldn't answer her. I honestly didn't know. I knew how I felt about abortion from the outsider's perspective. It's easy told say no when you're not the one faced with this inevitable change. Was I selfish enough to get an abortion just because it wasn't how I dreamed I'd be having a baby? Because I wanted someone else to be the father? Before I could answer, Anthony walked over to me with his uncle in tow.

"Ay, yo excuse me, can I talk to you for a minute?" Anthony asked his eyes lingered on Jaycee for a minute.

"What is it Anthony?" I asked drawing his attention back to me.

"Oh Uh, come here." he said pulling up from my seat and over to the side.

"Have you met my uncle?"

"Yes, and clearly he can't take a hint."

"Ay, he likes you. He's cool. You should get to know him, you know? Stop being so mean" he said hinting at something.

I looked at him in disbelief. I knew what he meant by "get to know" I had refrained from popping off at Anthony for weeks now, trying to keep myself calm. I held my tongue because I didn't want to fight. I even defended him when the roommates called him stupid and made fun of him. I thought maybe he was dealing with this in his own way. He barely talks to me unless he wants to have sex and even then it's not because he's attracted to me, it's because he's been unable to get in touch with the girls he actually likes and he thinks I'm a sure thing. If that wasn't enough, this moment made it absolutely clear that he has no respect for me as a person or as the woman carrying his child. It's unbelievable almost because just last month he was telling me I couldn't have sex with any other man but him and now he's trying to pass me off to his hobo uncle like a plate of leftovers.

"Excuse me?" I asked daring him to repeat himself.

"You should be nice to my uncle and get to know him you know? He thinks you're sexy."

*There is no way I would ever let that man touch me. I said on screen There isn't enough alcohol in the world. He's lucky he got a polite smile from me. He's dirty with a head full of nappy hair underneath a dirty du-rag with a beard so thick and messy that a bird could nest in there comfortably. I may have lowered my standards once for Anthony but they aren't so low as to let **this** nigga anywhere near me.*

My voice got so loud and so angry that the entire house went silent listening to the profane things that were being unleashed on Anthony.

"MiMi, breathe." Jaycee said standing up next to me.

"Geez, what's wrong with you?" Anthony laughed as if all of this was just some big joke.

"What's wrong with me? Are you really that stupid?"

James, DeVon and Athena had walked up to see what was going on.

"Hey there ain't no need to be callin the nephew stupid." His uncle said

"He is stupid." I argued "He's a stupid insensitive pathetic excuse for a man! A jack rabbit f--k with a little ass d--k."

"Woah what happened?" James said.

"My d--k isn't little!" Anthony defended.

"It's a baby penis, nigga."

"You trippin!"

"I'm pregnant with your motha f---in child and you tryin to pass me to your uncle like I'm a ho or some s--t!"

"Woah!" his uncle laughed "I ain't this one nephew... I can't help you. You ain't told me that was you."

"Anthony, you dumbass. Are you serious, man?" DeVon asked.

"She's not my girl though." Anthony defended.

"How many times do I have to tell you I don't want to be your girl?? NOBODY WANTS TO BE WITH YOU!"

"It doesn't matter if she's your girl or not," James said calmly. "You got her pregnant and you need to have some respect."

"Who are you?" Anthony said "Why are you in this?"

"James is 'Ric's cousin." DeVon introduced.

"Oh." The intimidation in his eyes was evident as he realized that a dude this size had my back. He probably thought with Trey locked up I didn't have anyone else. "Look I'm sorry alright? I didn't mean to piss you off." He put his arm around my shoulder trying to be nice all of a sudden.

I glared at him from under my eyelids "Dont. Touch. Me." I growled snatching away, my hands curling into fists at my side.

"You look kind of scary right now." He commented "Relax, it's ok."

"No, actually it's not."Jaycee said "Come on MiMi let's get your stuff you're going to stay with us tonight."

"MiMi? Who's MiMi?"

SAMANTHA SANCHEZ

Six

I never hated someone so much in my entire life. It truly amazed me how little respect someone could have for a woman to treat them as a pass around to their friends or their relatives. And to do it to a woman who was carrying your child? Who even does that?

I spent the night with James and Jaycee that night, it was nice to get away from the suffocation of the clubhouse. I was so pissed that I even started talking about abortion. All I could think about was how I didn't want to ever deal with Anthony again. How I didn't want his baby. How I just wanted to drink and be numb that this wasn't how I planned my life. If I was going to have a baby out of wedlock then it would be with a guy who, at the very least, respected me if not loved me. James didn't like that idea. He and Jaycee both agreed that, though it was my decision, it shouldn't be made in anger or for the wrong reasons. Hating my baby daddy was not the right reason for an abortion. They advised me to pray about it. I was too stubborn to pray but I weighed the pro's and con's of having one in my mind. The biggest con outweighed the biggest pro. I heard my child's heartbeat. That was a living child inside of me. That was my child, my baby, despite who the father was, I loved my child and I wouldn't be able to live with myself if I silenced that heartbeat because of my anger toward Anthony.

When I came back to the house the next day, I didn't speak to or even acknowledge Anthony. He tried to come and talk to me but I never responded. He tried to pull on my arm to stop me from walking away and I snatched away, warning him for the last time not to touch me again. There was nothing he could say, no apology sincere enough to excuse the way he's treated me. I wasn't the only one giving out the silent treatment either. Athena and DeVon were fighting again.

Athena's ex boyfriend was at the Halloween party and the fact that Athena is still close to her ex irritated DeVon. In his mind exes can't be friends unless they're still somehow involved. This was Athena's first love, the first guy she'd ever had sex with and with DeVon being so insecure, the fact that when he wasn't next to her she was engrossed in conversation with her ex didn't make that any easier. I personally saw it as Athena being a good hostess. Her ex didn't know anyone at the party except for her and she wanted to make sure that he was ok. DeVon saw it as the ex boyfriend still being in love with Athena and Athena didn't mind it. So in DeVon's mind that made Athena a cheater. He started screaming at her and storming away from her not even trying to hear a thing she was saying. Worried that DeVon might get violent Roman advised Athena to get out of the house that night too.Athena, tired of the arguing, and desiring separation from the negative energy that was being put out, left with her ex. He dropped her off and she spent the night alone in a hotel. When she came home the next day, DeVon was ready with accusations of sexual misconduct. She swore she spent the night alone but he didn't believe her. He believed that she had sex with the ex. I understood Athena's need to separate herself from the situation but leaving with her ex was probably a bad move. It took the whole day but DeVon eventually forgave her, but he never really got over it. He told his family about it and they hated her for it throughout their entire relationship. Once they made up, and if Monroe was occupying the guest room again, DeVon would kick Anthony out of their shared room and he'd have nowhere to go but mine. As usual, he tried to be nice to me and talk to me and touch me and I'd ignore him. Everytime he touched me I'd snatch away or hit him or push him away from me. For someone who claimed not to want me he sure was persistent. I couldn't stand the sound of his voice so I'd put on my headphones and drown him out to the Queen of the Damned soundtrack, it was loud, it was angry and somehow it seemed to calm me, help me internalize my feelings and be blank to the outside.

"So you hate me now huh?" He asked one time when we were all gathered in the living room. I was trying to study but I couldn't focus. I didn't respond so Monroe would ask for him for entertainment purposes.

"Lyric, do you hate Anthony now?"

"Yes." I responded.

"But why though?" Anthony asked. I stayed silent.

"Lyric, why do you hate Anthony?" Monroe repeated.

"He's an insensitive, unintelligent, jerk who doesn't know how to use a condom and thinks I'm his toy that can be passed around to his friend or picked up and played with whenever he gets bored and if he touches me again he'll get stabbed in the throat." The boys laughed but I kept my face straight.

"Monroe, can I move into your room now since Chris is gone?" I asked

"Why?"

"Because every time DeVon and Athena start f----in in DeVon's room, Anthony gets sent into my room and I don't want to slit his throat and end up having my baby in prison."

"Sure." Monroe said.

"Cool, that means Athena has her own room now," DeVon laughed.

Close to Thanksgiving, DeVon's temper and jealousy became extreme.

Contributing to the hostility was DeVon's sister calling Athena from Detroit to cuss her out. Since DeVon's phone was stolen by a guy on campus, people had to call Athena to get in touch with DeVon. DeVon was never too far from Athena. He would walk her to class and wait for her to get off work. Even if he wasn't on the schedule that day, he would hang around the restaurant while she worked. He was supposed to go to Detroit for Thanksgiving, but had suddenly decided not to go. DeVon's sister blamed Athena for DeVon not wanting to go and visit his family, Athena was called all kinds of names, her character was attacked, and they had never even met. I don't know what DeVon had told his family about Athena but it must not have been nice at all. Even still, DeVon didn't want to leave Athena. Partly because he was so in love with her, he couldn't stand to be away from her for five minutes and partly because he was worried that she would spend time with her ex. Athena urged him to go, told him he needed to go see his family. Truthfully she also needed a break from him, some breathing room, although she'd never actually say that to him. It would only set him off again.

Anthony's jealousy was as bad as DeVon's except he was quieter about it. Trey wasn't around, he was in prison but when I moved into Monroe's room and started spending more time with him, Anthony didn't like that too much. He didn't say so but it was in his eyes. Monroe was considerate of the fact that I was pregnant was more attentive to my well being than Anthony was. He policed my eating habits not letting me have too much salt or caffeine. It wasn't out of romance or attraction, Monroe was just a decent guy. The entire house was that way toward me except for Anthony he just didn't take notice until I started actually hanging out with Monroe.

While Athena and DeVon were busy with their drama Monroe and I were the only actual single ones in the house. So we'd go to lunch after class or to the movies. He'd tell me about the girls he was talking to and I'd open up about my history with Trey and my feelings for him and any feelings I may have had for Anthony.

"It's not even that I want to be with him." I explained.

"Thank God."

"I just wish he wouldn't act like I was the last person in the world he would want to be with." I said "Stop pretending like I'm some obsessed thirsty chick who's trying to trap him with a baby."

"That makes sense."

"Yea. I'm sensitive."

"Super sensitive on top of pregnant sensitive," Monroe joked.

Monroe even helped me learn to drive and even went with me to take the driving test. It was nice to have a male friend where there was no sexual tension or romantic attachment. Just fun and mutual respect. Just to see what Anthony would say or do Monroe would tell him that we were sleeping together. I played along and so did Athena and DeVon. It was obvious that it did bother him, his whole body would tense up and he had to force out a "Cool." Everyone teased him about it. Asking him how he really felt, asking him why it seemed to bother him that I could be sleeping with Monroe when he was trying to pass me to his relative on Halloween. He continued to repeat that he didn't care at all.

Come Thanksgiving, despite my mother's plea for me to come with her to Lake Elsinore, I stayed home. We were on break for the holiday, Monroe went to Las Vegas with his mom. Athena went to be with her family, DeVon finally was convinced to go to Detroit and Anthony was supposed to go to Long Beach with his aunts and cousins. I wasn't in a celebratory or thankful mood. I told my mom to just bring me back some Macaroni and Cheese and A peach cobbler. I was still nauseous at the sight and smell of most foods. The only exception being pickles. The saltiness from the juice helped ease my nausea, but when I got my appetite back I was heading for those two things first.

I was content to sleep the day away. If it weren't for Talia, begging me to come and Joanna begging me to go black friday shopping I would have stayed home and binged on my slasher movies. I was on my way out the door, my mom had left her car for me and rode to Lake Elsinore with my Aunt Judy, I grabbed the keys opened the front door and there was Anthony.

"Oh. Where are you going?" He asked.

"How did you know where I live?" I asked, breaking my imposed silent treatment out of shock and surprise.

"DeVon told me."

"What do you want?"

"I didn't have anywhere to go, and the Eagles game is coming on…"

"So you thought you could come over here and watch a football game?"

"Yea and I thought we could talk."

"I don't watch football and I don't want to talk to you."

"I know but I wanted to apologize. DeVon said I should apologize."

"Do you do everything DeVon says?"

"No, but I do feel bad about what happened at Halloween, I wasn't trying to make you feel bad."

"What were you trying to do?"

"I don't know…can I come in and we can talk?"

I had an idea. I had decided to tell my dad that I was pregnant and it would be much easier if Anthony was there with me.

"No, we'll talk in the car, come on." I said moving him backwards out of my doorway so I could lock the door.

"The car? Where are we going?"

"My dads house."

"Your dad?"

"Yes and he doesn't know that I'm pregnant yet so when I tell him it will be easier for me if you were there."

"Why? Is he going to try and kill me or something?"

"No," I laughed at the idea. Who did he think my dad was? "You don't have anywhere else to go, you know you're about to be hungry, so you might as well come get some food and watch the freakin' game like you want." I decided to lie to my dad. In order to make myself not look so bad, I would say that Anthony was my boyfriend that we had been dating for a while prior to being in the house and just got cast together. Daddy wasn't going to watch the show so he wouldn't know what the truth was and it wouldn't be so bad that way.

"As long as he doesn't try to kill me."

I was nervous the whole way there. I was halfway paying attention to Anthony as he prattled on a half apology/half excuse for his behavior. That DeVon and Athena explained to him how it seemed like he was treating me like I was his ho and trying to pass me to his uncle who hoped to have sex with me was wrong.

"So what I'm hearing is, you're an insensitive jerk," I said.

"I'm not insensitive."

"Yes you are."

"No, I'm not. Look this is going to sound bad, but I forgot you was pregnant."

"That's bull."

"No seriously I mean I was cross faded and wasn't even thinking about it."

"How could you not have been thinking about it?"

"I don't know. I just forgot for a minute."

"Well I guess you have the luxury of forgetting. I, on the other hand, have this life growing inside me draining all of my energy making me nauseous all the damn time, so I can't forget."

"I'm sorry."

"Whatever."

There was a moment of silence.

"So here's what's going to happen." I said "When we get to the house, I'm gonna lie and you're going to go along with it."

"Lie about what?"

"I need you to act like my boyfriend."

"What do you mean? Like kiss you or something?"

"No you don't have to do anything, you don't have to even hold my hand. Just if they ask I'm going to tell them that we're dating and I need you to back me up."

"Ok, why though?"

"Because the narrative is better."

"The narrative?"

"What sounds better to you, that I'm pregnant by my boyfriend whom I've been dating a while or that I got drunk and sloppy and had sex with a guy I barely knew?"

"Yea, the boyfriend sounds better." he laughed.

I pulled up in front of my grandma's house, the house driveway and curbs were crowded with cars. I sat there across the street, nervous, scared to go in. I hated having to lie, but I felt like my dad's opinion of me was already low that I didn't want it to get lower so it was necessary.

"Ok so when we get in there, remember my name is Naomi to them."

"M'kay. Where did you get Lyric from anyway?"

"I made it up."

I guess Anthony could tell I was nervous and he put his arm around my shoulders and squeezed me to him comfortingly. "It's gonna be ok, breathe." he said. We walked into the house and I was greeted with a rush of hugs and kisses from my aunts and uncles and cousins. I introduced Anthony as my boyfriend and everyone greeted him warmly except for Talia and Joanna: they already knew what was up. The rest of the family was shocked because I had never brought a guy home before. Since Anthony was my guest/ "boyfriend" I went ahead and fixed his plate and brought it to him, dessert as well. I wasn't naturally domestic, I had to remind myself that this is what women do for their men. I would have let him do it if we were at home. I hated gender roles and even if Anthony were my real boyfriend, I wouldn't serve or cook for him at home.He didn't deserve to be catered to like that. Maybe If I was making something for myself I'd ask if he wanted some and make extra but other than that, he had two arms and two legs he was capable of getting his own food.

At first, the night seemed to be going well. Anthony sat there and watched the game and talked with my cousins and my dad. Anthony minded his manners and didn't say anything ridiculous he wasn't rude or dismissive of me for once, I almost believed he cared and I was grateful for that. When My dad went into his room I decided that it was time for me to tell him.

"Hi daddy," I said upbeat.

"Hey baby," he responded.

"So I have some news to tell you," I said with a fake smile.

"What's that?"

I pulled out a sonogram from my doctor's appointment the day before.

"You're pregnant?" my dad asked.

"Yep."

I couldn't tell where the conversation was about to go but I was hoping he would take it well. When he sighed and lowered his head searching for the words. I knew he wasn't going to congratulate me.

"How far are you?" he said plainly.

"14 weeks."

"Are you taking care of yourself?"

"Yes, and the roommates are making sure I stay away from harmful foods."

"What about your boyfriend?"

"What about him?"

"How do you guys plan on taking care of the baby?"

"We'll figure it out."

"You better figure it out quick, cuz once that baby comes there goes the tv show and the whole acting thing."

"Why would my acting thing be over?"

"Because you need to take care of the baby, you need to get a real job. A career. There's no guarantee that you'll be successful with acting. I know it's your dream but it's time to be realistic now."

"I am being realistic, I'm in school, I get paid to do the show."

"How long can it last though? Do you know how fast that money you get is gonna go? Babies are expensive."

"Why can't you be supportive?" I asked.

"I am being supportive. I don't know what you want me to say, Naomi, I mean I don't know what you're going to do with a kid. You can't even take care of yourself."

"Yes I can."

"What about your boyfriend? Does he at least have a backup in case TV doesn't work out for him?"

"We're both being paid $10 thousand an episode. Even after taxes that's still a lot," I said.

"Well I don't know what you want me to say then." He said "I hope you're saving your money."

"Whatever, I just thought you should know, you're going to be a grandfather."

I thought I would cry at any minute. My dad just basically told me my life was over that I was never going to amount to anything and if I tried then I'd be a horrible mother. I didn't want to be in the house anymore. It was time to go, I shouldn't have come. I walked into the indoor patio where everyone was gathered watching The Bourne Ultimatum and told Anthony that I was ready to go.

"Ok can we wait until the movie is over?" he asked his eyes fixed on the tv.

"No. I wanna go now," I insisted.

"Wait a minute," he said.

"No, Anthony. Now." I urged getting impatient. I didn't want to lose it in front of my family. They wouldn't understand.

"Let him finish this." My cousin Jonny insisted "It's almost over. Just sit down."

"Anthony, I have this movie at home, we can watch it there, please I want to leave, now."

It was taking everything I had not to start yelling at him to get up so we can leave. I was panicky and I wouldn't be able to fight back the sobs much longer. I didn't want to stay here.

"MiMi, what's wrong?" Talia asked "I thought we were gonna go shopping later with Joanna."

"I changed my mind. I just want to go home. I don't feel good. Come on, Anthony."

"Alright." he said clutching his backpack but still staring at the TV screen.

"You're not moving," I said more angrily.

"Naomi, relax what's wrong with you?" Jonny asked.

"I would just like to go home now."

Anthony still didn't move. I felt helpless. It took every ounce of self control I had not to walk over and turn off the TV, to not go off in front of my family because they wouldn't understand. I wanted to cry but I refused to shed a tear in front of them because then I'd never get out of here and my dad would call me ridiculous.

"Ok you know what? You got five seconds to get up or you can take the trolley home." I turned around and headed for the door. I walked out without saying goodbye and three seconds later Anthony was rushing out behind me.

"You're not even going to say goodbye to your family?"

"Next time I say let's go, get the f--k up and let's go," I said.

The ride home was silent except for the E-40 album blasting through my speakers. Anthony bobbed his head along to the music seemingly oblivious to my tense posture and death grip on the steering wheel and if he wasn't, he refrained from asking about it. I pulled up in front of the clubhouse. He'd told me the producers were allowing him to stay here since he didn't have anywhere to go after his Aunt decided to go to Atlanta to visit her husband's family for Thanksgiving.

"Thank you for going along with it." I said turning the music down. No matter how hard I tried to hold it in tears ran freely down my face. I stared ahead at the street hoping with his poor eyesight combined with the dark that he wouldn't notice.

"No problem." He said "Your people are cool."

"Yea, they're awesome," I said and sniffed.

"Are you ok?"

"Yea, I'm fine."

"This is really affecting you huh?"

"Well what did you expect Anthony?" I said defensively "You get to pretend it's not happening, you don't have to carry a baby, nobody is going to look down on you the way they do me right now."

"Woah, calm down, who's looking down on you?"

"Nevermind. Have a good night," I said. He took the keys out of the ignition

"What are you doing?" I asked "Gimmie my keys I'm not in the mood to fight with you."

I don't know what went down with her pops but she's super emotional about it. Anthony said in his confessional. *I haven't exactly been supportive lately and I feel kind of bad about that. Honestly, she actually is kind of cute even when she's mad at me even when she yells at me.* He laughed *I could start paying her a little more attention. It couldn't hurt.*

Anthony got out of the car and walked around to open my door for me. I was shocked and confused when he pulled me out of the car and into a comforting hug.

"It'll be ok." he said "We got this."

"We?" I asked trying to pull away.

"Yes. We. From now on, I got you," he said refusing to break the embrace.

"Yea right." I chuckled rolling my eyes. It was strange being held by him. It's new. I never thought I'd be thankful for him, but I was. We stood in silence for a minute.

"Why won't you admit that you like me?" he asked.

"I never said I didn't like you." I corrected "I said I didn't love you, and I wasn't trying to be in a relationship with you."

"I don't remember you saying that."

"When are you going to admit that you like me?"

"You already know I do."

"I do?"

He leaned his face down and kissed me. It wasn't a passionate full blown open mouth kind of kiss. It was a smooch, an uncertain but determined, substitute for words kind of kiss. I laughed a little and wiped the tears from my face trying to figure out what it meant. What our next move would be.

"You wanna go inside and..." he asked. It was always sexual with him.

"No. I'm not really in the mood." I was emotionally exhausted and wasn't really in the mood to be sexual.

"Are you sure?" he asked pressing his pelvis against me.

"I'm sure. I don't want to be alone though. So how bout we just go lay down? We can watch a movie."

I'd bought a TV and DVD player a month ago so I could catch up, I was behind on my study of filmed plays class and needed to watch some movies that were based on plays and write papers about them in order to keep from failing. Everyone in the house and in the streets knew that Anthony sold bootleg DVD's which meant that we now had a selection of movies to choose from. The producers didn't like us watching the TV too much because it wasn't engaging enough they needed us to interact with each other, provide the drama that in turn made the show as popular as it was.

"M'kay." He said still pressed against me he pinned me between the car and himself, bent down and kissed me again. Harder more insistent. It excited me but It wasn't arousing. It was just nice to be kissed again and to feel desired in any way. "Are you sure you don't wanna..."

"I'm sure." I laughed "I'm tired."

"Ok. So what do you wanna watch? Pinky?" He joked. It was no secret in the house that I was the only one who hated porn. Call it a result of my upbringing, but porn made me feel awkward and uncomfortable. I didn't understand the excitement of it.

"Umm do you have Twilight?" I'd seen it in theaters with Monroe the day it came out and while the book was way better, I still liked seeing the visualization of it on screen. I was obsessed with the Twilight world. We made a pallet upstairs in front of the TV and after giving me one of his

T-shirts to put on and get comfortable, he pulled me into a cuddle. It was surprising, that he would be so intimate and affectionate. It was nice. We stayed like that all night and I thought, maybe, he wasn't such a bad guy after all.

SEVEN

Anthony and I had a great weekend together holed up in the clubhouse by ourselves. He was attentive and affectionate and funny.

*We actually **talked** and I realized underneath the attitude and bravado and jerkish front, was a guy who was masking a lot of deep hurt, fear, and resentment especially toward women.*

His birth mom was addicted to crack the whole time she was pregnant with him and was missing from his life for the first couple of years and then he was bounced around foster homes until the last one when the foster mother that raised him told him he wasn't really apart of the family. He didn't stay there long, his aunt was finally able to get custody of him. He used to be "in his feelings" about it until his uncle and his cousins told him to "man up", to "suck it up" and that "emotions were for punks" and he "ain't no punk." He wanted to do better for his baby than what was done for him. There were a couple of times that he even lay his head on my stomach. He really seemed to care but once the rest of the roommates started trickling back in and filming started full swing again, he became distant and cold once more.

Going into December, whatever connection Anthony and I had seemed to go and come back again on a whim. There were days when Anthony seemed to like me, and was softening up toward me, when we had, at the very least, mutual respect for each other. He even helped me find a used 1998 Red two door mustang so that I didn't have to take the bus anymore. I used the rest of my first season advance to buy it. The days when he was fond of me, Anthony always talked about our future. He'd accepted the fact that we were going to be apart of each other's lives for good now. Something I was still struggling to accept myself. He even seemed excited and happy at the prospect. He would talk on end about what kind of parent he wanted to be, and constantly hoped aloud that it was a girl so he could give her a princess name. As much as I hated it, on those days I caught myself feeling more for Anthony than I wanted to.

Then there were days when he would rather not deal. He was still a follower, grasping at the table for crumbs from whomever he was aspiring to emulate. Whether it be one of his numerous "cousins" or DeVon or a

SAMANTHA SANCHEZ

rapper whose song he was stuck on. I didn't understand how anyone could so wholly submit to an image of what someone told him he was supposed to be, how he was supposed to act and become so convinced that it was the only way to be. Anthony didn't even realize that people were laughing at him and not with him. He was their pet monkey.

DeVon found my predicament extremely amusing, DeVon would always be the one to put Anthony on blast about the baby. He never let anyone forget how it happened and always informed anyone who didn't know "Yea, she was drunk and this nigga blasted six times and now she's pregnant." Especially if we happened to run into Anthony in public with his "boys" and he tried to pretend I was just a roommate. Which was pointless because once the show aired everyone would know the truth. I was invisible to him most times, but then that was his game; knowing me, and acting like he didn't. I was irrelevant, just another one of his many "fans" was his way of being cool to the people he was trying to impress. The fact that it angered me was a bonus. Pissing me off and making me yell at him whether in English or Spanish, was his favorite game. I knew but I still couldn't stop. He would say something mean about me for a laugh and I would say something back just as mean if not meaner. He even tried to say once that there was no actual proof that the baby was his. That I could have had sex with someone else before him and was just trying to pawn it off on him. To which I responded,

"Why would I pick you to be my baby daddy? Who in their right mind would ever want to have a baby with a b---h ass piece of s--t like you? I *wish* this was anybody else's baby but yours."

I gave into my violent urges toward Anthony more and more often. Whenever Anthony said something condescending or degrading, I probably should have sat back somewhere and prayed through my frustrations, but I was pregnant and emotional and throwing an apple or an orange or a plum or a cup or a book or whatever I could get my hands on, was more cathartic. For good measure, I'd threaten to throw a knife at him if he said one more thing. I actually pointed one at his throat once and threatened to slice his adam's apple in half if he didn't get away from me. I would never actually do it, but the fact that he was scared that I just might be that crazy, gave me a little bit of happiness.

DeVon and Monroe had stuff thrown at them too when they pissed me off. The difference was, they would throw it back and a food fight would erupt. DeVon and Monroe weren't scared of me like Anthony was. When Anthony got mad, he would threaten to have his homegirls beat me up as soon as I gave birth. I laughed and dared him to. The laughter kept me from crying sometimes, other times I had to lock myself up in the bathroom to keep from being seen. I hated crying, I tried not to but I just couldn't help it. I wanted a drink so bad, being pregnant really sucked.

In between the fighting we did have sex, after which he immediately jumped up got in the shower put his clothes on and went about his day like nothing happened. I sometimes found myself being a tad bit domestic in my relationship with him at times. Whenever I did my laundry I'd ask if he wanted me to include his clothes. If I was in a good mood, I'd even drive him places sometimes. At first I did it to be nice, I didn't like being hostile all the time. It was exhausting and I was already tired all the time, then he started expecting it. He was under the impression it was my job to cook or clean for him. It was obvious that Anthony wanted all the perks of being a boyfriend or a husband with none of the commitment. So I stopped doing things for him. I let him take care of himself from then on. I blamed Athena for Anthony's expectations of me. She was very "housewifey" in her relationship with DeVon, causing Anthony to badger me to take care of him. I stood firm on the belief that a woman doesn't take care of a man. In my mind you take care of a child, you take care of your parents when they're old and can't take care of themselves anymore. What you don't do is take care of a man who is capable of doing things himself.

"Athena does it for DeVon," He whined.

"I'm not your girlfriend though, remember?" I pointed out using his favorite phrase against him. DeVon laughed at us. He claimed that he didn't know why we acted the way we did. How it was so obvious that we were in love with each other and we might as well make it official because it was bound to happen eventually anyway. It wasn't that simple for me.

Do I care about Anthony? Yes. Do I want his attention? Yes. Would I be his girlfriend? Probably, I'm pregnant with his child it's not like I can date anyone else right now. Would it last? No. Did I love him? No. Did we have a future together separate from the baby? Probably not.

Anthony didn't love me either. I don't believe he even loved himself too much or he wouldn't be trying so hard to be like someone else. Anthony didn't want to be with me exclusively because he didn't want to give up the possibility of someone better being interested in him. He liked the video hoe type of girls, someone that looked like she'd be a finalist of Flavor of Love. When he hugged up on me it was for one of two reasons. Either DeVon told him to because I was feeling depressed, or because he wanted some. That wasn't a good foundation for a relationship.

As the semester wound down our contracts for season 2 were reviewed and finalized. Apparently, the footage that had been put together so far and shown to the big wigs, looked promising and they anticipated success. I was offered an additional $10,000 per episode for season 2 because the drama between Anthony and I was so intense that the focus groups believed that we were the most interesting storyline of the entire show. As a result, Anthony and I were approached for our own spin off about the baby to be filmed in the summer after the birth, depicting us getting adjusted as new parents. They would rent us a condo and pay us thirty grand each per episode. Anthony was excited about it. He jumped at the opportunity. I signed for season 2 but I was hesitant to agree to a spin off. I wasn't sure about bringing a new baby into an environment where the parents didn't even get along most of the time but were forced to live together. It wouldn't be healthy. I would prefer it if I lived alone with my mom and the baby and Anthony could come over and visit from time to time. I told them I would think about it and get back to them.

"Why not?" Anthony asked when I told him I didn't agree to it.

"Why would you even want to?" I asked him.

"It's $30,000 an episode!"

"This is our child's well being!"

"Our kid will be good."

"*We're* not good. You and me. We're not a couple. We don't get along. You don't like me."

"I didn't say that I didn't like you, I just said I didn't want to be with you."

"So why would you want to live with me? It's too confusing."

"I'm just there for the baby though."

"Yea, cuz that's original. We need to think about the welfare of our baby not money."

"How else are we going to provide for the baby without money?"

"I don't know, Anthony. We'll get jobs."

"You wanna go back to regular jobs?"

"Well no, but what choice do I have? You can still do the third season, but I'm gonna be raising a baby on my own."

"On your own? What are you talking about?"

"Do you honestly expect me to believe you're going to be around? If The Breakfast Club takes off and you start bringing in groupies by the dozen do you really expect me to believe that you're gonna want to be saddled with the responsibility of being a father? I'm not going to be one of those nagging baby mamas begging you to be around, harassing you for money. I already know I'm gonna be raising this kid alone."

"What are you talking about? I'm gonna be there to take care of my kid. You won't have to nag me. And you won't have to go back to regular jobs if you would just agree to the show with you, me and the baby."

"I'm not comfortable with it. End of story."

"Just think about it." He said putting his arm around me "It could be fun."

After the negotiations were settled and our checks in hand for the second season, it was time for the photo shoot. Christopher returned for it, which makes sense seeing as he's in half the episodes. He explained his absence by confessing that he'd been in jail for the last couple of months on some bull that his aunt cooked up. He wouldn't go into detail about it. The photos would be used to promote the show, which was set to air at the end of January on Wednesday nights. These were the pictures that would be seen on television, on billboards on the internet. I wasn't necessarily showing yet, and I wore a waist cinchers under my outfits to make my stomach look a little flatter. We had professionals doing our hair and makeup and dressing us. I felt beautiful and fun and worry free... until they decided to play up the couples angles. I was fine with it but Anthony, I could tell wasn't here for it.

DeVon and Athena were the cutesy, happy, in love, kissy kissy couple. She sat on his lap, he lifted her in the air, they hugged and kissed for the cameras. Athena wasn't sappy like that but she went along with it because technically it was her job. With Anthony and I, it wasn't as mushy. We didn't look into each other's eyes longingly, we didn't kiss. He was posed to hold me but I was directed to look into the distance longingly and he was to look over my head like he was bored. Then we were back to back glaring at each other, then alternately rejecting each other, then simultaneously rejecting each other.

Our individual pictures were different. They were more about us displaying our personalities and having fun. The boys were all posed like they were the flyest guys alive. Anthony held his shirt collar up on both sides like he was poppin his collar, DeVon and Monroe posed with their shirts up showing off their abs. I posed with Christopher and we were silly dancing doing the waltz. We finally posed altogether as a group and Anthony couldn't stand far enough away from me. Which was disappointing but not entirely unexpected.

A crowd had gathered around during the photoshoot outside the school, curious about what was going on. When he wasn't in the pictures, Anthony was trying to talk to the girls, doing his best to boast about himself. I wasn't

55   SAMANTHA SANCHEZ

his girlfriend but it bothered me that he seemed to give them the kind of attention that I wanted but didn't get from him. I was prettier and way classier than most of those chicks. I, at least, knew how to dress for my size. I knew what to cover up, and what I could get away with showing and yet Anthony couldn't get away from me fast enough. My ex was now married, Trey was locked up and out of touch, and I was left with Anthony, my baby daddy, who often treated me like I was the last person on earth he'd want to be with, and I just couldn't understand why. What was wrong with me? What did I do? Why didn't they love me?

"Wouldn't it be funny if I went to New York and I came back and Lyric had another dude?" Anthony asked DeVon on our last night in the house. We were having our last family dinner of the semester. I sat in silence sliding my food around on the plate. I had no appetite. I just wanted to be home already and away from all of this. Six weeks of peace and quiet that's all I longed for.

"Yea that would be funny." DeVon agreed looking at me to assess my reaction. I didn't react. I was tired of reacting to Anthony. I wasn't in the mood to fight tonight.

"I hope she do find a new dude." Monroe added. As if that were likely while I was pregnant.

"I'd be like 'Oh so you're new the one?'" Anthony continued in a laugh "And if he got hostile I'd be like 'woah, back up homie. You got the wrong one, don't you know I will kill you?'"

"Wow, you gonna kill him huh?" DeVon asked trying not to laugh.

"What would you care anyway?" Monroe asked "You always sayin' that she's not your girl, Are ya'll even f----in still?"

"No," I answered.

"But still, I'm just sayin..." Anthony said.

"Just sayin what?" Monroe asked.

"That's my seedling, she got in there," he reached over to touch my stomach but I pushed his hand away

"Don't touch me," I said calmly.

"Geez, what's wrong with you?"

"Nothing I just don't want to be touched right now."

"Well I just gotta let people know who's daddy." He said reaching over again I blocked his hand. I got the feeling that he wasn't referring to the baby exclusively. It felt like he was implying that he was *my* daddy in a way. That, as his baby mama, I was his property.

"Touch me again and I'll stab you with this fork." I said holding my fork pointy side up. "I'm going to go read." I said getting up from the table.

I didn't feel like fighting or getting mad or getting loud. It was pointless by now. All he would do is laugh at me and my emotions again. It never changed anything, I was tired like always and I felt empty inside like always and I thought it would never go away. I picked up my plate and sat it inside the fridge and retired to my room. I opened my very worn copy of twilight. I needed to get lost in the story of the hot guy that everyone wanted falling for a plain awkward girl and wanted nothing more than to be around her even when she slept. A lot of people say it was creepy but I understood Bella's fondness for it. It must have been nice to have someone want to be around you all the time and to want you to be around them all the time.

"You're so stupid," I overheard Monroe say to Anthony.

"What?" Anthony asked innocently. I put in my headphones to try and drown their voices out. I didn't want to hear their conversation.

You either want her or you don't make up your mind. Monroe said in his confessional

In all honesty. I don't think Anthony knows WHAT he wants or how he feels. He's confused. Athena commented. *And Lyric is feeling a lot of things and I think she just wants to feel cared about.*

He tryin to keep her in his pocket. DeVon laughed *That's cool and all but that dude need to be careful. Pregnant women are crazy, Black women are crazy, Mexican women are crazy and Lyric is all three so you know she gotta be psycho and I got a feeling this semester was only the beginning.*

SAMANTHA SANCHEZ

EIGHT

Filming for season one wrapped the day after finals. It couldn't have come at a better time. The frustration and stress from being in that house had my blood pressure raised a little too high. I needed a bit of sanity and solitude. DeVon stayed in San Diego with his mom for Christmas. Athena stayed too. Monroe went back to Vegas, Nobody knew what happened to Christopher and Anthony went to Brooklyn to visit his family missing another doctor's appointment. Making it the 2nd out of 3 he's missed. Well considering he left in the middle of the first one I could argue that it was the 3rd out of 3 that he'd missed so far. My mom went with me though. We were supposed to find out the sex of the baby but it wasn't in the right position to be able to see.

I'd gotten enough money so far to be able to put a down payment on a house for me and my mother to move into. I didn't want to bring my baby home from the hospital to a ghetto apartment complex with neighbors constantly screaming at each other and police cars lining the block every weekend. My mom found a house in Paradise Hills that had been foreclosed on and we were able to buy it for less than the previous owners had paid for it. It was in a nice residential neighborhood, one story 3 bedrooms, the master bedroom, which I'd claimed for myself because I could set up a nursery on one side, had a bathroom attached to it. It also had it's own entrance through the backyard. The house came with a garage and a built in den attached to the living room. From the thunderbolts painted on the walls, it was obvious this used to be a man cave to the previous owners.

DeVon and Monroe, along with James and a few other men from the church helped us move in. By Christmas Eve we were 100% moved in. I usually went to my dad's house on Christmas Eve but I didn't go that year I didn't want to answer a bunch of questions about my plans for the baby and about Anthony. Truth was I didn't know what I was going to do. How I was going to provide any more. I'd save the money from the second season as much as I could but I didn't know how long that would last. A year maybe? So I stayed home with my mother and got a feel for our new home. Once everything in our bedrooms was put away, my mother and I climbed into her bed like we used to do when I was growing up. We started in on our collection of Christmas movies and while we laughed and sang along to "Snow Miser" and "Heat Miser", from "The Year Without a Santa Claus", I realized that next year there would be a little bundle in between us watching the movie too. I pictured a seven month old baby bouncing and laughing, throwing toys off the bed. The baby would probably just be learning how to crawl and I'd have to catch him or her before they crawled off of the bed. Then he or she would get tired and curl him or herself into my arms and I'd rock my baby to sleep. I smiled at the prospect of it. I had been so focused on the bad elements of this situation, worrying about Anthony and his attitude that I had never stopped to realize the good things that come with having a baby. Yes, it was going to be a lot of work and the work wouldn't be easy, but I was going to be a mother. I was going to have a child that would love me always. As much as my mother and I clashed about things, I loved her so much that I couldn't imagine being without her. She was my blessing as much as I was hers and I will be my baby's blessing as much as he or she will be mine, just like finding this house for the price we did was a blessing. God was going to take care of all of us, all I needed to do was trust and rely on him.

Apparently, Anthony had a revelation while in Brooklyn as well. He called me a couple of days after Christmas and told me he was sorry for being such a jerk. He'd had a talk with his mom and she told him that, no matter how he feels about me, he needed to be more supportive of my situation and be the best man he can be to set an example for his child.

"If it's a girl." he explained "When she grows up, I want a dude to respect her and be there for her. So I'm going to try and do better for her by being that kind of guy for you. I'm gonna be getting a spot of my own so the baby can have some place to kick it when I'm taking care of her." I'd heard all of that from him before and nothing ever changed. I think his intentions were good but his follow through left a lot to be desired. I don't know if he was just scared or what but I knew that I wouldn't rely on him for anything or expect anything from him. Maybe things would change when the baby arrived and maybe they wouldn't but for the duration of my pregnancy, everything he said I would take with a grain of salt.

New Years Eve came and my mom was at church for Watch Night Service. I chose to stay home. Watch night service was too long for me and too boring. I'd been to plenty in my lifetime to know that it's not how I wanted to spend my New Years Eve. I had ran a bath and was about to step in when my door bell rang. No phone call, no text, no warning, just "Surprise."

"Who is it?" I yelled walking up to the door wearing the Biggie Smalls T-shirt that Anthony had given me to wear on Thanksgiving. I never gave it back because I liked it, I liked wearing men's oversized T-shirts. They're roomier than regular Tees, plus it hid my ever expanding stomach. So I felt sexy.

"It's me Ric, open the door." DeVon said from the outside. I groaned and unlocked the door and when I opened it, of course, he wasn't alone. Anthony was standing behind him.

"Hey. Happy New Year 'Ric. Anthony needs a place to stay." DeVon said in one breath walking in past me. Anthony followed suit.

"What?"

"Yea, he's homeless."

"Is that my shirt?" Anthony asked.

"No, it's mine now."

"What?"

"How are you homeless? You just said you were getting a spot."

"Not happenin'." He said cooly "That is my shirt"

"Why isn't it happening?"

"The manager at this one place I looked at yesterday was trippin'. I think he's racist. I've been lookin for that shirt too. Hey, what else do you have of mine? Cuz I'm missing some stuff. He put his bag down and went further into my house in search of my bedroom.

"No! Stop!" I shouted. I turned on DeVon "What the hell is going on?!"

"Anthony needs a place to crash, until he gets his own place." DeVon explained or until next semester starts and we move back into the clubhouse."

"He's not staying here." I insisted "Why can't he stay with you?"

"Hey! Are these my basketball shorts?" Anthony called out.

"Anthony!" I shouted "Get OUT of my room!"

"Ant, stop lookin' through her s--t, man! That's rude!"

"DeVon I don't want him staying here. Let him stay with you."

"Can't."

"Why not?"

"I got into an argument with my step dad and my mom's kicked me out."

"So then get a hotel. You can afford it." I called out to Anthony. I walked down the hall DeVon in tow to find Anthony with his shoes off on my bed watchin TV "You not stayin' here." I told him knocking his feet off of my bed.

"Yes I am." he said in a dismissive tone and put his feet back up. Why weren't either of these dudes listening to me?

"No you not! Get up!"

"Ric, just let him stay."

"No! Ya'll can't stay here."

"Ima stay at Athena's I'm just dropping him off."

PRODIGAL   60

"Then take him with you there!" I pleaded.

"There's not enough room. It's just a studio."

"He's gotta go somewhere. He can't stay here."

"He's your baby daddy." DeVon laughed "Don't be like that."

"No. You gon have to go back to yo aunt's in Long Beach or one of your cousin's. Get a hotel," I said turning to Anthony.

"I can't."

"Why not?"

"My aunt won't let me, my cousin's girl don't like me and why would I get a hotel that's what you for and I don't have any more money left anyway."

"How do you NOT have money left for a hotel?"

"We haven't gotten paid for the rest of the episodes yet."

"We got the first 3 and the advance for season 2, what happened to all that?"

"Christmas presents for my family and stuff and I haven't cashed my advance yet."

"You have nothing left over from the restaurant all semester?"

"Nope."

"Why not?!"

"He fell in love with a stripper like Akon did," DeVon chuckled.

"What?!"

"Ya'll females are expensive. Hey what you got to eat?"Anthony asked "Can you make me something to eat? Please? Thank you."

"I am *not* taking care of him!" I said to DeVon. "Go stay with the stripper!" I yelled back at Anthony.

"He can't. she don't want him no more."

"That's *his* problem."

"Stop being mean. Ya'll finna live together anyway when you film your spin-off."

"No we're not because I didn't agree to the spin off."

"You will," Anthony predicted.

"No I won't."

"Whatever you say, Lyric," DeVon patronized. "Anthony is gonna stay here and he's gonna be nice. Right Ant?"

"I'm always nice."

"Ok, good. Alright, I'm gonna go back to Athena's I'll see ya'll". He walked out of my bedroom and I followed him.

"DeVon, take him with you, he can't stay here."

"Bye! Have fun!" He laughed.

"DeVon!" I stomped my foot crying in frustration "No!" he walked out and shut the door behind him leaving me and Anthony alone.

"Hey can you bring me my bag?" Anthony asked.

I felt so helpless. I wanted a drink so bad but the solid mass protruding from my stomach prevented me from doing so. How do I get railroaded in my own home? We were on hiatus. I'm supposed to have six weeks before I have to deal with him again. It was bad enough that I wouldn't be able to escape him next year or any year after that, if he planned on being around for his child, although I get the feeling he's one of those guys that will talk about being in his child's life but will be inconsistent about it. However, the six weeks between the end of fall semester and the beginning of spring were supposed to be just for me. To regroup, to relax, to wind down from all the drama of living in the clubhouse and to brace myself for the next wave. If I didn't need the money, I wouldn't even go back to the drama. I walked back into my bedroom crying, wishing I could reason with Anthony but knowing what I wanted never actually mattered when he needed something.

"Why are you crying?" Anthony asked "Relax."

" Get off of my bed!" I ordered. He didn't move. I grabbed his ear tight digging my fingernails into the part that attached to his skull and pulled. "I TOLD YOU TO GET OFF OF MY BED!" I yelled. "GET OUT OF MY HOUSE! YOU ARE NOT STAYING HERE! THIS IS MY PERSONAL SPACE! YOU CANNOT BE HERE! I DO NOT WANT YOU HERE!"

"Ahh!" He cried out swinging his feet over the edge of my bed and I let go when he stood up.

"Calm down. Come here." He grabbed me by my waist and pulled me to him. "I been thinking...we should start our arrangement again."

"No." I said trying to push his hands away "You don't want me, remember?"

"I wouldn't be here if I didn't," he put his hands on my bottom and tried to kiss me but I turned my face and moved his hands.

"You're so full of s--t". You're only here because you have no place else to stay." I reminded him.

"No, not just that. I could go to Long Beach if I had to. I wanted to be here. I missed you." He tried to kiss me again but I turned my face again.

"What part of 'No' don't you get? You cannot live here." And it wasn't fair for him to be playing with my feelings. He missed me right now but soon he wouldn't. As soon as I gave in or even if I didn't, his attentions would wander and I'd no longer be enough.

"Just let me stay tonight then. Tomorrow if you still want me to, I'll catch the greyhound to Long Beach." I felt so defenseless and weak. The heaviness in my heart deepened.

"Ugh! Whatever! You're sleeping in the living room. There's a blanket and pillow in the hall closet." I walked away and into the bathroom slamming the door behind me. My mom would be home soon and she was not gonna like him being here. Yes it was technically my house, I paid for it but, as a licensed minister it would look bad to allow her pregnant unwed daughter's non boyfriend to stay in the house she lived in. It would already be bad enough when the show aired and everyone found out the details of my situation, but I couldn't let him sleep on the street either. I wasn't that cold hearted.

This was going to keep happening I already knew it. Baby or not. The fact that Anthony and I had a very public sexual relationship, past or present, has condemned me to be stuck in this cycle with him and I really didn't know how to stop it. Clearly. "No" didn't mean a thing. I slid down in the hot bath, as hot as was medically acceptable to keep the baby from going into distress, and really cried. Not the weak simpering tears of frustration but sobs of hopelessness and emptiness. He was never going to care about me. I don't even know why I wanted him to so much. Either way we're permanently linked because of one stupid night.

I took my time exiting the bathroom. I dried off and combed out my hair and then I just sat there til the steam faded off of the mirrors. I didn't want to go out there. I didn't want to see him but I knew eventually I would have to. I heard the front door open and then close but I was too lost in my own thought processes to really register it.

"I'm home!" My mom called out. Then the tone of her voice changed to shock and anger "Naomi!" she yelled. It was loud enough to shock me out of my reverie. I jumped up and walked out of my bathroom fully dressed in my pajamas to find Anthony completely naked on my bed covering his junk with his hands clearly my mom surprised him as much as he surprised her.

"What the hell?!" I asked outraged. Not only was he naked, he was watching porno on my TV. He knows I don't like porno. They're disgusting and degrading and give men unrealistic expectations. It was clear that he expected me to just fall back into bed with him because he was there.

"Why are you naked?" I asked completely annoyed. He was speechless and frozen in fear. If I wasn't so irritated right now, I might have laughed

"Why is he here?" my mom asked.

"Because he's stupid." I said venomously "Put your clothes back on!" I shouted at him. I turned, took the movie out of the DVD player, broke it in half and threw the pieces at him. I walked out of the room closing the door behind me to give him some privacy.

"DeVon dropped him off and left. Apparently he's homeless until he can find a place."

"He can go to a hotel."

"I said that. They didn't listen."

"He can't stay here," Mmy mother said.

"I said that too and DeVon left him anyway." I explained "He's going to Long Beach tomorrow. I don't want him here either but it's late so I'm just going to let him stay the night."

"You guys are NOT having sex in this house."

"I don't want to have sex with him. I didn't tell him to get undressed. I was taking a bath."

"Sleep in my room tonight. I'm not comfortable with you two sleeping in the same room."

"I'm not a child mom" I argued. I hated being told what to do by my mother. The idea of me sleeping in her bed, as if I were a child, to keep me from having sex was ridiculous to me. Even if I hadn't already told Anthony to sleep in the living room.

"MiMi…."

"I'm not going to have sex with him. He's sleeping in the living room."

"But still…have some respect for me."

"I'm not sleeping in your bed. I'm already pregnant, the damage is done. Chill out." I walked away back into my room before she could reply, I wouldn't sleep in her room, and Anthony wouldn't sleep in mine. The conversation was going to go in circles and I wasn't in the mood to argue. I walked into my room and he wasn't there but my shower was running. How did "put your clothes on" translate into "take a shower?" This is why I was always fussing at him. This blatant disregard is why I was always so pissed off.

Fuming I bit my tongue back waiting for him to get out of the shower. I made up the pull out couch with extra blankets and a pillow off my bed. I moved his bag and put it next to the couch minus his CD case full of movies and albums that I wanted. I was serious about him not sleeping with me, whether he knew it or not. About 20 minutes later, he danced his way out of the bathroom, thankfully dressed, if only in a fresh pair of boxers. I had no idea what on earth he had to be so happy about. He saw the look on my face and froze.

"What's wrong with you ?" he asked.

"I said 'get dressed' I didn't say 'take a shower.'"

"I needed a shower though. I had sex with this girl in her car earlier and

I didn't get to take a shower after. I felt dirty," he explained.

Pretending I didn't hear that last part, silently I walked toward him. He backed up scared like I was going to hurt him or something. I grabbed his wrist and led him away from my bathroom, through my room and down the hall to the living room and over to the pull out couch and pushed him down into a sitting position.

"Good Night," I said.

"You were serious about me sleeping in here?" he laughed.

"Yep and you leaving tomorrow like you said even if I have to drop you at the Greyhound myself." I started to walk away and he grabbed me by my wrist and pulled me back and wrapped his arms around me.

"Why you being like this? Come on let's go back in the room."

"No that is done." I said pushing away but he wouldn't let go.

"Why?" he leaned in trying to kiss me but I put my hand over his mouth and pushed him away.

"Cuz I'm over it," I said. "You're only doing this because it's what you think I want, or because DeVon told you to. So no." He knew I needed to feel wanted, He knew I desired affection and he was trying to use it against me. I wasn't falling for it.

"No it's not. I told you I missed you."

"You *just* told me that you had sex with someone else before coming here."

He laughed "You can't be mad at that though, and it wasn't *right* before coming here. That was at like 2 o'clock."

"I'm not in the mood."

"I heard pregnant women always want to."

"And my mother is in the house. It's not happening." I stopped struggling and looked him in the face "Let go of me." He released his grip. Probably intimidated by the look in my eye telling him that I was about five seconds away from becoming violent.

"Good Night." I said with finality and walked back into my room. I locked my bedroom door for good measure. I wouldn't have put it past him to try and sneak in during the night. My mom slept with her door open so even if he tried she'd shoo him back into the living room.

SAMANTHA SANCHEZ

NINE

The show hadn't even aired it's first episode yet and there was already controversy from conservative groups across the country. We were a representation of all that was wrong with young black people in America. We used the "n"word, we were vulgar, crude, disrespectful, violent and we were immodest. Word had already gotten around that one of the two girls had gotten pregnant in the house. We were a disgrace. However, the more conservatives shouted against it the more the not so conservatives and the common folks whose lives were just like ours wanted to see it. Ninety percent of test audiences polled said they would tune into the show every week that our drama was so captivating that they had to see it play out. However, with that, the black females in the audience didn't like what Monroe said about why he prefered white women. "Because black women are too dark down there." However, it was the controversial statements and actions from us that made the show the success that it became.

The supertrailer for the show premiered at midnight during the network's New Year's Eve countdown. Throughout the night there were snippets of pre recorded interviews with The BFC. We filmed them just before leaving the house in order to promote the show. We weren't allowed to go into any kind of detail about our storylines, but we answered questions about what it was like to live in a house with near strangers. A little bit about our lives before the show and what we're studying in school, generic, getting to know you type stuff. Then we were shown the trailer. It started off with views of the San Diego skyline and landmarks, Coronado Bridge, Belmont Park, SeaWorld, Petco Park, Qualcomm Stadium and finally the college campus. Then came the individual introductions of our "characters".

Athena was the studious one so she was filmed browsing through the library looking for a book that she brings back to a table where a laptop and other books already lay open. DeVon, wanted to be a rapper, he was seen on an empty stage "rehearsing". Monroe was a dance major so he was filmed in a dance studio with a bunch of other "students" practicing some moves. Christopher was a musician so he was seen in a recording booth playing guitar. Anthony was the "hustler" he was shown slapping hands with some random guy and freezing to stare at a beautiful girl who walked by. I was the party girl so they set up a scene for me in the club, wearing an extremely busty dress and sipping a cocktail and making flirty eyes with a guy.

Then they cut to scenes from the show. I had the first line of the trailer

"Who wants shots?" A succession of very active scenes. Partying in the club, dancing in class, DeVon and Athena agreeing to date, DeVon daring me to go kiss Anthony and me immediately straddling him and locking lips while he held onto my behind. Then there was clips of fight scenes between DeVon and someone else and Monroe lunging at Anthony who flinched. Then there was a scene where Anthony telling me that he didn't want a relationship with me but that we could be "Cuddy Buddies." Then DeVon telling me that I couldn't be mad at him talking or looking at other women because I wasn't his girlfriend that he was free to do what he wanted and so was I.

Enter: Trey; Rubbing sunblock on my shoulders in the pool, kissing me against the wall, While Anthony looked on fighting the jealousy in his expression. Cut to Athena and DeVon arguing about his family and me throwing fruit at Anthony, Monroe going upstairs with a girl, and Christopher tuning out on his headphones playing air guitar and then stop and freeze on the ultrasound while not revealing which girl was pregnant. You just hear Monroe sayin "Oh s--t" as the screen cut to the title card. It looked good. I have to be honest. I wasn't exactly sure how they were going to edit the storylines. I hoped they wouldn't make me out to be a hoe or something.

The trailer played intermittently throughout New Years Day as well. I would get calls and texts throughout the day from family members talking bout it.

"It's so weird seeing my cousin on TV." Talia texted "The show looks crazy."

"Haha I just saw the commercial for your show." Joanna texted "What is it with you and throwing things at people's heads?"

"Naomi," a cousin from Texas said when he called me "I just saw a preview for this new reality show on TV, was that you I saw sitting on some dudes lap?"

"That was me," I admitted.

"First of all what you doing on TV?"

"Gettin paid."

"Second of all you better get off that nigga lap like that."

"Hahaha shut up, boy, I'm grown."

New Year's Day was always marked with a family dinner. Everyone has their own families for Christmas so we don't all get together on Christmas Day like we used to so my grandma came up with New Year's Dinner. Since we finally had a house, my mom had invited everyone over and decided to host at our home for the first time. I hated family gatherings. My entire family was coming. My grandma, my aunts and uncles a bunch of cousins including James, Jaycee and my cousin Aisha, James' sisters. It would serve as both a New Year's Celebration and a housewarming party. I had invited Athena to come and keep me company. Most of my mom's friends were church folks who would talk about the bible and God all day. Even though my cousins were close with my mom, I wasn't exactly best friends with all them. When they're all together, James included, I was the odd one out majority of the time. I really didn't want to feel alone in my own home. Athena was the only one in the house who didn't tease me about my situation with Anthony. As supportive as Monroe was at times he still always says "Well that's your fault, you shouldn't have f---ed Anthony." DeVon's go to was "Anthony really cares about you, he just doesn't want to show it, he's a dumbass." Christopher, when he was around, constantly looked at me and said "Eww you f---ed Anthony. You're nasty. You're tainted now." and even when he wasn't verbal about it, he would give me the look that said it all. Athena was the only one who didn't say anything about it. She cared how I felt, and if I was taking care of myself. Athena policed my food more than Monroe did and came up with an eating plan. Which, although was a nice thought, reminded me of my adolescent years when my mom did the same thing, trying to help me lose weight. Both of their intentions were good but I still chafed against it.

The plan was for Athena and I to hide in my room alone. I should have made it clear when I invited her that the invitation was only extended to her. I'd expected, like me, that since the season was wrapped, she'd want a break from her significant other. However, after last night I knew that wasn't the case. I'd have invited DeVon but he was too closely linked to Anthony in my mind and I didn't want to think about, talk about, or be around Anthony until the semester started. Unfortunately, that wasn't the case either. When I woke up and opened my door, Anthony was just about to knock. My mom had been up for a few hours already cooking her dishes and my aunt and grandma had come over to help set up. Most likely the noise woke Anthony and sent him to my room.

"Oh. Morning," he said casually.

"You on your way out?" I asked remembering his declaration to go to Long Beach. I turned around and walked back to my bathroom, to brush my teeth and prepare for the day.

"No, your grandma, actually invited me to stay. She's cool, she told me to call her Nanny."

"Don't call her Nanny and you're not staying," I said. Mentally stomping my foot at Nanny. It's not her fault though, she doesn't know. All she knows is that I'm pregnant and this was the father.

"Why not?"

"Because I don't want you to."

"You don't?"

"No." I said scrubbing my teeth. I couldn't help but think his eyes and long eyelashes would be so pretty on a baby girl.

"You don't want me to meet your family? I mean like you said on Thanksgiving, we're having a kid and I'm gonna have to meet them eventually anyway."

I spit the toothpaste foam out of my mouth. "You're hungry, that's what it is right?"

"Kinda," he laughed.

"Fix yourself a plate to go," I said brushing my teeth again.

"Why can't I eat here and meet the fam? I like your peoples."

"Because I don't want you to," I reiterated.

"Why though?"

"It's complicated," I spit and rinsed and put my toothbrush away.

"I just don't want you to be here, so can you please just go?"

I really wanted him gone before my female cousins came. I knew him and with my cousins being so beautiful and made up and fashionable, he would drool. I never liked bringing guys around my family because I low key felt inferior to the other women in my family. Ever since I was 12 years old and a boy asked me if Aisha and I were cousins then why is she so beautiful and I'm so ugly. I knew it was 10 years ago and boys were stupid and I was beautiful too but that still stuck with me and now that I'm pregnant and getting bigger my insecurities were getting worse with each week. My baby daddy already gawked at every other chick that wasn't me, I didn't need him jizzing his pants over my own family.

"You really don't like me any more huh?"

"No. You flip flop too much."

"What? Flip flop?"

"Yes." I said plugging my flat iron into the wall. "First you don't like me and you don't want to be around me, telling me about other girls you've had sex with. The next minute you do and I'm the only one you want. Then I can't even touch you to brush something off of your shirt without you pushing me away and accusing me of being in love with you. Then you're back to wanting me." I separated a layer of my hair at the bottom and tied the rest up into a bun at the top of my head. I bounced the closed flat iron in my palm to see if was hot enough to straighten. Anthony laughed at my description of his behavior.

"See? That!" I pointed out "You laughing when I tell you what bothers me? I don't like that. It pisses me off."

"You can't get mad that I'm with other girls though. You're not my girl."

That statement was beyond annoying now.

"I swear to God if you say that one more time, I'm going to heat up my curling iron and shove it up your ass."

"I'm just sayin…"

"I f---in know I'm not your girl! We've been over this a thousand times. I don't want to be your girl. And that you f--k with other girls isn't what bothers me. What bothers me is that you brag about it. It's rude. I'm pregnant, and super sensitive and you don't give a s--t."

"That's not true. I care. I'm just not trying to be held down in a relationship right now. Especially now that the show is about to take off, I mean we can still do our thing like we always do though."

"I don't wanna keep doing 'our thing' you're the only one getting anything out of it. You can keep yourself open for the groupies, you can run through them two or three at a time, I really don't care. I want to be more than somebody's bed mate. I wanna feel cared about, I want to feel supported emotionally. "Our thing" doesn't give me that."

"What you mean more though? Like married? I mean you're definitely wifey material and maybe when I'm like twenty seven or twenty eight, if I haven't decided on anyone else we could…"

"No." I smirked at the misunderstanding. Like I was really going to sit in his pocket and wait to see if he chose me. "I don't wanna marry you and I don't wanna be your girl. I honestly wish I wasn't having *your* baby."

"That's f--ed up." he commented.

"No, the way you treat me is what's f---ed up."

"What do you want then?"

"I want to be *someone's* girl. I want to be someone's wife. Pregnant or not I deserve to be with someone who is satisfied with just me and doesn't feel the need to keep their options open just in case someone else comes along."

"M'kay." He shrugged "Good luck with that." he laughed. Clearly, he didn't believe that was possible for me. Did he think no one would want to be with me just because he didn't? "Cuz truth is, you havin' *my* baby. I'm gonna be a part of you forever and you gon be a part of me forever. No one is going to be able to take my place with that."

"No one will be able to take your place in your child's life but you have no hold on me."

"We'll see."

Nanny insisted that Anthony stay and eat, much to his smug satisfaction. She wanted to get to know the father of my child. Everything was cool until James and Jaycee arrived. They remembered him from Halloween and were cold to him. They looked at me like I invited him here.

"No, he showed up last night and wouldn't leave," I explained. "I made him sleep on the couch he was supposed to take off this morning but Nanny told him to stay so he stayed."

"What you mean he wouldn't leave?" James asked.

"I mean he wouldn't leave, DeVon dropped him off. He said he didn't have anywhere to go. Cuz he hasn't cashed his checks yet. I don't even think this nigga got a bank account."

"Oh hell no," Jaycee said. "Has he at least been treating you better."

"On and off. Mostly off," I said honestly.

"This nigga gotta go." James said "I'll drop him off at the bus stop or something."

"Let him eat," I said. "I don't want to cause a scene in front of Nanny."

The atmosphere didn't get any warmer when the rest of my cousins arrived. Jaycee had told Aisha who had told our other cousins, who told our aunt, about how Anthony tried to pimp me to his "uncle" on Halloween and they all looked at him like he was the lowest P.O.S that ever walked the earth. I'd never had such support from my family before, it was comforting and empowering. It was good to know that no matter my issues with my cousins they knew I deserved better.

I was serious about Anthony not staying another night. He may have thought he could walk over me like he always did but not with my family here. Someone told Nanny about how Anthony had been treating me and how much I didn't want him here and she pulled me aside and apologized for insisting that he stay and agreed that he needed to leave. It was only after James offered to drop him off somewhere that his cousin was conveniently on his way. I think Anthony was worried that James was going to take him somewhere and beat him up. James stayed until Anthony left and then told me to call him if he came back.

I was so tired of dealing with Anthony. I didn't really want to go the rest of my life having to put up with him. I knew what kind of mother I would be and who my child would be around but if Anthony doesn't care enough to take care of his child while the child lives within me, how did I know that he would step up and be an actual parent when the baby was born? I felt that it would be better for everyone concerned if he wasn't involved. He told me before that he wasn't ready to be a father and I told him I wouldn't force him. My child deserves better than a dad who's self absorbed, so I decided that I would give him an out, after doing some research and talking to a lawyer, I found out that the easiest way to get full custody of my baby would be not to name him on the birth certificate. We weren't married, so I would have legal custody and all right's anyway, but I wanted full sole custody. I wanted to leave it up to him to establish paternity and file for visitation and jump through whatever legal hoops he has to in order to gain parental rights, and be in the baby's life. I doubted that he would. If he was the kind of guy I thought he was, he'd take the out. My life and my baby's life would be better off without him involved.

Ten

By the end of January my baby bump had become very pronounced. I was 22 weeks and I looked about 30 weeks. Anthony was built like a bear (hairy as one too) so I guess the baby would be big too. Aisha and her mom, my Aunt Judy surprised me the day before the new semester and took me maternity clothes shopping. My clothes had stopped fitting a while ago and I was always wearing sweatpants. Whenever I went shopping I hadn't really thought of buying myself anything other than movies. Most of my attention was spent on buying stuff for the baby. I bought a crib and a bassinet, stuffed animals. As much as I could without knowing the sex of the baby. That wouldn't work for TV so the two of them got together with my mom and other aunts and nanny and took me shopping. They bought me really cute baby doll dresses, sun dresses, house dresses and the clothes didn't make me look like a bag of potatoes with no shape. I couldn't wear jeans anymore so I had to get leggings and long tops to hang down over my butt so that my underwear wouldn't show. When I had bought enough clothes to last me a couple weeks, I promised myself that I would come back once I got paid from the restaurant. It's not that I didn't have the money but I was trying to save. I had insurance for both the house and my car to pay and gas. I wasn't a bottomless pit of money and I needed to be as frugal as possible until my other checks came rolling in.

"Why are you even going back?" Nanny asked when we sat down for lunch.

"When I signed up for season 1 I signed the option for season 2 which meant that if the show was picked up for a second season I was obligated to do it."

"I'm concerned that being around the baby's father and with him treating you the way that he does, it will cause unnecessary stress." My Aunt Judy said "You need to take care of yourself mentally as well as physically."

"I can handle Anthony," I said.

"If you can't call me," Aisha said. "I'll come over."

"When do you find out if it's a boy or a girl?" nanny asked.

"I find out on Valentine's day at my next appointment."

"What are you hoping for?"

"I don't know. I want a girl but I'd be ok with a boy as long as he or she is healthy."

"Do you have any names picked out?"

"If it's a girl I've always liked the name Tiana. If it's a boy... I don't know. Adan maybe."

"Tiana is pretty," nanny said.

It would be a lie to say that I wasn't at all concerned about moving back into the clubhouse. My doctor had told me that I needed to be mindful of my blood pressure and stress level at my last appointment and this last few weeks without Anthony were refreshing. I felt like I could breathe when he wasn't around, when DeVon wasn't dumping us on each other. It was a constant battle, to try and be understood and not criticized for being emotional. Now it was time to go back into the gladiator pit. I'd been talking to Athena and She agreed to room with me again and to keep her and DeVon's sexcapades confined to the Boom Boom Room so that it didn't push Anthony into our room or me into theirs to get away from it. She also suggested I take Yoga with her to help me stay calm and relaxed this semester. It wouldn't hurt, so I figured why not? DeVon was the opposite of Athena, he wasn't as pro-active about helping me stay calm and centered. He insisted that everything would resolve itself. He said Anthony really did care about me and the baby and just was scared of the commitment. DeVon swore that Anthony confessed his feelings for me to him but when confronted with the confession Anthony would deny everything. Even if Anthony did have feelings for me, I didn't have time for the foolishness. I was having a baby in a few months and I needed some stability in my life and that wasn't anything close to what I'd get if I continued to deal with Anthony. I hadn't even planned on speaking to him the rest of the semester if I didn't have to. I was resolved to remain indifferent toward him. I wouldn't allow his indifference concerning my pregnancy, his smug smile whenever I talk to him about what bothers me, that laugh that makes me feel like I'm on the outside of an inside joke about me, his false bravado and cockiness get to me.

"Lyric!" Christopher exclaimed when I walked into the house. I was the last one to arrive again. I wasn't sure Christopher was going to be there. I thought for sure his absence most of last season would cause him to get fired. I was happy that he wasn't. Christopher always made me laugh whether I wanted him to or not.

"Holy f--k you're big," he said reaching for my stomach. I grabbed his hand before he could reach

"Yea, I don't like people touching my stomach," I laughed but hugged him.

"Do you know what it is yet?" Monroe asked as I made my way through the group with hugs. Stopping when I got to Anthony.

"No. My next appointment is on Valentine's day. Hopefully I'll be able to find out then."

"On Valentine's Day, that's cool," DeVon laughed looking at Anthony.

"Yea." I said. I turned to Athena "Which room are we in?"

"Yea...about that?" she started to explain.

"You're rooming with Anthony, this semester." DeVon laughed "You guys get the room with the bathroom since you're pregnant and you have to pee a lot."

I turned to Athena silently.

"I'm so sorry, Ric." she said "I tried but the boys had already decided on the rooms, I just got here, right before you." I could have cried right there.

"Nobody else wanted him." DeVon said. "And he's your baby daddy, so yea." I felt the annoyance bubble in my stomach. The sobs caught in my throat and burned there. Anthony stood there silently. Clearly this wasn't what he wanted either.

"No. Somebody switch rooms with me," I demanded.

"You his baby mama, you live with him."

"Forget it. I'm going home." I said heading back to the front door with my bags."

"No, Lyric don't leave," DeVon said grabbing my purse.

"Give me my purse. I need to go. I'm not doing this."

"You'll be fine. Calm down," Christopher insisted.

"My doctor told me not to put myself in stressful situations and sharing a room with him would be the opposite of unstressful."

"He's not going to stress you out." DeVon said "He's going to be nice and help keep you calm. Ain't you, Ant?"

Everyone except me turned their attention toward Anthony waiting for an answer.

"I guess." He said sounding confused. It was obvious he wasn't thrilled about the situation either.

"See?" DeVon pointed out.

"No, This was a bad idea even coming here. Give me my purse."

"Look, I'll switch rooms with you," Monroe offered.

"No, I don't want to be in the room with a pregnant lady and all the complaints and farts and emotions." Christopher said. He was joking but I wasn't in the mood to play. All I felt was panic. I was trapped in this house and now they were trying to trap me in the room with the root of all my current insecurities. They wanted me to kill him.

"Look you ain't gotta leave, Lyric, everything is gonna be alright you'll see," DeVon insisted.

"Forget it. I'll hot wire my damn car." My cousin Kendrick taught me how to do that a couple years ago. I grabbed my suitcases and carry on bag and made my way back outside. It had started raining. I stood next to my car, realizing that without my keys I couldn't unlock the door to even try and hot wire the thing. I walked away from the house across the street and onto a long wooden bridge that led over a deep valley of trees and plants. I stood there in the rain and cried and sobbed and screamed. The whole situation was just messed up. It's not funny. It's not a joke. It became serious the minute that stick turned pink. I prayed to Lord God for the strength not to murder these dudes. I also wondered if, since I was pregnant, I could beat the charges pleading Extreme Emotional Distress.

"What are you doing out here?" Anthony asked.

They sent him out here? He is the last person I'd want to see.

"Go away," I pleaded "Just leave."

"I don't want you to get sick."

"Like you give a f--k"

"Why do you always say that, it's not true."

"GO AWAY!"

"Come back inside."

"Why?"

"Because if you get sick, it's dangerous for the baby."

"You stressing me out is dangerous for the baby."

"I'm not trying to stress you out ok? I promise. Look, I already took your luggage inside let's try and at least be friends... no benefits."

"I don't trust you."

"Can you try to? For the baby at least?"

I agreed to try and as the semester got going Anthony was true to his intent. He tried to be my friend, at least for a couple of weeks. There was no fighting, no arguing, no frustration. But underneath that from the way he looked at me, I could tell there was something there. He was the guy from Thanksgiving weekend again only without the sex. Although, I could tell he wanted to. I knew it wouldn't last. It's like there's a switch in his brain that flips when things are calm that tells him to mess it up. DeVon started poking fun at our peaceful coexistence saying that we should just be together already because it's clear we want to be. It wasn't long after that, that Anthony reverted back to the pompous, self centered poser that he'd always been. Anytime it seemed like he was feeling something real, he backed away from it and chose to be a jerk instead. The peace between us was doomed as soon as the premiere of season 1 showed.

The network had promoted the premiere party all across town. It was hosted at DECO's nightclub next to TGI Friday's in the gaslamp. I was practically forced to go, I was pouty that it was a nightclub and there were drink specials and I couldn't drink. But I dressed myself up and the guys dragged me out. I didn't expect such a big turn out. But there were people lined around the corner by the time we got there. I wondered how so many people could be so excited over a show that no one had even seen yet. We all posed together for pictures, and the executives from the network came to San Diego to see how things were and to meet us. Everyone was so buzzed about the girl who got pregnant on TV. Obviously they couldn't show the actual sex act but, still, I was a novelty for some reason.

When the episode aired, I finally found out what really happened and how I ended up naked beside a naked Anthony. I mean I was told about it, but seeing it was something completely different and it still didn't jog any solid memories. The last thing shown that I remember is finding out that my ex was getting married and downing my drink.

So first my boyfriend breaks up with me, now I find out that he's getting married? This is too much. I can't deal. I feel like I'm going to fall apart.

After we all left the club, we went and bought a couple pizzas to take home in order to soak up the alcohol. Which would have worked had I chosen to stop drinking.

Anthony had struck out with every girl in the club and he said it was my fault. That I blocked him.

Lyric was on me all night, she scared all the girls away because they thought I was with her.

I had been walking barefoot since we left the club. Everyone, except Anthony was drunk to an extent but I was the drunkest and most wobbly of us all. I didn't seem to care. Monroe left the club and went straight to the house with two white girls he managed to pull. We could hear them in the Boom Boom Room when we got home and we laughed. I dropped my shoes at the door and wobbled into my room to pull out the two thirds full bottle of vodka from my suitcase. I took the lid off and started drinking. I walked back out and everyone else was on the patio passing out plates and pizza.

"Hey Ric, why don't you put the bottle down and eat so you don't throw up," Athena suggested.

"Yea throwing up would be bad, man," DeVon agreed.

"But I don't want to feel anything," I slurred.

"I know Love, but how bout you eat first and then you can drink some more after."

Anthony snuck up behind me and took the bottle from me and replaced it with a water bottle.

"How bout you drink this now?" he said.

I pouted then giggled and patted him on the face "Aww you're so sweet." I said. He didn't laugh but he didn't look mad either.

"Hey, Lyric" Athena said once Anthony excused himself to make a phone call. "I think you should get to know Anthony tonight."

"Yea, man, you guys should have sex. Maybe some d--k will make you feel better. You said it's been a minute right?"

"Anthony doesn't like me," I said.

"Yes he does."

"No he doesn't, he doesn't even talk to me. He hates being around me."

"He totally does like you." Athena slurred "He just needs a little nudge in the right direction, he's shy."

"And, besides you know what they say, the best way to get over someone is…"

We just trying to help both of them out. DeVon said in his confessional *Ant needs some p---y and Lyric need some d--k so she can stop being sad. It's win-win for both of them. They should go for it. It's just sex.*

"I dare you to go kiss him right now." DeVon laughed.

Anthony was sitting on the bench in the alcove under the stairs but he was still on the phone. Who was he even talking to at 2am? I asked in my confessional and then shrugged Why not? He isn't completely unattractive I mean when he wears his glasses he's downright adorable. He barely talks to me though. And when i try and speak to him he looks at me like he's scared. Like he thinks I'm going to eat him or something.

I took a drink of water to wash down the food and got up from the table. Anthony watched me walk over to him. His eyes were worried but he didn't move to get away from me.

"What are you doing?" he asked when I took his phone out of his hand and hung it up. I didn't say anything I just straddled him and met his mouth with mine. He resisted for a second and then he melted into it.

I'm on the phone trying to talk to this girl I met tonight, and Lyric just comes over and jumps on me. Anthony explained in his narrative *I knew she wanted the D, she's been smiling at me and being all nice since we got here.*

Grabbing on my behind as the kiss got deeper, he started to lean forward and I had to pull away before we both fell on the floor. His face was still inclined toward mine, eyes closed, his lips searching after I pulled away. DeVon and Athena cheered in the background.

"You want to go in the room?" I asked him. I thought it would be an automatic yes but he hesitated and then he said "Nah, That's ok."

"You want me to get off you then?" I asked.

"Yea," he said.

I was shocked and hurt at the rejection but I got off of him like he wanted. I looked back over at Athena and DeVon. "I told ya'll he didn't like me. I'm going to sleep though, so good night."

"What? Anthony, you dumbass." DeVon exclaimed "No, Ric don't go to sleep. If that nigga won't f--k you I'll f--k you and Athena both."

"No that's alright." I grabbed my bottle of vodka off the table. Feeling humiliated, I retired to my bed. I had just taken my corset off when Athena came in to check on me. I sat there completely bare chested and didn't even notice.

"You ok, mamas?"

"Yea I'm fine." I said taking a big swig out of the bottle "I'm just really sleepy." I climbed under the covers in panties.

"I like how your bra and panties are all matchy matchy," she laughed.

"Thanks," I laughed climbing under the covers.

"So what happened?" She asked sitting on the side of my bed "Cuz it looked like it was going well."

"I don't know. I asked him if he wanted to go in the room and he said no."

"That doesn't make any sense."

"It's typical actually. Why would he want to?"

I started to cry. Oh God, I was so embarrassed when I saw this. I was the drunk crier. How humiliating!!!

"Obviously he finds me repulsive, like everyone else. No one cares to stay in my life. No one wants me. My own boyfriend is marrying someone else."

"Oh no, sweetie." Athena said dropping down next to me "Men are just stupid." She rubbed my back comfortingly.

Outside, DeVon was fussing at Anthony for rejecting me. "What is wrong with you?!

When a female that you are obviously feeling says she wants to f--k you, you take her in that room and d--k her the f--k down."

"She's too aggressive." Anthony gave as an excuse.

"So?"

"I don't like that."

"Anthony, you the one that told me that you thought she was cute and you'd give her the D if she didn't have a boyfriend. She doesn't have a boyfriend anymore, she's askin for the D, go give it to her."

I think Anthony's scared. DeVon laughed in his confessional *I don't know why, maybe he's just been frontin this whole time about bangin all these females. I mean maybe he's a virgin, or maybe he's used to making the first move all I know is if he doesn't go in there and get that p---y he is the stupidest nigga alive.*

I don't want her to get stuck Anthony explained *It'll be awkward, we gonna be living together and then what happens if I bring another girl home? I can't have all that jealous drama, so it's just better to not even go there.*

"Look all she wants is to feel better, her dude just dogged her out, go in there and help her forget about him, or at least just lay down with her, give her some attention."

"I'll lay down with her but I'm not going to f--k her," he said.

"Anthony said he'll cuddle with you." DeVon announced coming in the room "You going to bed nigga? Woah! You cryin?" He asked seeing Athena comforting me.

"My boyfriend doesn't love me anymore," I said angrily. "I'm sad."

"Don't be sad, you got Ant and he wants to cuddle."

Anthony stood at the doorway looking scared to move.

"Why would he want to do that?" I asked "He doesn't want anything to do with me."

"I never said that," Anthony said.

"You didn't have to say it."

"Alright well it's up to you," He said.

"Look, ya'll gonna stay in here and cuddle. And me and Athena gonna go do the same in the other room. "Come on Thee Thee". DeVon grabbed Athena's hand, pulled her up and out of the room, while shoving Anthony further in and lowering the privacy curtain.

They ended the episode with Anthony, kicking his shoes off and scooting into bed next to me and then cut to a few minutes later using the night vision. Anthony and I were laying on our sides kissing, I'd heard stories from everyone about what happened as the night went on but I honestly don't remember it at all.

The rest of the night was spent posing for pictures with fans and as a group for fans. It was weird that I had fans now. Some of the people coming up to me I'd known since elementary school, some were members of my cousin's extended family. The producer of the show pulled me aside to see where my head was at regarding the spin off featuring Anthony and I. Anthony had already signed up for it the only thing they needed was me. Considering that I hadn't planned on sharing parental responsibilities with Anthony, I don't think a show would work. I certainly wasn't going to allow Anthony to use my baby to cash in. I politely told them that I wasn't interested in doing a show with Anthony. It just wouldn't be a healthy environment for a newborn. That wasn't the answer the network wanted but it's the one they were getting. Anthony wouldn't be too happy about it either.

Once classes started, I don't know if it was my mood swings or if I was depressed but I started feeling isolated and unmotivated. I went to work, I went to class but while I was there physically, I wasn't mentally or emotionally present. I was empty inside. I felt like I was a bother to everyone. If it wasn't for Christopher and his disdain for the club scene, I'd have been completely without company on weekend nights. Athena wouldn't always go either but she still had DeVon to attend to, one way or another. While the rest of the house got drunk, and sloppy Christopher and I went out to dinner and bonded. We became closer friends that semester and it was nice to have at least one of the guys in the house who wasn't into instigating or fanning the flames of the drama in my life. Like with Monroe last semester, my closeness with Christopher made Anthony suspicious and jealous, DeVon even speculated that maybe Christopher wasn't gay like we all thought, just to see how Anthony reacted.

It's funny because Anthony tries so hard to pretend he doesn't care about Lyric when it's obvious to everyone except for him and Lyric that he has some real feelings for her. DeVon said in his commentary.

After a couple of weeks with Anthony primping in the mirror everyday, telling himself he was the "Freshest Nigga Alive" and telling me that I was "lucky to have a fly ass nigga like him in my life." I was at my wits end. I took advantage of Monroe's man whorish ways and when he had "guests" over, I'd sneak upstairs and take his bed in the room with Christopher. Some nights I even preferred to sleep on the couch than in the same room with Anthony. When Monroe was in his bed, Athena and DeVon were in the boom boom room, I slept in Athena's bed. One night , a week before Valentine's Day, I decided that it was time to move Anthony out of my room. I was tired of climbing the stairs to stay in Monroe's bed at night. I was tired of hearing Anthony talk to other girls on the phone and looking to see if I was reacting. He had already went back on what he said about not wanting any benefits from our friendship. He'd come home horny and sexually unsatisfied and, to him, "No.", "Get off me.", "Move.", "Don't touch me." was the start of a negotiation not an actual rejection. He thought if he kissed me it would convince me but I would always move my face out the way. "You my baby mama, you can't say no." He laughed. I wanted to move him into DeVon and Athena's room, it would be a tight fit but it could work.

"You're not supposed to do any heavy lifting." Christopher reminded me as I flipped Anthony's mattress over and started dragging it across the floor.

"Do you want your room back? And It won't be that heavy if you help me," I told him.

"Ugh! Fine," Christopher whined.

We couldn't move the bed frame but the mattress and box spring were easy enough. I was nice and made up the bed for him and neatly stacked his clothes next to the closet. I had showered and changed into some pajamas, rubbed Cocoa Butter on my belly to help keep the stretch marks away, and climbed into my nice warm bed. I had just closed my eyes and began drifting to sleep when everyone piled in from the club. I didn't move to see what was going on, I just waited.

From what I could hear, DeVon was wasted and Athena was trying to get him to calm down. He was throwing a fit and accusing her of flirting again and ranting about how dude was going to catch a beat down if he ever saw him again.

"What the hell?!" DeVon exclaimed "Ant, why is your s--t in my room?"

I pulled the cover over my face trying not to laugh out loud.

"What are you talking about?" Anthony asked.

"Lyric done moved you out of your room nigga," DeVon said.

"Why?"

"Because your girlfriend don't like you," Monroe said.

"Girlfriend?" An unfamiliar woman's voice asked. "You have a girlfriend?"

"She's not my girlfriend," Anthony defended.

"Just your pregnant baby mama," Christopher chimed in.

"Ay! Yo!" Anthony asked walking into my room. I pretended to be sleep "Yo! Wake up! Ay!"

"What?" I asked feigning annoyance at being woken up.

"Why is my stuff in DeVon and Athena's room?"

"Because I don't want you in here," I said.

"I don't want to be in the room with them. They're going to have sex."

"Maybe you'll learn something. Think of it as a live porno. You like porno." I laughed.

"No." DeVon said bringing one of Anthony's bags back into my room. I got out of bed and grabbed the bag and tossed it back out.

"Woah." The girl said taking me in "You're super pregnant." I surveyed the room. Anthony was standing closest to me. Monroe and his latest girl, were standing in the kitchen. Anthony's date was standing in the kitchen next to Monroe's girl. She wasn't really that cute. She was kind of plain in the face, but she looked like a size 5 so I'm sure Anthony thought he was lucky right now.

"I know right?" I laughed "Be careful with this one, he doesn't like to use condoms. It only lasts a couple minutes, anyway so I guess I can see why it would be a waste of one." I rubbed on my stomach "But, still, make sure he pulls out."

"Wow. Umm I think I'm gonna go."

"No Don't go," Anthony said.

DeVon tossed more of Anthony's stuff out and I threw it back.

"He's your pet monkey, you keep him," I argued.

"No, he's your baby daddy, you keep him."

"I'm gonna go," the girl said.

"What about the jacuzzi?" Anthony asked trying to pick his clothes up off the floor.

"I'm good," she said. She looked at her friend who looked like she didn't want to go.

"Nah, don't leave," Monroe intervened. "You can suck my d--k too. It's way bigger than his." Monroe's girl looked at Anthony's girl as to suggest it. Anthony's girl shrugged her shoulders. She was for it.

"For real?" Monroe asked shocked.

"Sure," she said looking at him in a kind of hunger.

"Let's go!" He said excited. He grabbed his girl by the hand who then grabbed Anthony's girl by the hand and they ran up the stairs and slammed the door to the boom boom room.

"What?!" Anthony asked, mouth gaping open. There was a moment of shocked silence and then everyone else started laughing. Anthony looked at me like a little kid who's balloon just flew away.

"Well, you shouldn't have brought her here." I shrugged.

In the end I won the struggle for the room. Anthony was so pissed off at me for blocking him that he didn't want to be in the room with me either, especially if I wasn't going to make up for it by having sex with him myself. DeVon insisted that Anthony couldn't stay in there either, so Anthony ended up moving his bed to a corner in the living room and keeping his clothes in DeVon and Athena's room. He didn't speak to me for a week. I relished my small, if petty, victory and Monroe boasted about it at every possibility. Bragging about how good it was and the tricks she knew how to do. He probably exaggerated just to piss Anthony off more. All I did was laugh. It felt good to laugh. I was glad I still could.

I didn't at all feel bad for messing up Anthony's plan with the girl. For once, I was surprised at his behavior. I never thought he would actually bring a girl home. He talked to them in my face, and flirted with them but he had never been bold enough to bring one back and try to have sex with her in the house that I live in too. It was like he was actively trying to make me feel bad. DeVon said Anthony didn't think I'd see her. He thought I'd be sleep and he could get her in and out before I woke up.

"Well he finishes so quick," I said back " It might have worked."

Valentine's day came and my mom and Nanny met me at my doctor's office. Today was the day I hoped to find out if I was having a mini me or mini him. Anthony wasn't there, which wasn't surprising. He didn't care enough to be there. I was certain he knew about it because not only was he present when I moved back in the house and told everyone that Valentine's day was my next appointment, I was talking to Athena and DeVon about it the night before and Anthony was in the room. Plus I'm sure DeVon, who was always a go between with Anthony and myself whether we wanted him to be or not, had mentioned it to him at some point between now and last night.

I was so relieved when I found out the baby was a girl. Looking at the monitor I realized we now had 4 generations of strong willed women in the room. The doctor told me my blood pressure was still a bit higher than normal and stressed the importance of ease and relaxation.

"Why didn't you tell me you had another doctor's appointment today?" Anthony asked later on at the restaurant. I guessed he decided to come to work today.

"Shut up. You knew there was an appointment today," I said placing an order ticket on the rack for the cooks.

"No I didn't." He said as I walked past him back to my section.

"Oh. Well thought you knew. It's not like you care anyway," I said.

"I need you to stop saying that."

"You never care what I need so why should I care what you need? You haven't been to any doctors appointments that I've told you about before. How was I supposed to know you'd want to go this time?"

"You still could have told me."

I rolled my eyes at him "Whatever." I walked past him back into my section where an elderly couple were sitting.

"Hi. My name is Lyric and I'll be your server today," I smiled.

"Lyric?" the man asked. "Like the words to a song?

"Yes sir." I smiled wide.

"That's pretty," his wife said.

"Thank you. Can I get you something to drink?"

"I'll have an Iced Tea with a splash of Lemonade." The man ordered.

"Ok and for you ma'am?"

"She'll have a Lemonade with a splash of Iced Tea," the man ordered for her.

"How do you know what I'm going to order?" the woman asked.

"Because that's what you always order."

I smiled and laughed. It must be nice to have someone pay attention enough to know something so small as what you like to drink.

"I'll be right back with that," I said and walked away. I wondered what it would be like to have a partner in life. Someone who loves me and wants to be around me. I thought about it a lot actually. I saw the comfort and ease Athena and DeVon had together in their relationship, and it made me think about Trey. Sure DeVon and Athena had their dysfunctions. Their personalities were so drastically different from each other but they seemed to make it work. Trey and I were on the same level for the most part. An unspoken understanding of the way the other one thought. I wondered, if Trey weren't locked up, would we be together? I knew for a fact that he'd make sure I felt beautiful despite my growing mid-section. Trey would rub the cocoa butter on my stomach for me when my skin started itching from the stretch. I knew that Trey wouldn't miss any doctor's appointments, if he were here. He'd make sure that I had nothing to worry about except staying healthy and making sure the baby stayed healthy. The back and forth, game playing and fights, the laughing and playing on my insecurities, just to get a reaction wouldn't be an issue with him at all. Pregnant or Not. Even if we weren't together and were simply friends with benefits, he would respect me enough not to constantly bring up other women just to remind me that we weren't a couple. I missed Trey, I loved him, whether he knew it or not. I prayed for him to be well, more than I've ever prayed for anyone besides myself.

"So is it a boy or a girl?" Anthony asked interrupting my thoughts. He was waiting for me by the soda fountain. I hadn't even realized I was smiling until my face dropped as Anthony came into view. The sight of him ended my happy daydream and I became annoyed with the reality.

"Huh?" I asked pouring lemonade into a glass and splashing Iced Tea into it last.

"The baby," he clarified.

"Oh. A girl. I'm naming her Tiana." I filled the second glass with Iced Tea and splashed lemonade onto it.

"Shouldn't I get a say in what we name her?"

"No." I said. "Look I'm giving you an out. I can handle it by myself."

"What do you mean?"

"I mean that it's obvious you're not really into the idea of being a father, so I'm going to stop asking you to be. Go live your life, and do you. I'll leave your name off of the birth certificate and once the semester is over, we'll go our separate ways." With a straw pinned between each cup and my palm, I made my way back to the table. "Are you guys ready to order?"

I asked "Or would you like more time?"

"Lyric, let me ask you somethin." The man said "What's with the cameras around here?" He referred to the cameras that followed both myself, Athena and Anthony.

"Oh, we're filming a TV show."

"You mean, we're going to be on television?"

"If you're uncomfortable with it they'll blur your face out."

"Oh. Isn't that somethin'?" the woman asked. "Are you famous or somethin'?"

"Not yet," I joked. "Right now I'm just a college student doing what I can to get by."

"Oh isn't that nice. What are you studying?"

"I'm majoring in Theater."

"Theater? So you're an actress?" The woman said impressed "Can you sing as well?"

"Well with a name like Lyric of course she can sing," the man said. "Can't you?"

"Umm I try," I laughed shyly.

"Can we get you to sing a little somethin? You know any church songs?"

"Oh. No. I'm not ready to sing in front of people yet," I laughed.

"Don't embarrass the girl like that," the woman chastised him.

"I'm sorry sweetheart. I didn't mean to embarrass you."

They were a sweet old couple. They seemed happy, radiant. They'd lived for so long, been through so much and yet they still could sit there as if life was great. I wondered how they did that. They both ordered the catfish lunch. One had a side of macaroni and cheese, the other had collard greens. When I came back to serve them their food, they started in on another round of questions. Normally, I would be annoyed at nosey people asking me a bunch of questions, but I was at peace with them so I didn't mind at all.

"So tell me, Lyric. Are you married?" the woman asked. "I can't help but see that you pregnant."

"No ma'am, I'm not. My baby was unplanned."

"Oh well don't worry about it, A pretty girl like you? You ain't going to have no trouble attracting a husband." The man said "It takes a strong woman to handle a baby without support from the father. I have a feeling you are going to do just fine. You will make a great mother."

"Aww thank you," I smiled.

"Oh yea, you going to be blessed and your little angel is going to be blessed too." The wife said "God is going to take care of you sweetheart. If you believe in anything, you can believe in that. Just keep smiling that beautiful smile, baby."

"I will. Thank you."

As I walked away I realized that I had never told them, I was having trouble with the father. They were too far away to have heard me and Anthony. So how did they know? How did they know Anthony wasn't supportive? I turned around and they were gone. Their table empty of the food I had just served them. All that was left on the table was a bible, bookmarked to a scripture in Joshua.

BE STRONG AND COURAGEOUS. DO NOT BE TERRIFIED, DO NOT BE DISCOURAGED FOR THE LORD YOUR GOD WILL BE WITH YOU WHEREVER YOU GO.

SAMANTHA SANCHEZ

ELEVEN

"Y ou told him what?!" DeVon exclaimed as we all sat around the dinner table inside the clubhouse. As it was Valentine's Day, I expected Athena and DeVon to go out and be romantic but Athena wasn't into all that crap. She was satisfied with a box of chocolates and a Teddy Bear. Seeing as how the rest of us were single, the roommates, went in on a Giant Pizza (All except Anthony, who'd probably set up a date with a stripper, who wanted to get her face on TV), I ordered a side of potato skins, and wouldn't share. Potato skins were all I ever wanted to eat.

"I told him I was giving him an out. He doesn't have to be involved."

"Why though?" Athena asked "I mean there's still time, Anthony could still step up"

"No, Anthony is too concerned with himself to be held down by anyone, even his daughter."

"You don't know that for sure, though." DeVon pleaded "You just gonna rob your daughter of a father? That's f---ed up, 'Ric"

"Better to not know him than to be disappointed and heartbroken by him later" I said. "I'm just protecting her from the inevitable. I mean do you really think Anthony is really going to sacrifice anything for anyone?"

"I'll talk to him again. Maybe once she's born he'll come to his senses."

"I doubt it."

"Me too," Monroe agreed.

"He likes to bounce back and forth between the idea with being around. Being absentee and fickle with me is one thing, being like that with your own child is completely different."

"I'm sorry Ric." DeVon said "I feel like this is all my fault. I'm the one who set you guys up.

"Don't be." I said "You didn't tell that dude not to use a condom so it's not your fault but it's best for everyone involved this way."

"Are you sure, it's what's best for her and you're not thinking about what's best for you?" Athena asked.

"I don't want her growing up seeing the way Anthony treats me, and one day think that it's ok for men to treat women with complete and utter disregard and disrespect. So in the long run, I feel it's best for her if he wasn't around."

"Kids need their father tho," Monroe argued.

"No kid should have Anthony for a father right now, he's not ready and it's really going to be up to his decision. If he wants to be in her life, it'll be on him to establish paternity and get his name on the birth certificate to gain his parental rights."

"I still think ya'll are gonna end up together." DeVon laughed "You guys are like that couple in How To Be a Player, that were fighting through the whole movie"

"You need to let that go," I said.

"No, I can't." DeVon laughed "You guys are just like that though. Dude would front and like he didn't care, like he was a player too, but when no one was looking he would call her and try and beg for her forgiveness. The girl was trying so hard to be done with him from the beginning and was always yelling at him. In the end he realized how special she was to him, that he loved her and she realized that despite it all she loved him too and they got back together."

If Lyric and Anthony would both stop frontin and admit they both have feelings for each other, it'd be all good. He said in his confessional

I just rolled my eyes and took another bite of my potato skins convinced that it was never going to happen.

"So what are you naming her?" Athena asked sensing my annoyance.

"Tiana." I answered grateful for the change in subject.

"After that thing in the new Disney movie?" Christopher asked coming back from the restroom and reclaiming his seat next to me.

"Why you gotta say it like that?" I laughed taken off guard.

"Because I heard that movie is completely racist."

"Walt Disney was a racist," Monroe chimed in.

"He was not." I argued

"Yes he was. You ever seen Fantasia?" Christopher added.

"Or Dumbo?" Monroe asked. "That crow named Jim Crow?"

"Whatever, but that's not why I'm naming her Tiana. I like the name, it's pretty. Stop touching!" I said popping Christopher's hand. He was squeezing my boob. Christopher had been obsessed with my boobs from day one even more so now that they were getting bigger.

"Ehh" He whined "I wanna see if milk's gonna come out."

"It's not." I informed him "Not until she get's here."

"Well I wanna see anyway." He said squeezing again. Again I popped his hand "No."

"Hit me again" He dared "I'll slap you all up and down this house."

"You'd harm a pregnant woman?" I asked feigning horror.

"B---h, I don't care if you pregnant." He insisted, his voice going up a few octaves. "It ain't my baby."

An hour or so later, I hopped into the shower and when I came out an hour later,Anthony had moved back into the room and pushed our two beds together.

"What are you doing?" I asked getting impatient.

"I wanna show you something, Come here," He said.

"Anthony, I'm tired I'm not in the mood for any more of your s--t."

"I'm not trying to give you any drama I promise. Just come look."

I followed him out into the living room and A giant teddy bear with a big red bow tied around it's neck sat on the ground next to the couch. That wasn't all though. There were baby clothes displayed everywhere onesies that said "I'm cute, my mom's pretty, my dad is lucky."or "Daddy's Princess", "Mommy's Angel", "Spoiled Rotten", and other cute quirky sayings. There were also poofy dresses and toys and baby jordans in very girly pastel colors. A baby swing and a bassinet still in the boxes of course.

"Back on the baby train, I see." I said unimpressed. Except for the teddy bear, I wanted the teddy bear for myself.

"I don't want an out. I want to be there . I want to raise my daughter with you."

"You realize being a parent requires more than just buying things right? You have to actually be there mentally."

"I will be. Just give me a chance to prove it. I don't want to never not see my child, or you either actually."

I was very aware of not only the cameras watching what was going on but the roommates were watching to see what I'd do next too.

"Anthony... I don't have the energy for this anymore; the back and forth. One minute you want to be there, the next you won't even go to a Doctor's appointment. I can't do that anymore."

"This time is different though."

"How?" I asked skeptically.

What on earth could he say that I hadn't already heard from him before? I asked in my green screen *What? Are we gonna be friends that co-parent? Does he wanna be a better example of a man for his daughter by treating me better? What does he have that's new?*

"Remember in the beginning when I told you that I couldn't fall in love? Well maybe I can and maybe that's with you."

That was new.

"Oh wow, you really are full of s--t." I said turning to walk away "I am so sick of your f---in' emotional manipulations that it's not even funny."

"I'm not trying to manipulate you, I'm serious."

"Just stop, ok?"

"I'm for real. I really do think that we could maybe be something. We should at least see what's up and try to be a family."

"No, I don't trust you and why would I want to "see what's up" with a man, who only wants to "see what's up" with me because I'm pregnant."

"Well what do you want me to do? I'm trying to give you what you want."

"What is it that you think I want?"

"You want me to do and be better, You want me to be more supportive of you emotionally."

"That sounds like something Athena told you," I said looking in her direction.

"Hey, I didn't tell him to say or do anything," She laughed.

"Yea this is all him Ric" DeVon added "give him a chance."

"I can be a better man, and I really do have feelings for you and I want to start over, like I want to be with you."

"You brought a random chick into the house a week ago, but now all of a sudden you want to be with me?"

"That was messed up, I know. but can we please start over? Give me one more chance? Here. I got these for you." He picked up a dozen long stemmed red roses and a box of chocolates from Sees Candy off of the breakfast bar "It's all milk chocolate covered marshmallows and cream filled and white chocolate truffles. I know those are your favorites."

I started to soften up. He knew my favorite chocolates. How did he know my favorite chocolates?

"How did you know what kind I liked?"

"I pay attention. You think I don't but I do. I want to try and be a family. I don't want my baby to grow up without me."

I didn't trust him. I didn't trust that this wasn't a manipulation. An attempt to lure me back into bed with falsehoods. I wanted to believe him but I just couldn't yet. Too much has happened in such a short amount of time and I didn't know if I would be able to let it go or even if I should let it go.

"Whatever." I said taking the candy "Put the roses in a vase. I'm going to bed. I started to walk away then hesitated turned back around picked up the teddy bear and then went back into the room.

"So is that a yes or a no?"

"Shut up," I replied. "Come in here and separate these beds back."

Anthony walked into the room a few minutes later and, thankfully without argument, separated the beds. He thought it was a step in the right direction that I didn't kick him out of the room again.

"Things are gonna be different now. Watch." He laid a kiss on my cheek and moved back to his bed.

"This is not a yes." I clarified "If you wanna be there for your daughter fine, I'll give you a chance with that. But as far as me and you and being a family....this is not a yes."

"But It's not a no either right?"

"Shut up." I said. And then there was silence and then sleep.

I couldn't trust my emotions when it came to Anthony. I wasn't sure what I was feeling other than confused. The next morning I had him explain where his head was at because after months of telling me he didn't want to be with me he comes in and suddenly wants to be with me.

"When you told me that you weren't going to let me see my baby, I called my aunt." He explained. "I told you how my aunt is more of a mom to me than my mom and my aunt knew, she knew without anyone telling her, that I'd been a jerk for six months, despite all the advice she'd given me I still wasn't supporting you emotionally. She yelled at me about it and told me how dangerous it was for you to be really upset while you were pregnant and that she actually understood why you would want to cut me out."

At least I knew where he got the "emotionally supportive" line from.

"She told me that I either A.) needed to prove that he wanted to be there or B.) I could wait until the baby is born and take you to court. I told her at Christmas that I cared about you but that I wasn't ready for a relationship and a family and she told me that I needed to man up and handle my responsibilities and not let my child grow up without a dad like I did."

"I have never asked you for a relationship." I repeated for what felt like the millionth time.

"I know, but it still seems like you want one."

"I feel depressed. Of course I want to feel cared about by the man who got me pregnant but I wouldn't want you to care about or be with me only because I'm having the baby," I explained.

"Well I care about you."

"If I hadn't gotten pregnant though, would you want to be with me?"

He thought about that for a minute. "I don't know. Maybe," he replied honestly.

"Exactly. And no matter what happens with you and I, of course

I don't want my daughter growing up without a father, Daddy-daughter relationships are the best. They set the example of how a girl should expect to be loved and I don't want to deny my little girl that. So, as long as you stay consistent and show me that you're all in when it comes to her, then of course I want you to be in her life. I just don't want to be disrespected, I don't want her to think that being disrespected by a man is ok because daddy did it to mommy."

I was absolutely convinced that this change in him wouldn't last, it never did. To his credit he stayed consistent from that day forward and even stayed trying to pursue me. There were no other females on his radar , as far as I knew it was just me he was after. He was sweet, attentive and caring. He would go on late night runs for food or ice cream whenever I asked, he was ideal. Especially when James or other members of my family came around. I still didn't agree to be a couple. I didn't trust his reasons. However I agreed to give him a chance to be a decent father with one caveat: the first time he tries to back out of his responsibilities, I would be filing for full custody and child support. Anthony didn't like that idea at all. Especially the child support. To him it was the worst thing in the world.

"Do you know I could go to jail over child support?"

"Sounds like a fair punishment for being a deadbeat dad."

"But I'm not going to be a deadbeat dad."

"Then there shouldn't be a problem."

It was cute how amazed he was the first time I let him feel the baby kick. He signed us up for child birthing classes and even drove us there himself to make sure we were there on time. He and I both freaked out when we saw a video of a woman giving birth. The rest of the roommates laughed as I cried at what I would have to face. I was immediately convinced to use drugs for the birth. I didn't want to feel not one thing.

Aisha and my other cousins had become close with me since New Years. They were quite supportive of my situation, having gone through bad relationships and situations themselves. We finally began to form a kind of bond so much so that they planned a baby shower for me at Ski Beach. It was co-ed. Anthony was active in registering for gifts. He was excited about all the toys and clothes, he loved the idea of not having to buy this stuff ourselves.

"You know we're probably not going to get ALL of these things right?"

"Why not?"

"Because people are broke." I explained. "We're in a recession. They'll get what they can but what we don't get, we'll have to come back and buy ourselves."

"Aww man."

"Stop pouting, we can afford it."

"We could afford more if you would sign for our spin-off"

"I already told you…"

"I know, but things are better now." He said "We can function together."

"We've only functioned together for two weeks. That doesn't mean we can live together."

"We been living together for over six months already." He laughed

"And we only get along every other week. I don't want that kind of energy around a newborn."

"What if we got them to get us a two bedroom?"

"No, Anthony." I snapped "I just want time to adjust to being a parent and bonding with my baby. I'll allow them to film the baby shower and the birth but that's all I'm comfortable with right now so stop asking."

The producers were still adamant about doing the spin off as well. Upping my per episode salary, to 45 thousand an episode. I needed to have some source of income and I couldn't bare the thought of going back to retail after this. I didn't want to revert back to obscurity, so I agreed on the condition that I have say on when they can film the baby. I was already very protective of my child and I didn't want her to be too exposed. The show would be about Anthony and I developing some sort of relationship whether it be strictly coparents or romantic and that it would have to be a two bedroom somewhere quiet and safe. My terms were met. It was the first time I was so desired that I could set terms and have them met. This drama between Anthony and I was at least good for something. I decided then that I should get an agent to help me in the future beyond the show, milk this for as much as I can.

I signed the contracts for the spin-off the next week and that same day we had our photoshoots for the season promotional. I hated that day, I thought I looked like a sweaty pot belly pig. My nose had spread and my lips were swollen like I'd gotten injections. Sure we had stylists and makeup artists but I still felt like a beached whale. The BFC and the production team tried to convince me to come out of the bathroom telling me I looked good, but it wasn't until Aisha came to the house, that convinced me that I looked beautiful. The BFC would say anything to get me out of the house but Aisha wouldn't lie to me about it and have me out there looking an entire mess for the world to see.

The photographer played up the pregnancy had me stand in the center with everyone touching my stomach. I had to fight the urge not to slap everyone's hands off of me. In one photo Anthony stood behind me his hands on either side of my belly his face buried in my neck while I looked toward him and in the same pose he would smile at the camera while I just smirked. In another picture they had him on his knees in front of me hugging my stomach while my hands rested on his head. Another one where he kissed the belly. I thought the image they were trying to put out there was a complete lie, Until just a month ago Anthony never really cared as much. I wondered how they would play it out in the season.

I'd heard about the first season as it came on from Talia and Joanna who watched the show. I guess the show made it seem like there was a love triangle between Anthony, Monroe and I. It was funny and gross at the same time. When It came time to film the reunion, Monroe and I explicitly denied any romantic or sexual connection.

"Anthony was acting like he didn't want her, Christopher was gone, Athena and DeVon were wrapped up in each other, she needed a friend that she wasn't a third wheel with. That's all it was." Monroe explained. Whether or not we were believed, was a different story.

Sitting on that stage for the first time, I was 33 weeks pregnant. It was so hot under those stage lights and we were there for hours: takes and retakes, getting everyone set up, keeping me hydrated. I sat next to Anthony on the stage his arm was extended behind me on the back of the couch. He wore a black and white Scarface shirt with some brand new jeans, a new haircut with an ill advised star shaved into the back of his head, and a new gold chain hanging low from his neck. I wore a sleeveless royal purple maternity dress that connected at the collar which was gold. I wore black eyeshadow and liner for that smokey eye look and a colorless gloss on my lips. I wore gold bangles on my wrist to match the collar and purple high heels to match the dress. I couldn't walk in them but I didn't have to. All I had to do was sit there and look gorgeous. Anthony was back to being slightly distant again and it upset me. I felt like he was putting on for the studio audience. We filmed on campus inside the little theater. It was more intimate in there and the stage was just a platform elevated a couple of steps from the audience. I invited Talia and Joanna to come to the taping. Everything seemed to go on without a hitch. The nature of DeVon's relationship was discussed, and the touchy subject was his family's treatment of Athena around Thanksgiving.

"My family is very protective." he laughed "What can I say? They don't like her."

"But they don't even know her." The hostess pointed out "They only know what you tell them."

"True, I probably shouldn't have told them anything."

Then they came to me and Anthony's relationship…

"So Anthony, 'is she your girlfriend tho?" The hostess asked making fun of Anthony's annoyingly consistent declaration. The editing together of clips of the history of Anthony and my relationship from season one brought up the frustration and irritation with him. He laughed when it played back and I couldn't help but dramatically roll my eyes.

"No, she is not my girlfriend." He insisted with a laugh, the audience laughed with him. I didn't. Hadn't he been bugging me for the last few weeks about being his girlfriend? Asking me to have sex with him, to give him a chance to be better and now he was happily declaring that I wasn't.

"Lyric, there was another man that occupied a place in your heart this season and it seemed to shake Anthony's confidence."

"My confidence wasn't shaken."

"Yes it was, stop lying," Christopher called out.

The hostess bringing up Trey was the first time I genuinely smiled all night. I now regretted signing on for the spin off with Anthony. Although Trey would respect the monetary motivation, behind the decision, I again found myself wishing that I were carrying his baby and doing a show with him instead.

"No it wasn't. I don't care about that nigga, he ain't got nothin on me, that's my baby, I'm daddy, ain't I?" he pulled me to him.

" Baby's daddy, that's it."

"Stop lying, you know that p---y mine too."

The audience "Ooh'd"

"You wanna get busted in your jaw? Keep talkin talkin s---t." I threatened.

"So Lyric, have you heard from Trey?"

"I have not. His brother was supposed to get in touch with me, to give me Trey's information but unfortunately that hasn't happened."

"So you don't know when you're going to see him again?"

"Nope."

"So does that mean there's room for you and Anthony to try and start something real?"

"Nope. Anthony and I will be co-parents and that is it. As everyone saw in the clip, neither Anthony nor I want a relationship with each other, but as long as he's around for my daughter then we should be cool."

"And what happens if and when Trey comes back, will things still be cool?"

"I don't see why not."

"Man, f--k that nigga. Lyric always gonna be mine til I decide it's time to let her go. Trey can kiss my ass, Monroe can kiss my ass too."

"Don't say no s--t like that, nigga." Monroe warned "You don't want this ass whuppin."

"Man, you can try, me and my cousins will beat the bricks off you."

Monroe stood up from his seat. "Why you need your cousins? Handle it yourself, nigga!"

Security rushed the stage and held a slowly encroaching Monroe back from where Anthony and I sat.

"I can't move, Monroe, save that s--t for later!" I called out. I didn't want to get hit in the mele. Anthony just sat back laughing his arm around my shoulder. I pushed it off and scooted over a bit. Why was he so bold today? I looked to the audience and saw that A couple of other guys were being blocked in their seat by security. Their eyes on the stage. Anthony nodded to them and it became clear. He was frontin for whoever was there watching him. I looked at Talia and she shook her head disgusted by Anthony. Apparently Anthony forgot that he had another month left in the house with us.

"Wait! wait! wait!" The hostess shouted over the roaring of the audience "Anthony, how you gonna say that Lyric is always going to be yours when you claim to not even want a relationship with her?"

"Because he does now and she doesn't," DeVon answered for him.

"No that's not it." Anthony clarified "Look, i'm not gonna lie, Lyric do got some good p---y, if I could get her to suck d--k then we could hella make money."

"What do you mean make money?"

"How bout you grow a mother f---in d--k and then maybe I'll suck it," I told him.

"How bout you hop on a mother f---in treadmill as soon as you pop the baby out and lose some weight. Then maybe I'll give you more attention. I'm not DeVon you can't play me, like Athena be playin' him, I don't care how good your p---y is, I'm not gonna roll over and do what you want me to do if you ain't doin nothin for me."

The audience "Oooh'd", then cheered as my fist connected with Antony's jaw. I continued to punch him. A couple of security tried to pull me off of him and that's when Monroe and DeVon swooped in. I stood and continued to swing at Anthony and he pushed me off of him with such force that I lost my balance as I tried to regain it my foot slipped off the top stair and I fell down into the audience.

SAMANTHA SANCHEZ

TWELVE

I was rushed to the hospital after my fall, to make sure I was ok. Anthony wasn't allowed anywhere near me. The doctor said my blood pressure was way too high and that I needed to calm down so I didn't go into labor too early. I did have a sprained wrist and they wrapped it but that was the least of my concerns. They did an ultrasound and said that everything looked ok, and told me to come back if I started to feel any pain. I decided that I would move out of the clubhouse for the rest of the season and first thing monday, I would call the producers and see if they could make some changes to the spin off. I didn't want to be in the same city as Anthony after the disrespect at the reunion, let alone the same apartment.

"Are you sure, you're going to be ok?" Talia asked as she pulled up to the clubhouse.

"Yea, I'll be ok. If I know the boys, no way is Anthony coming back tonight. I'll go home in the morning. I still need to pack.

"Ok, call me tomorrow and let me know you're ok? Should I tell your dad?"

"No, I'll call him and tell him tomorrow. He might freak out and call me and I just want to sleep tonight."

"Ok cool. Love you."

"Love you too." I managed to hurl myself out of the car, having spent about 5 hours in the emergency room. I was exhausted and ready for bed. What I walked into was a complete storm. Anthony wasn't there but his things were thrown all over the place. His bootleg CD's and DVD's broken into pieces his bed and his clothes were floating in the pool his shoes were in the jacuzzi. His mini DVD player was broken in half, his shower products in the trash. I couldn't have done it better myself.

"Ric! You aiight?" DeVon asked as I walked through the door barefoot my heels in my hand

"According to the ER doctor yea. They said if they had any pains to go straight back. What happened here?"

"We kicked Anthony out the house."

"Where is he?"

"He left with his 'peoples'," Christopher mocked.

"Have you heard from him?" Athena asked.

"No."

"He hasn't even called to check on the baby?"

"No, he still tryin to front, cuz he got some friends or relatives or whoever in the audience watching."

"Damn. I'm sorry 'Ric, I wish we had never hooked ya'll up. If I'd known he would end up like this"

"It's whatever." I shrugged "I'm moving out early though. My blood pressure can't take anymore spikes and my mind can't handle anymore bulls---t."

"Don't go Lyric." DeVon pleaded "F--k Anthony, he can leave."

"He can stay or he can go I don't care anymore, I'm gonna stay the night but I really think I should go home and relax until it's time."

I promised my mom I would go to Easter service with her. She'd been bugging me for months about coming to church so I finally agreed. I got a couple hours of sleep and then I had to get up and make myself pretty for church. I felt like I had been missing that radiance that was attributed to most pregnant women. I looked dull and lifeless, the circles underneath my eyes betrayed not just my physical exhaustion but my mental and emotional as well. Since it was too difficult to do much without my wrist hurting, Athena helped me get ready by flattening my hair and curled the tips. I wore a black knee length dress with black flats and a white sheer overcoat to cover my arms I had just finished packing my bags as James and Jaycee walked in. I was too pregnant to drive my Mustang comfortably, so they were my ride to church. Jaycee looked gorgeous and extremely fit in her beautiful white dress with pale pink flowers and her matching pale pink six inch heels and pale pink lipstick. She was flawless and I was just a mass of fat imperfection.

"What happened to your hand?" James asked outraged.

"And what happened in here?" Jaycee asked surveying Anthony's tossed clothes and bed in the patio.

"I punched my baby daddy in the face last night. The angle was off cuz I was sitting next to him. And the guys trashed his stuff and kicked him out.

"What did he do?"

I gave them a brief run down of the night's events; what I was around for and what I wasn't.

"Why are you fighting and you're seven months pregnant?" James asked.

"Yea you need to calm down and stop lettin that guy get to you." Jaycee agreed "That can't be good for the baby."

"It's easier said than done. But the doctor said everything was fine and I'm moving out of the house tonight and going back home."

"Good. Let's go."

I hadn't even realized that I missed being at church until I walked into the place. I missed my best friend Sasha who'd been impossible to keep in touch with since she, moved to Virginia after joining the military four years before. Her contract was up and now she was home and without her husband whom she'd secretly married three years ago. I was happily surprised to see my cousin, Hennessy, come in with Nanny and Aunt Lucy. Lucy was Nanny's sister and Henn was her granddaughter she was a few years older than me and way more street savvy than I was. I hadn't seen since her brother's funeral five years back. She'd had a rough time adjusting to life without him, she'd started doing drugs from what I heard. She looked clean now and It looked like she was trying to get back on track with her life now so that's all that mattered. Kyanna was there but she barely spoke to me. She was fake nice but something was off and I couldn't figure out what it was. Surely, it still couldn't have been because I was cast on the show and not her. It almost seemed at times like she was laughing at me about something. I didn't have the emotional energy to worry about her right then. I figured whatever it was it could wait until another time.

The Pastor was alright with cameras depicting the service as long as it didn't inhibit anybody's praise or become too much of a distraction. It's amazing how some things can just never be forgotten. I hadn't recited the statement of faith in months yet it was ingrained in my memory as if it were the letters to my own name. "We believe in the ministry of the holy spirit, who convicts, regenerates, baptizes, indwells and enlightens believers for Godly living and imparts spiritual gifts for the edification of the body of Christ."

I sat next to Sasha and Hennessy in the back row of the sanctuary and we laughed and sang along to the songs we'd sang for so many years together in the choir. We sang the three part harmony of "How Much We Can Bear."

"If in your life you are going through, and you don't know, really what to do, just call on Jesus he will see you through. For he knows!!!! Jesus he knows! How much... we can bear!!!"

Later during the sermonic hymn I felt the holy spirit move in a way that I hadn't felt since I was fifteen years old.Later during the sermonic hymn I felt the holy spirit move in a way that I hadn't felt since I was fifteen years old. It felt kind of pointed at me that both the A selection and sermonic hymn were about being able to handle the things God puts on us. I stood fighting tears by the second verse of Kirk Franklin's "More Than I Can Bear". As the song started to build tears ran free down my face belting out the words almost louder than the choir. Sasha and Henn both stood next to me rubbing my back in comfort both dropping a few tears themselves over their own struggles and situations. I was trying not to loose it in front of the cameras but at that point I didn't care.

I had said it to myself before over and over that God had me. No matter what Anthony did in regards to our daughter God would always do right by her. I'd said it but I didn't truly feel or believe it until that Easter. It had always been just something to say when I didn't know what to say. It seemed the right thing to say to get people to shut up and stop preaching at me or trying to minister to me when I didn't want to be preached at or ministered to. I didn't feel God's love surrounding me as consistently as I had when I was fifteen. I'd been too focused on how I was being perceived by the world, by the BFC by Anthony, trying to convince them that all I wanted was for Anthony to be a man, to care if not about me than about the baby. I'd forgotten that there was a God that loves me and cares for me, and that he would never have allowed me to get into this situation if I couldn't handle it.

Before that Sunday, I had never really been able to connect with a sermon. Nothing really resonated with me, not since the Gods Young Women's Conference. I was sent there for a week in Palm Springs the summer between 10th and 11th grade. I usually spent my Sundays zoning out in the choir stand or helping in children's church to get away from the long drawn out messages in the sanctuary. It rarely felt like it was a message for me. However, this time I was still in my seat. I was uncomfortable in the pew but I was always uncomfortable anyway.

"Some people seem to think that Jesus, knowing he was The Son of God, knowing what his future held, had it easy." The Pastor preached. "He didn't. No, as a matter of fact he had it worse because he DID know. Matthew 26:39 says..." He put on his glasses and looked down at his bible "H e went on a little farther and fell face down on the ground praying: 'My father, my father if it is possible let this cup of suffering be taken away from me. Yet I want your will not mine." The Pastor looked up at the congregation "Jesus was afraid…" he paused letting that sink into our minds for a minute. "He begged his father to let him off the hook." He paused again "How many of us knowing that we were going to be whipped and beaten and humiliated and killed tomorrow, wouldn't run and hide from it? Show of hands. How many of you wouldn't leave town knowing that some people were coming for you looking to end your life?" Hands stayed down as everyone looked at each other knowing that they'd avoid death at all costs if they could. "Jesus was God made flesh. He hurt the same way we hurt. He didn't want to die, he could have not gone to that place, he could have avoided it, he could have called down a multitude of angels and proven himself to be The

Messiah, but he didn't....because his death was necessary for us to live."
The congregation murmured in agreement. "If you read a little further in
Matthew 27: 46 when Jesus is on the cross he says 'My God, My God
why have you forsaken me?'" He paused again "Surely, Jesus, as the son
of God would know that he wasn't forsaken right?" He looked around the
congregation,who was quietly and actively responding "Right? Wrong. In
that moment before death, Jesus really felt as if God had abandoned him.
How many of us have felt like that in our lives?" The entire congregation
raised their hands in agreement "Did you know that, while Jesus was on
the cross, he was thinking about each and every one of us? Yea. He knew
exactly where we'd be physically, emotionally; today, yesterday, tomorrow.
The Son of God could have gotten down off that cross at any time but he
didn't. He thought about you, and he endured for you. Because he loved
you. As an individual, every experience, every quirk, every flaw from the
tip of your toenails to the end of the longest strand of hair on your head. "

I can't explain the feeling but I was glued to my seat like metal to a
magnet, trying my hardest not to cry again but failing. I felt an aching in my
soul burning like peroxide being poured over a wound. When they asked
for people to come up for prayer I was somehow released from my seat
and being followed by cameras down the aisle. I was taken to the back and
the altar worker who went in the back with me asked the cameras to stay
outside the door. The room was full of people crying softly, sobbing loudly
all while being prayed for and ministered to.

"Naomi..." The woman sighed with a smile on her face. I knew her, she
was my mom's best friend, Karina. "You are named after a leader... You
are a leader ." I kept my eyes downcast. I was always afraid to look people
in the eye when they were praying for me or speaking to me about God. I
didn't want them to see through me, and the facade of happiness that I put
up. "You have the power to lead millions of people to Christ. When they
see you, people will see an example of God's love and mercy and blessings.
You are anointed, your child will be anointed. Your baby will be a powerful
leader. I know that you are going through a lot and that you are hurting but
if you let Him, God can ease your suffering. Life isn't going to be easy, you
still have more that you're going to go through, but no matter what happens
lean on God and He will see you through. When you're ready, you will have
a powerful testimony, of strength."

After church I didn't feel so drained. I felt refreshed and renewed in
the spirit. I always knew God was there I just got so caught up in the chaos
that I couldn't feel Him, I felt Him now. For dinner, my entire family, plus
DeVon, Monroe and Athena met up at Golden Chopsticks in National City.

It was nice to be around family and not feel angry or tense. I felt somehow free that evening. I was safe in the knowledge that God had me, like maybe my future wasn't as bad as it seemed to me.

My cousin Kendrick was back in town from Atlanta. He was 12 years older than me. Apparently he knew nothing about the show or that I was pregnant and was incensed at the fact that my wrist was sprained and even more so that my baby daddy was disrespectful enough that I had to punch him in the face. I was his sweet baby cousin, his favorite, he taught me to fight when I was 12 years old after I had gotten jumped by a boy in 7th grade.The same boy got beat on the street by Kendrick when she found out. Kendrick didn't allow his face to be seen on the show. He would rather have it blurred out and his name bleeped out because there were people looking for him. Kendrick was an OG from the set who didn't want his little brother following in his footsteps, or his actions coming back on his family so he left town when we were 13 and only visited on the holidays if that. When I was 16 he taught me how to hotwire a car. I relished every visit with him. He kept asking where Anthony was, and why he wasn't there taking care of me. I told him I didn't want to talk about it but he kept pressing the issue until Nanny told him to shut up.

I was exhausted and so full by the end of the day, my stomach hurt. Kendrick and James wanted to go back with me to the house just in case Anthony was there. Kendrick hoped he would be because he had a few words for him. DeVon and Monroe didn't think he would've come back yet but, nobody knew for sure. I still hadn't heard from him after I was rushed to the hospital. He didn't come check on me, didn't call me, nothing. Pulling up to the house, we noticed about 2 other cars in the driveway. One old busted looking grandma cars, and one old green Toyota Corolla with gold rims. There was music coming from inside the house. I sensed this was a bad situation and I should have just let the boys go in and get my stuff, but I urgently had to use the bathroom. I felt like the Chinese Food had given me bubble guts or something. We walked in and I immediately recognized Anthony's bushy faced "uncle" from Halloween sitting on the couch with a girl on his lap. Another dude with a faded black t-shirt, a black du rag and gold capped teeth was over at the stereo, blaring new music from a rapper I wouldn't know even if I saw him in person. There were a couple of other guys outside on the patio. The chicks they had with them were nasty too. they wore booty shorts and sneakers, a couple of them didn't look any older than 16 maybe 18 but somebody should have told them that shorts tight enough to give you a camel toe and a wedgie were NOT cute.

"Hey mama, how you doin'?" His uncle asked "You bout ready to pop huh?"

"Where Anthony at?" DeVon asked.

I scanned the room looking for that smug cocky smirk that he always wore on his face when he believed he was untouchable. There was food and bottles of Henny and 20oz coke bottles all over the counter in various stages of empty but I didn't see Anthony anywhere. The sheet over the doorway to our room was lowered.

"I know he ain't got no chick in my bed." I thought to myself. His mattress was still in the pool so the only bed in the room was mine.

"Ay yo Ant! Incoming!" the guy in the black shirt shouted in laughter as I approached the room. I could hear his grunt as the music broke. I pulled back the curtain and there was Anthony laying underneath a -- the only way I could describe her as was a werewolf. This thing had an overbite that made her mouth look like a dog's muzzle, a mustache and stubble on her arms and legs. I should have known Anthony was into animals. They looked like a bear and a coyote humping each other. They didn't stop when I walked in. In fact she looked at me and smiled, like she had won something over me. I didn't know this chick but it seemed like she knew me.

"ARE YOU SERIOUS?!" I shouted. Seeing nothing but red feeling nothing but hatred, I walked over to my bed grabbed the thing on top of him by the back of it's head. The force of the pull hurt Anthony too because he was still inside of her.

"Ow!"he screamed as I dragged her off of him and across the floor. She kicked and reached for my hand but my grip was too tight, she dug her nails in but I didn't feel it. She called me every name in the book but I was unphased. DeVon and Monroe squealed with surprise and laughter as a dragged the creature naked into the living room. Kendrick ran to me and told me to relax and let go.

"Everybody GET OUT!" I shouted. Everyone outside by the pool looked to see what the commotion was. A couple of girls tried to rush me to defend their homegirl but security blocked them.

"What is your problem?" Anthony asked laughing coming out of the bedroom with his boxers on.

"Ugh! Anthony put some clothes on," Monroe winced.

"Really Anthony? You smashin Alpo now? In my bed?" I asked my hand still gripped around the animal's sewn in hair.

"My bed is in the pool!" he laughed "Ay, let her go." Anthony said reaching for me. Kendrick blocked his access to me. Security was already around me trying to get me to release her. When I did, they escorted her back inside the room to get dressed.

"You can't even be mad, you're not my girl. You won't even f--k me anymore, I'm done with you." He looked around the room for approval from his audience. The music had shut off and everyone he brought with him was smiling and laughing at the situation. Kendrick said something to Anthony and Anthony argued back. I couldn't hear the conversation over the ringing in my ears. All I saw were people laughing at me, Anthony laughing at me. The phrase "You're not my girl" played over and over in my head. It's all I'd heard from him and everyone in the house since I'd gotten pregnant. I wasn't his girlfriend so I didn't have the right to be upset about his constant disrespect. For seven and half months I was made to feel like some crazy obsessed stalker for demanding respect and consideration. All I wanted was for him to step up, to show me some kind of sympathy for the situation that he created, that I had to deal with. If I hadn't gotten pregnant, I wouldn't have been on him at all about anything and he never understood that. My entire life from then until now ran through my head like a cartoon filmstrip. I didn't say a word. All the yelling and the screaming, he expected it, he thrived on it. It made him feel like he was "The Man". He could push a woman to the edge of her sanity time and time again. To him only a real man could do that, it was all just a game and I was sick of playing into it. I was sick of him.

There was a voice in my head that told me to walk away, let it go and another voice tellin' me that all I'd ever done was walk away and people never stopped. Naomi would walk away and go cry about it somewhere, but

"Naomi isn't here right now" the voice said "Your name is Lyric and you can't let this slide anymore, he needs to learn what happens when you come disrespectful. Last night wasn't enough. It's time to teach him and everyone else that you ain't the one to play with."

I was only half aware of James trying to lead me away. My hand flew fast and hard against the side of Anthony's head. The 40oz bottle of Steel Reserve that had been on the counter beside us shattered at his temple upon impact. Gasps and exclamations "Oh s--t!" went around the room as Anthony collapsed to the ground. Pieces of glass and beer covered him as he bled from his head wound. I reached for a knife that was in the sink, wanting to make sure he was dead but James and Kendrick, as well as security rushed me away. They tried to escort me to my room to get my stuff so I could go but again had to restrain me from attacking Fido and she from attacking me.

There had been a dull pain in my stomach since I left the restaurant, I thought I had eaten too much and needed to go to the restroom but the dull pain had now become a sharp pain. I felt like a chainsaw was ripping through me. The dinner I had enjoyed made it's way back out of me and I fell to my knees on the floor. I screamed when I saw blood coming from between my legs and curled up on the ground in fetal position.

"Call an ambulance!" Somebody called. It was the last thing I heard and passed out from the pain and exhaustion.

THIRTEEN

I was in and out of consciousness, weakened, tired from the blood loss and the vomiting. I tried not to cry but at times the pain would get so severe that I couldn't hold in. I heard the echoes of sirens and people calling my name talking to me, telling me to relax. The doctors told me that I had a placental abruption and needed an emergency C section to get the baby out because she was losing oxygen. I called out for my mom but she wasn't there yet. James said he had called her and she was on her way. I wanted her in there with me but I couldn't wait. I was in too much pain to stay awake so they put me under.

When I woke up, I didn't recognize where I was. It took me a minute to register my surroundings. When I tried to move I felt pain in my lower stomach and that's when everything came flashing back at once. I winced from the pain, loud enough to get my mother's attention.

"Oh, try not to move honey." My mom said to me "Vic." she called out my dad came in through the door.

"Let me call you back." He said into his phone "How are you feeling baby?" he asked me.

"Where's Tiana?" I asked looking around for my baby. I looked at my mom who was searching for the words. I started to panic. "Daddy?" His eyes reddened and started to water. My dad never cried.

"I'm so sorry, baby," He said.

It came on slowly. The whining tears, the protests in denial that soon turned to heavy sobs. The doctors said that they don't know what necessarily caused the placental abruption. It could have been my blood pressure; it was extremely high on intake, or it could have been caused by the fall at the reunion. It could have been too small to even pick up when I was in the ER. They did everything they could but she died in my womb.

I'd felt her move inside of me, I'd heard her heartbeat, it was prophesied that she would be anointed, how could she be dead? This was a nightmare. A nightmare I had to wake up from. I was dreaming, this wasn't happening to me.

I stayed in the hospital for a week. I went into a mildly catatonic state. I didn't want to see anyone at all. If I could have kept my mom away, I would have. I just wanted to curl up inside myself and die right along with my baby. When I was released home, the only way my mom could tell I was alive was from the sobs coming from behind my door. I didn't want her or anyone around me but she forced her presence on me in order to change the dressing from my C-section. I was bedridden for a month recovering from the surgery. I only moved to go to the bathroom. I broke all the mirrors in my room, I hated looking at myself. I hated that I let Anthony get me to that point. I was warned to relax, to stay stress free. I shouldn't have let him get to me the way he did, affect me the way he did but I couldn't help it. I couldn't control it. I tried but I must not have tried hard enough.

The first two semesters in the house changed me. I started the show thinking that a man I am sexually involved with is supposed to respect me. Even if he didn't love me or want to be in a relationship that he would, at least, be mature and respectful. I believed that I was exceptional, because I didn't have any expectations like a lot of other females. I didn't equate sex with love. I walked through life believing that I was allowed to have feelings. That I was supposed to, at the very least, matter to someone that I was having a child with. I guess I was wrong. Being an affectionate friend to someone I'd had sex with made me clingy. Having basic human decency meant that I was in love. If I wasn't a girlfriend, it wasn't my place to be upset when the father of the child I was carrying cared more about impressing other women than making sure I was alright. I was supposed to not care that strippers and women who could make their booty cheeks clap were more worthy of attention than I was because I was just a cuddy buddy or baby mama. The entire house would always remind me of my status that, because I didn't have the title, I had no reason to expect respect and sensitivity. I didn't love Anthony. I didn't want to marry him, I didn't want him to be my man, I didn't even want him to be my baby daddy but it still hurt when he went out of his way to remind me how little I mattered to him. I was only a warm place for him to lay. I was supposed to take care of him, to listen to his problems while my feelings were trivialized and diminished. The whole thing began because I had an emotional void that I needed to be filled. Anthony was supposed to make me feel better about myself but all he did was make me feel so much worse.

Anthony was so far beneath me on every level, I never should have let him touch me. I called myself trying to do him a favor and now look what happened. I was so stupid to believe that Anthony would ever man up and be there for me, at least while I was carrying his kid, but he hadn't even bothered to call. Everyone else called, not that I answered, but not my baby daddy. Trey had reached out to me. On my last day in the hospital a nurse handed me a letter that she said a young woman had dropped off for me. Since I didn't want visitors she had to leave it at the nurses station. He told me he was sorry for my loss, and that he couldn't be here for me. He said that his brother had gotten arrested before he could give me Trey's information and that his sister was bringing me the letter. He said he was going to keep his promise and take care of me, that he would be out soon and he would come and find me. He knew that Anthony was to blame and he would handle it. He reminded me that I was strong and that I could get through anything and to trust and rely on God. He promised, once he got out it would be me and him and nothing bad would happen to me anymore, not if he could help it. He asked me to write back and as much as I wanted to, I didn't. I wasn't ready to be cheered up and communicating with Trey would do just that. I wanted to wallow in my misery.

The news of the premature birth and subsequent death of my child, spread over the gossip blogs and entertainment news channels and at the end of the reunion the words on the screen read:

> FOLLOWING THE TAPING OF THIS REUNION, LYRIC WAS RUSHED TO THE HOSPITAL TO ENSURE THE WELL-BEING OF THE BABY. UNFORTUNATELY, THE NEXT DAY BABY TIANA WAS BORN PREMATURELY AND, DESPITE ALL EFFORTS, DIDN'T SURVIVE.

After the reunion aired Anthony was vilified by women on Facebook and Twitter. I had the sympathy of every baby mama in America who got pregnant by an inconsiderate, disrespectful deadbeat, bum. Guys thought Anthony was hilarious, the stupid men loved him. The real men considered his disrespect toward the woman his child's life depended on reprehensible. And so Team Anthony and Team Lyric emerged. T-shirts were sold with his quote "You're not my girl tho'" and my quote "Grow a mother f---in d--k."

I was angry, I was humiliated, I was hurt. I'd been hurt for what seemed like an eternity. I found myself wishing Anthony was dead. I wished that he would die, that a great defender would rise up and strike him down forever. I wished security hadn't stopped me from jamming the knife into his throat, so I could have watched him choke to death on his own blood. I couldn't justify how it was fair. How God Almighty would allow this pathetic excuse for a man to go unpunished for what he had done to me. My mom tried to talk to me, to help me see that this loss was apart of God's plan, that it was all for a reason, even though we couldn't see it. I wasn't able to understand why God would give me the promise of a child, just to take her away from me. What kind of God was that? Merciful? Mighty? Awesome? Just? How was it "just" to allow my daughter to die but allow Anthony to live? I suffered while he was probably out celebrating and that thought burned a rage inside me like I had never felt before. The book of James, Chapter 1 verse 8 says that "A double minded man is unstable in all it's ways", My instability began to manifest that summer.

Sometime in May, word got back to me that Anthony was beat to hell on the streets. Someone or someones, broke his jaw, his arm, his nose and his leg. One of his eyes was swollen shut while the other was just black, and a couple of teeth had been knocked out. He wasn't dead but the news that he was hurting made me feel a little vindicated. He had to be hospitalized for a few weeks. It was speculated that maybe I had something to do with it, but I could honestly say I knew nothing when questioned by the police. I hadn't been out of bed in a month, I hadn't answered my phone or made any phone calls other than to the pizza delivery place so there was no evidence to support the theory that I had anything to do with Anthony's attack.

My thoughts wandered back to Trey's letter. He said he would handle it, maybe this was his way of letting me know he got me. He couldn't tell me directly that he was going to beat him up or have him jumped because the letter was screened before being sent out to me, but could it have been what he meant? I finally decided to write back. I let him know that I was happy to hear from him and thanked him for reaching out. I also apologized for not writing back sooner and explained that I wasn't in the right head space at the time. I told him that Anthony had gotten jumped and that people seriously thought I had something to do with it. I told him I found it laughable. I also said that I couldn't wait to see him when he got out. The letter came back a week later. I assumed he had already been released.

By June I was tired of being depressed, I hated crying so I refused to do it anymore. My weight was the topic of negative conversation by a lot of viewers that first season. So that was first on the docket, I would get back at Anthony and all my critics, I would let my hatred and anger fuel me. My baby belly had gone down, I only ate when I was about to pass out and spent hours at the gym with James while he trained for the upcoming football season, pushing myself as hard as I could. The producers approached me about a season 3. They wanted to pay me 50 grand an episode for season 3 and if I signed for season 4 in Mexico, I'd get 60 and episode. The Team Anthony vs Team Lyric trend was growing and they wanted to capitalize on it. Before agreeing, I talked to my Aunt Yvette, she had recently married a talent agent who was supposed to be helping her with her singing career. According to her he was the best. So he agreed to handle my career. Both my aunt and her husband, my uncle Ivan could get me where I wanted to be, beyond reality TV; Theater, Movies, scripted TV, music. He boasted friendships with some big names in the industry, none were my contemporaries but I'd heard of them so that's what mattered to me. Uncle Ivan got the show's producers to agree to my terms and conditions, that Anthony and I never be place in the same room again, that I would not ever have to be around him unless filming with the group. Apparently Anthony had made the same request so it wouldn't be that difficult to maintain. Uncle Ivan also got them to agree to 80 grand an episode for season 3 and 95 grand an episode if I signed to do season 4. I was getting more than anyone else in the show, I was the character that most females related to. Everybody in my family thought I was nuts for going back, even Yvette and Uncle Ivan wanted me to quit, they hated reality TV anyway, thought it was trash. I even heard someone say that I enjoyed the drama. I told them that I was in it for the money. Money makes things happen, money helps me move forward in life. If they understood anything, they understood that. It was time to work toward something.

In July my physical determination had paid off. I'd lost 15 pounds total, 10 in baby weight and 5 of my own and dropped to a size 13. That was also the month that Ivan booked me my first gig outside of The BFC. I was to be the new spokesperson for Audi. For my first commercial, they dressed me in red couture with slits going all the way up my left thigh. The commercial was set up sort of like a James Bond movie and I was the bond girl behind the wheel. Audi agreed to be my sponsor for the show and gave me a brand new dark gold Audi R8. It was next years model and I was the first one to have one. All I had to do was talk about the car on the show and be seen driving it on camera. I didn't know much about cars but I knew it was sexy. James had a fit when I drove up to his house showing off. He begged me to let him drive it.

The car was too sexy for me to look drab driving it. I needed a new look. Jaycee, Aisha and all my other female maternal cousins were very much on board for a makeover. It almost turned into a real fight when Aisha tried to throw out all of my black make up. I was sort of Goth the first season and a little during the second season. All of my clothes were black, as was my make-up. It wasn't an intentionally Goth look, I just didn't look as big in black as I did everything else. Also, bright happy colors weren't me. I agreed to incorporate other colors into my wardrobe but not nix the black altogether. I didn't do any promotions for the second semester/season of the show that summer. I wasn't ready to be around the rest of the group yet. I was still avoiding their calls and when they came over, my mom told them I still wasn't ready to see anyone. I did show my face though, I went to the beach with Joanna and Talia, to get out and "have fun". I ran into a couple fans of the show who asked to take pictures with me. I obliged.

"How's Anthony?" The guy with the camera asked.

"Who cares?" I answered in a laugh.

"Hey is it true you have him jumped?" the guy next to him asked.

"No. but good lookin out to whoever did."

They laughed and by Monday it was on TMZ. They caught what I said on video and then sold it to the gossip site. I didn't care though. It's how I felt.

Half of the commenters loved it and laughed at what I said others said I was insensitive, uncaring, bitter "because the nigga didn't want me". Some even believed that I was lying and paid to have Anthony attacked. It was all very amusing. Monroe, DeVon and Athena were the only ones who went on the promotional tour. Anthony was still rehabbing his leg and couldn't travel and probably didn't want to be seen as less than pristine in front of audiences. My absence fanned the flames of controversy, nobody knew if I was coming back for season 3 some people believed I was fired, others said that I quit. Some actually guessed correctly that I just didn't want to be around everyone yet. I wasn't surprised that Christopher was fired he didn't really like interacting with us too much and he didn't have a storyline. It made me wonder if they would leave us as 5 or if they would add another roommate to the mix.

The end of August came, and so did the start of the new semester. I decided I wanted my own place. I didn't want to live with my mom anymore. She didn't understand me, the fact that she was always preaching to me about God's plan and praying and trusting him, made me believe that she couldn't understand what I was going through at all. I put in applications at apartments downtown and just waited. I hadn't really built up any credit yet but I was hoping my monthly income would be enough to persuade them to give me a chance.

Without the pregnancy weighing on me, I felt more balanced and mellowed out. The heights of emotion had subsided. I was angry but I didn't want to cry all the time. The last two semesters I wore my feelings on the outside. That would be different this time around. I wasn't hurt anymore. I was pissed. I was the first one in the house this time. I wouldn't stay in a room downstairs and certainly not the room I spent the last two semesters in. I did peak in there and saw that they did change the carpet, the last carpet had been blood stained. Even with the new carpet I felt that the room was tainted and haunted by ghosts of everything that transpired there. I liked the upstairs bedroom with the balcony so I claimed it for myself, I could easily hide myself up there. Everyone usually congregated downstairs so up here I would most likely be in a land of my own. Neither Anthony nor DeVon would be sharing a room with me. DeVon was the biggest reminder of what

I'd been through, next to Anthony. He'd been Anthony's cheerleader and advocate and I didn't want to hear Anthony's side of anything anymore. Anthony didn't have a side, there's no excuse. I was glad that I didn't have to raise a child with Anthony, I was free but I hated myself for being relieved.

I stopped by a mirror, I hadn't really looked at myself in admiration in almost a year. I lost another 10 pounds and was down to a size 10 waist. I didn't look as heavy as the scale said but I had hips and I was loving myself and my body more and more. I smiled at my new and improved figure. My hair which had previously hung to the center of my back and dyed black, now barely touched my shoulder and was brightened to a medium light red. My top hung low over my shorts, (I was finally ok with wearing shorts that showed my thighs) and slid off of my left shoulder revealing a fresh tattoo on the inside above my heart.

TIANA, I NEVER KNEW YOU, BUT I'LL ALWAYS LOVE YOU

Was written on my shoulder blade. It was the same words I had inscribed on her urn at home. I used some of her ashes and turned them into diamonds and placed inside a small, dark, almost black, silver cross that stretched over my middle finger and connected to a diamond bracelet with a bigger matching diamond studded cross necklace. I felt beautiful, sexy. It didn't cover the grief that I carried with me and would carry with me everyday but looking good at least made me feel better about myself.

"Hello?" A female voice called. It wasn't Athena. Was the newest member of the BFC a female? I wasn't surprised that the show runners would add a new female in the mix to shake up the "couple's" well couple in the house, since there was no longer any connection between me and Anthony so there was no drama to be had on that front. Athena didn't like females she got along better with guys, believing most females to be vapid and annoying. I was the only female she could stand because I wasn't a shallow, wanna-be video hoe with no sense what so ever. Superficial females would be difficult to avoid considering we lived in a house with not one but three superficial guys, who liked to bring home stupid thirsty females. I was the same as Athena in the sense that I didn't get along with girls. Not that I found them annoying, I just never fit in with them after grade school, due to my lack of knowledge about boys and things of the world. I always felt like I was the victim of a practical joke they were planning and tended to shy away from them. Athena was one of the few "knowledgeable" females that didn't laugh at my sexual naivete. I was curious what kind of female this new roommate was and I walked downstairs to introduce myself. I was overjoyed when I saw the new roommate and recognized my childhood best

SAMANTHA SANCHEZ

friend Ruby. I hadn't seen or spoken to her in years. We gasped and ran to hug each other.

Ruby's dad and my dad were best friends as kids, they lived across the street from each other and stayed friends way into adulthood. Ruby and I were a year apart and basically inseparable since we were babies. She was always bolder and more flirtatious than I was. The Latina Princess that she was, made it hard for any guy to resist her. She had the type of body that cholos painted a likeness of on the hoods of their low riders. Although she probably would have them paint her with bigger boobs instead of the barely there boobs that were actually attached to her chest. Unlike most girls growing up, Ruby never shunned me for my lack of appeal. She had my back against anyone who said anything negative about me and even taught me how to dress a little more sexy in order to catch attention. Of course, I had to change at school and back again before I went home. My mother never would have let me out of the house in low cut shirts and skin tight jeans. My dad on the other hand, while not liking my choice of wardrobe allowed me to explore and find myself in the way I dressed, instead of forcing me to cover everything up. She got pregnant when she was 18 and moved to Arizona with her boyfriend and we tried to keep in contact but phone numbers changed, email passwords were forgotten, and a whole lot of other stuff and we drifted.

"Oh I'm so glad you're here, Meems!" Ruby squealed "I missed you!"

"I go by Lyric now," I corrected.

"Oh right." She laughed "Oh my God! you look so good! How are you? I heard about the baby."

"I'm fine," I lied.

"We're gonna have so much fun this semester."

"I hope so, I sure could use it after the year I've had."

The front door opened and a familiar voice called out "Hello?" My stomach turned and bile rose in my throat. Anger shot through my body like an electric charge. I'd gone 4 and a half months without hearing that sound and now I wanted to reach down his throat and rip out his voice box, so I never had to hear it again. I turned to see him and when the recognition registered he was taken aback, looking me up and down he offered a pitiful "Hey, how you been?" It wasn't casual but cautious like he was scared of my reaction. That was good. Fear was good. He was all healed up now so his injuries couldn't please me anymore but his fear of me made me happy.

"You ok?" Ruby asked me in spanish, surveying Anthony with contempt and disgust. Finally someone in the house who was irrefutably on my side with no jokes or digs or diplomatic neutrality.

"No. I hate this dude," I replied back in Spanish.

"Come on, show me our room." She continued in spanish I grabbed one of her suitcases and headed toward the stairs. Anthony backed away as I approached and I smirked at his apprehension and led Ruby up the stairs.

"This is a nice house," she said.

"It's cool," I replied. I realized how fun it was going to be to have someone else in the house that spoke spanish. We could talk about people and they wouldn't know what we were saying. I was always cussing at someone in spanish anyway now someone would know what I was saying and could co-sign if I needed her to.

FOURTEEN

L et's go get in the pool." she said excitedly after unpacking. "Ayy! I don't want to go downstairs."

"No, I'm not letting you hide up here." She said "Not from that *payaso*. Put your bathing suit on let him see what he f---ed up and missed out on."

My stomach had gone down significantly since last year but it still wasn't as tight as I would like it to be. I still had a bit of a pooch, no where near bikini ready. I didn't want to see the comments after this episode talking crap about it like I knew they would. My C-section scar was still ugly and not the least bit sexy. When it healed up all the way I would get a tattoo to cover it up something creepy and gothic, maybe bloody vampire fangs. That would be cool. In the meantime I stuck with a low cut, black one piece with a purple hibiscus flowered wrap around my waist.

Ruby and I were the only ones at the pool. She stayed in the water, lightly splashing me as I floated in the inflatable bed. Anthony watched from afar. I didn't see him but I felt it. I'd become attuned to him enough to know when he's near or when he was watching me. Ruby told me how she and her boyfriend had just broke up again before she came here. "For good this time." She insisted. He kicked her out of the house and since she had no job and no place to live, he kept their son until she got steady. When I asked her why they broke up she said it was over some BS that she didn't want to get into. Now that she was back here though we were going to party and have fun. We were both sexy and single and getting paid. So why not?

After about 25 minutes at the pool Ruby and I decided to run to the store for some margarita mix. I was happy to drink again at any available opportunity. We slipped shorts on over our bathing suits, put on our sunglasses, put the top down on my Audi and headed to the grocery store. We went for tequila and stuff to make margaritas, we left with enough alcohol to fill a small bar. By the time we got back, made our drinks and went back to the pool, Monroe and DeVon had arrived.

"Lyric! You back?" Monroe asked.

"Looks that way!" I laughed.

In a surprising act Monroe grabbed me happily and hugged me from behind.

"I'm so glad you're back nigga!" he said.

"Happy to see you too Roe," I laughed.

"Ric you back, nigga? What the f--k?! you can't answer your phone or nothin?" DeVon asked in concern.

"I didn't feel like talking to nobody," I said dropping my smile.

"Guys this is Ruby." I introduced "Ruby this is Monroe, and DeVon."

"Nice to meet you, welcome to the club house." DeVon says looking her up and down.

"Nice to meet you too." She says meeting his gaze with one of her own.

Really? Is she attracted to him? Nooo. Really? I asked on green screen.

What? He's cute in a weird Ludacris sorta way....he needs to brush his teeth though cuz they lookin kinda cakey and yellow. That's not hot. Ruby said in her confessional

"Ruby." I said in Spanish *" Cuidado "*

"What?" she asks innocently

"You know what," I say narrowing my eyes at her. "I can see it in your smile. Don't do it," I warned. "Trust me."

"Hey that's rude cuz I don't know what you're saying." DeVon pointed out looking back and forth from me to her. Ruby and I laughed.

"Where's Athena?" I asked.

"I don't know I don't keep up with that b---h, we broke up."

"Why?" I asked genuinely shocked.

"Because she's a whore who wants to f--k her next door neighbor."

"I can see this is going to be an interesting semester." Monroe said

"Well I'm going to finish unpacking and come join ya'll in the pool." DeVon declared. "I'm glad you're ok Lyric."

"Yea," I said unenthusiastically.

"He seems nice." Ruby offered "Funny."

"Don't f--k him," Monroe warned.

"Who said anything about f---ing him?" Ruby asked innocently

"Mmm hmmm." Monroe said narrow eyed. "I'll be back though." With that he returned to the house.

Whatever, my name is Lyric and I don't wanna hear it. I said in my confessional *Ruby, I love you but don't come complaining to me and Von I don't want to hear it from you either. Keep that s--t between ya'll.*

Athena arrived just as Monroe, DeVon and Anthony come out to the pool a few minutes later. Of course DeVon had forgiven Anthony. He always did. They got into tiffs a few times the last two semesters. DeVon would want to fight him one day, and a couple of days later they were best friends again. When Anthony came out, I got up to go pour myself another drink and to say hi to Athena. We touched cheeks and hugged.

"Oh yay! You're back, I was hopin' you would be. How are you?"

"I'm good."

"Ok, how are you really?" she asked.

I smiled and chuckled a little. "I'm dealing as best as I can." I said truthfully. "I don't want to talk about it though."

"Alright well if you change your mind. Let me know."

"Uh-huh"

"So are we rooming together?"

"No, I'm rooming with Ruby. I think you're with Monroe."

"Who's Ruby?"

"New roommate." I nodded toward the pool where Ruby and DeVon were in full frolic and flirt mode.

"Oh." Athena said noticing the same thing.

"I heard you guys broke up." I said pouring more Margarita into my cup.

"Yea...it was for the best though, I'll tell you about it later."

"Ok. You want a Margarita?"

"Sure, I'll join you guys in a minute."

"OK I'll leave it right here, with the green straw." I said and headed back to the pool.

"Lyric, you look good," DeVon said as I walked back outside. "You look like you lost a lot of weight."

"I have."

"Oh, congratulations."

"You look different, besides that too." Monroe said inspecting me "Like something is missing about you."

"Yea." DeVon agreed.

"25 pounds is what's missing," I said.

"Wow 25 pounds?" Ruby asked "Good for you."

"No, it's something else," Monroe said.

"What do you think it is Anthony?" DeVon asked. And so it begins...

"She's smiling and not pouting anymore..."

"That's it! she doesn't look depressed anymore!" Monroe exclaimed

"You were depressed?" Ruby asked. "Why?"

I switched the conversation into Spanish "I was fat and then pregnant, and then dealing with this piece of sh---t over there..." I nodded toward

Anthony "I was basically by myself, feeling ugly and unloved, no one understood, no one really cared."

"Hmmph. Well I'm here now, I got you meems."

"My name is Lyric," I corrected.

"Aye I'm sorry, Lyric." she laughed.

When Athena came outside, she greeted both Monroe and Anthony warmly, introduced herself to Ruby, she spoke to DeVon who acknowledged her simply by giving a less than enthusiastic. "What's up?" She asked how everyone's summer was and the conversation went from there. Monroe met a girl and started dating her exclusively. Which shocked everyone. DeVon apparently whored around in Miami for a while in May with Anthony before he came back to Cali and got beat down and hospitalized.

"Poor Ant." DeVon laughed "First he gets bopped over the head with a 40 oz by Ric, and then he gets f---ed up by someone else and hospitalized then he can't go nowhere, do nothing or even talk for like 2 months. Nigga can't catch a break."

When my prediction that Anthony was out celebrating, while I was so distraught I couldn't get out of bed was realized, I was pissed off and couldn't keep up the facade of being ok anymore.

"Poor Anthony huh?" I asked "Anthony was out partying and celebrating while I grieved over the death of my child. The one he pretty much forced me to conceive and then tortured me for 7 months because of. Yea, poor Anthony," I stood up. "He deserved to get that bottle smashed, and I wish whoever f---ed you up had killed you."

Everyone was silent as I walked away from the pool and up to my room. I had to spend 16 weeks breathing the same air as him, living in the same house as him, seeing him every damn day. Eighty thousand dollars wasn't enough, there wasn't any amount that could make me feel better.

I sat on the floor leaning against my bed, not wanting to get the blankets wet by sitting on it. I played with the cross ring on my finger, turning it around a little thinking about what could have been. She would be four months old right now, making noises that sound like words. My Breasts started to feel full again, I'd hoped the milk would have dried up by now but every now and then I still leaked.

"You alright?" Ruby asked coming in.

"Yea. I just couldn't stay down there." I chuckled "It was getting a little hard to breathe."

"Was it that bad last semester?" She asked sitting across from me.

"It was humiliating and I don't know why I keep expecting him and everyone else to care about my feelings," I laughed to hide the hurt.

"They're stupid. Don't trip off them. I'm here now. I got you."

"I really don't want to be here right now. Can we go somewhere else?" I asked.

"We've been drinking, who's gonna drive?"

"We can call a cab, or take the bus, I don't care, I just need to be away right now."

We took off without a word to anyone that we were leaving, but they saw us leave. I thought about inviting Athena so she's not stuck here with her ex boyfriend, but she was a reminder of everything too because she was there. Ruby and I took a cab to the beach, it was supposed to be a trip to go let ourselves be seen. Once we got there we immediately caught the attention of two Mexican guys. One was really tall like 6 foot 3 and the other was average height with very big arms. They were wary of the cameras at first but soon learned to ignore them. The muscled guy's name was Gunnar, he was from Texas and the tall guy was his cousin Aaron. We stuck together the four of us, drinking & laughing. We walked around Belmont park and rode the roller coaster and other rides.

Aaron was a perfect gentleman.He chased me to the shore and through the water before pretending he was going to tackle me but instead scooped me up and kissed me. It was refreshing and validating to finally feel desired. Ruby took pictures on her phone of us hugged up. She crooned about how we'd make a cute couple. Ocean washed and air dried hair with the glow of the sun in the background, I looked gorgeous. and with Aaron's face inclined toward mine, his lips brushing my cheeks, it looked like we were a couple. Ruby uploaded it onto Facebook and by the next day, there was talk about a new man in my life. We did look good together in pictures. I'd never thought of myself with a Mexican guy before, they never seemed to be attracted to me. Aaron was though. He asked about my tattoo and without getting into the drama of it all, I told him that my baby died. He apologized and changed the subject.

Ruby and Gunnar were in a world separate from us. He was more cholo than Aaron, which is what Ruby liked. Aaron was an altar boy growing up. He worked at an Auto-body shop in Chula Vista. As the night went on, we exchanged phone numbers and the boys drove us home. When we pulled up, Ruby and Gunnar stayed in the car and Aaron walked me to the door. He kissed me goodnight and made plans to hang out again the upcoming Friday. I couldn't wait.

The first week of classes were interesting. Second year theater students had to take a Musical Theater Audition class and perform in the showcase in the theater in front of an audience. I was too scared to ever sing lead at church how was I going to sing in front of an audience? I joined the stage crew to keep me out of the house more often. Friday came and I was excited about seeing Aaron, I didn't know where I was going on our date, if it was a date. I wasn't sure, I'd never actually been asked out on a date before. I'd had a couple boyfriends that I hung out with but none of them ever took me out, we just kicked it somewhere. By going out with Aaron that night I would be bailing on "family" dinner night. It was an established BFC tradition that at the beginning of the semester were reserved solely for us, to celebrate the start and end of an adventure. Athena would cook dinner, or sometimes we'd order a pizza or someone would make a taco shop or chinese food run. I would bake a cake and hope it didn't fall apart. DeVon would get the drinks and chasers and Monroe would set and clear the table and at the end of it all, Anthony was left with the dishes. The only problem this semester was I hated being around Anthony more than I did the previous two. I was disgusted by him and it made me sick to even hear his voice. My storyline, I already knew was, again tied to Anthony and how I'm coping. I still avoided Anthony at all costs but I still saw him watching me cautiously every time I walked into the room. The last time I stopped speaking to Anthony, I was at least polite and obliged a request like "Can you pass the salt?" Now I wouldn't even do that.

The producers told me they didn't have enough footage of everyone together. Meaning I needed to stay in and have dinner with the family. There couldn't be drama if I left with Aaron. Since technically this was my job I had to cancel but Ruby had the bright idea to invite Aaron and Gunnar here to the clubhouse. That way we would fulfill our obligation to the show by having all the roommates together, and satisfy my desire to see more of Aaron.

The guys came over after we had finished eating and were in the "chill" portion of the night. The rest of the house wasn't too thrilled about company coming over but I was. I used Aaron as a shield all night. I instructed him that he wasn't to be friendly with Anthony and if he was then he and I would have a problem.

"Is he your ex or somethin?" he asked.

"Or somethin'" I said "It's a lot to explain. And I'd rather not talk about it."

"Is there gonna be drama cuz we can just go somewhere else."

"There's not going to be drama," I insisted.

I introduced the guys to the rest of the house. We sat somewhere by ourselves and eventually made our way into the jacuzzi. We made small talk in between making out. Apparently the rest of the BFC were feeling ostracized in their own house and were annoyed but I didn't care. The boys decided that if Ruby and I could have company they could too. Before long, two white girls and an Asian girl were walking in the front door. Clearly, they were Monroe's connection. DeVon only knew hood rats and Anthony couldn't pull three girls. It really was a party, everyone was paired up except Athena who didn't seem to care and just curled up in her room studying with her headphones on.

DeVon was overly attentive to his girl, he had one of the white girls. The way he spoke and laughed out loud it was clear he was just trying to make someone jealous. I just couldn't tell if it was Athena or Ruby whose attention he was trying to get. Monroe's girl, the other white girl was named Heather and apparently that was his girlfriend and not just a random. She seemed sweet; not a wanna-be black kind of white girl but not super valley either. Heather was just normal and comfortable with herself. I liked her. The poor Asian girl was stuck with Anthony, she seemed to like him a little bit. She was laughing. Whether she was laughing at him or actually thought he was funny, I didn't know and I didn't care. Anthony flirting with other girls was a sight I was used to and had become numb to. If I didn't have any right to be jealous before, I sure didn't have a right to be upset now. Especially not while I was sitting on the lap of my way more attractive other.

Aaron rubbed my arms and told me I should get B.D.A going down my arm. The letters stood for Big Daddy Aaron. I laughed at his suggestion. I would never call a man "daddy" except my actual daddy and I told myself I would never get a guys name tattooed on me unless he was my husband. Maybe not even my husband because marriages end, husbands leave. The night ended with Monroe and his girlfriend in The Boom Boom room, Ruby and Gunnar hanging out in his car and me with Aaron cuddling in my bed. We didn't have sex. I was curious about it, I wanted to know if sex was better than what it had been with Anthony, but I wasn't ready for anyone to see my body, not with the C-section scar still visible and my stomach still a bit loose.

FIFTEEN

I hadn't heard from Aaron since that night he came over. Gunnar told Ruby that he'd gotten back with his ex girlfriend so I figured that was that. I was disappointed but it wasn't a big deal. I deleted his number and moved on with my life. By the end of the first month I'd grown a bit tired of Ruby's habits. Ruby was Monroe with a vagina. In addition to seeing Gunnar, she had a long time boo named Big. Whenever she heard that her Big was hanging around some other girls, they would be on the phone all day arguing about it, or he'd come over and sweet talk and hug and kiss on her trying to make up. It confused me because for a month, she had been seeing Gunnar and even started having sex with DeVon because DeVon said she couldn't handle it and she didn't think he could really do anything so they called each other's bluff. I asked her about her relationship with Big because it was hypocritical to me, being upset that a guy is doing something, when you're doing the exact same thing. She told me that she loved Big, he treated her really nice when they were together and bought her nice things but until he started acting right and put a ring on her finger then she was going to keep doing her. That just confused me more because in my mind, If you are trying to be with someone, you get your relationship together before the ring not after. Maybe that was just me. Ruby also had a few "friends" that we'd hang out with, just hang out with nothing more. Still, I'd take my car though just in case. A lot of these dudes were unemployed, lazy, hustlers, with a couple babies who were just trying to get on TV. They were the type of guys Anthony tried to imitate only uglier.

Ruby may have liked and had sex as much as a guy did but that was her business. Unlike DeVon and Monroe, who had dubbed her "The Headmaster", I didn't judge Ruby for her sexuality. She was the only one in the house who understood the hurt that I felt and the need to do anything to not feel it. As long as she had my back I really didn't care who she slept with. I'd sit back with my bottle, and let her do her.

The last week of September, as usual, Ruby and I were having our own little party at another spot apart from the rest of The BFC. There were no cameras that night, it was our day free from a smothering entourage. Athena had chosen to stay home and get ahead on homework. She really liked her classes that semester. Ruby and I met up with one of her "friends" and his two friends were with us, Ruby was so drunk that we had been asked to leave. I was drunk too but I was fighting it to keep my wits about me and fight off the advances of the two guys that were left for me to choose from. I was too drunk to even remember their names. I forgot right after we were introduced. These guys were old and dusty and hearing them tell me about how they "put it down" wasn't going to make me any less disgusted. They were talking about going to a hotel but that's where I wouldn't be going and Ruby was too drunk to stand so I wasn't going to let her go either. "You need to stop touching me." I snapped as one of them grabbed my belt loop to pull me closer to him. "Hey!" I called up to Ruby and her friend "Get yo boy before I break his nose!"

"Stop being so mean." Ruby slurred as her dude held her upright, both laughing at me "Can you wait a minute?" I asked her. They were a full block ahead of us. I was in heels, my feet were hurting and I couldn't walk fast. I would have taken them off and gone barefoot but I was trying to catch up with Ruby first.

"Girl, hurry up." Ruby laughed. They turned the corner and by the time I caught up they had disappeared into the dark parking lot. I called after her but she didn't respond. Did she really just leave me alone with a couple of randoms?

"They aiight." The guy that was pulling on me said "They prolly jus went somewhere to get it in."

"Yea." The second guy said "Come on. We can go someplace else and see wassup."

His eyes never left my cleavage.

"No." I said pulling out my phone walking forward. I called Ruby but her cell went straight to voicemail. I called out her name again and still no response.

"Don't trip off it." The first guy said "She's wit my boy."

"I'm not gon leave her."

"Come on." the second guy urged pulling on my arm.

"No. Let go of me." I started calling again and still no answer. I hung up just as I got an incoming from DeVon, we were in the parking lot next to the building they were in.

"Hello?" I asked. They were trying to pull me toward the parking lot but I wouldn't budge.

"No. Stop. Let go!" I commanded.

"Yo Lyric, Where you at?" DeVon asked.

"I'm on 7th and Broadway, in the parking lot next door. I can't find Ruby."

"Just come on. We'll wait for them in the car." The second guy insisted

"I'm not getting in the car with y'all." I told them.

"What you mean you can't find Ruby?" DeVon asked "Where'd she go?"

"I don't know she walked off with this dude and I don't know where she is. She left me with these two dudes who won't leave me alone."

The guys kept pullin at me but I wouldn't budge. I tried to dig my feet into the ground like a child would to pull away from their parent, but in six inch heels I couldn't stand long against their force and my ankle turned to the side, I collapsed and dropped my phone. They helped pull me up off the ground but I couldn't stand. I fell again and the first guy put my arm around his shoulder. I was allowing him to lead me but I wanted to go back to the street and he was trying to take me to where their car was parked. My self preservation instincts kicked in. I panicked and I tried to pull away but I couldn't get far. The second one grabbed me.

"DeVon!" I screeched at the top of my lungs hoping he was outside and could hear me or was still on the phone and could hear me. The second guy covered my mouth. I struggled and screamed at him to let go. I tried to move my face so his hand would slip below my top lip and I could bite him. His other hand was wandering in unwelcome places. I'd never been so scared in my life. I licked the hand that was covering my mouth and as a reflex he moved it to wipe it off. I screamed out DeVon's name again. Just as he had run up Monroe and Anthony in tow.

"Hey get off her!" DeVon shouted. He threw a punch and dude released me. I fell forward into Anthony's confused arms.

Monroe and DeVon were fighting my attackers. I was vaguely aware of a crowd having gathered to see and the sounds of sirens approaching.

"Are you ok?" Anthony asked. The genuine concern in his voice was something I'd never heard before.

"My ankle." I whimpered. I was in too much pain and too desperate to care that it was Anthony who was helping me.

"Where's Ruby?"

"She left me," I said.

"Hey, she needs help." Anthony said as about half a dozen cops rushed in our direction.

"What happened?" One of the officers asked.

"I don't know. I think they were trying to rape her. We heard her screaming and when we came over we found her like this." The alcohol and the energy I spent trying to get away from them made me dizzy. I almost fell backward but Anthony caught me and scooped me up in his arms.

I didn't think I could be any more pissed off. The incident was all over the internet and news stations by morning with pictures of DeVon and

Monroe being put in handcuffs along with my assailants, and me being carried away from the brawl by Anthony. You couldn't really tell what was happening. It looked a lot bigger than an even fight between four people. With a dozen cops and paramedics all over the scene, it looked a mess. I was getting phone calls from everyone in my entire family. The reports said that I was raped and beat and unconscious as retaliation for what happened to Anthony, which got everyone in a panic. I avoided all calls except my mother and father and told them to pass along that I was fine and I didn't want to talk to about it, it was too embarrassing. I didn't even want to talk to the police. I just wanted it to go away. Unfortunately I had to tell them what happened, they were involved now and if I didn't DeVon and Monroe would get in trouble. I was so humiliated by it all.

Anthony vehemently denied the public speculation against him, outraged that anyone would even think he would do something like that. Despite Anthony's denial and my affirmation of his statement, speculation continued regardless and there was nothing we could do about it. You would think Team Lyric vs Team Anthony was Tupac vs Biggie the way audiences were going on about us in the comments, arguing with each other insulting either myself or Anthony depending on who's side the commenters were on.

I know what almost happened but it didn't, and I would really rather have forgotten the whole mess. I wouldn't allow myself to show weakness on the camera so I swallowed my feelings and put on a brave face for the audience watching at home.

I hoped Anthony didn't think just because he helped me that I would forgive anything or stop hating him. I literally threw up when he put me down, sick from the scent of him... or maybe the alcohol... maybe both or maybe from the whole situation. I found out that Ruby wasn't hurt at all. I worried about her the entire night I spent in the emergency room waiting to see if my ankle was just broken or sprained, but when she came home the next morning, ignorant of everything that had transpired, she said she actually went back to a hotel room with that guy. She left me with two strange men, thinking it was funny, and caught a bike taxi to the Ramada with the third. I refused to speak to or even hear her apology. Athena went in on her though. She hadn't liked Ruby from the beginning and was just waiting for a good reason to tell her exactly what she felt. Ruby tried to step to Athena. but security grabbed her before she could. Ruby didn't like her either, Mostly because DeVon still wanted her. Ruby thought that after being with her, DeVon would be thirsty for her instead. She made a good show of trying to attack Athena, screaming and cussing and swinging trying to move away from security. Athena was an advanced martial artist and would have had no problem embarrassing Ruby without even throwing a punch. Monroe jumped on the bandwagon and started clowning Ruby too while DeVon stood there and laughed. She looked to me to defend her but I was silent. I should have, but I didn't. I was too upset and honestly some of what they were saying was true. I'd thought them myself but I never said them out loud.

If you didn't want to be called a hoe then you shouldn't be spreadin em like peanut butter. You a trollop, hoe. Monroe laughed in his confessional

I laughed at his use of the word "trollop."

Who'd want to get serious with a chick that every dude on the street done been with? DeVon asked in his confessional. *I might smash again though* he laughed *just because I can.*

You call a cow a cow and a pig a pig and someone who has had more sexual partners than a porn star... what do you call them? She should at least get paid for it. Athena said in her confessional.

Now Ruby was on the outside and I clung, once again, to The BFC. They were sympathetic, at the moment, to my physical pain. I refused to use crutches except as a weapon against DeVon and Monroe. I still ignored Anthony and whenever he tried to join in I stopped laughing and hobbled away.

Grateful as I was for his assistance that night, it didn't make up for anything. It didn't undo anything. I knew enough about Anthony by now to know, his consideration of me never lasted and he never extended any courtesy without expecting a reward. My attitude made it clear that there would be no reward.

I was still hesitant to completely thaw against the roommates. If anything, with the absence of Ruby, I was more alone now than I ever was. It was frustrating not being able to go to the gym and work out. I couldn't really do anything aside from study. I had to quit greenpeace because I was unable to stand at the locations and make my weekly quota. I bought a wheelchair to move around the house more easily, and the boys built me a ramp to get up and down the stairs but whenever I wasn't in my wheelchair, the boys used it, as a toy. They'd roll each other down the ramp into things set up as bowling pins the more dangerous the more fun. They'd also run out the house pushing each other to the edge of the pool and then tip the chair forward tossing each other. I would yell at them about it because often my chair would end up in the pool as well. But they'd playfully tell me to shut up and relax.

Athena was the most considerate and we'd study together and she'd help me with math. We finally talked about things. I told her that I did appreciate her calls over the summer but explained that I wasn't in a mental place to answer. What would I have said? That was I ok? I wasn't ok. I told her that Anthony hadn't called not once the entire summer, I wouldn't have answered but it would have at least shown that he'd had the human decency to check on me. I asked her how she felt about DeVon's trysts with Ruby, she was unphased and unthreatened by the development. In fact she found it amusing because DeVon was so obviously trying to make her jealous. I wasn't surprised at her composure she was always more mature than him anyway. She told me that they broke up because his insecure jealousy finally got the better of him and Athena had had enough of his immature tantrums. He even gave her an ultimatum: Stop hanging out with her guy friends that like her and obviously want to have sex with her,(according to DeVon at least) OR they were done. She didn't choose him. Now he was dead set on making her jealous.

A couple of weeks later, I received two early birthday presents. First, I was approved for an apartment in Little Italy for $1,700 a month, I could move in on November first and the second present came in the form of a six foot tall golden knight, with deep cavernous dimples and a smile a mile long. I had been hoping that my Freakboy would find me for weeks and one day he just walked into the restaurant like it was nothing. There was a line around the corner of people waiting to get in the restaurant. People wanted to come in and take a chance at meeting one of the BFC. The girls would give out their numbers to the guys, if their guy of choice wasn't there, they'd ask us to pass it along. Even girls who thought that DeVon was still with Athena didn't care and wanted his attention. There were guys who came to see Athena and I as well, some commenting negatively on my weight loss saying they liked me with a little more meat, because they were BBW. Others were more inclined toward me because of the weight loss. Because of my ankle, and the boot around my foot, I was relegated to hostess rather than server. I had just clocked out and was heading out to go shopping for a dress to wear to the season 2 premiere party, that was the next night, when I walked out the door and someone grabbed me and pulled me into a hug before I could see who it was.

"What the?" I shouted pulling back to see who it was. The minute I laid eyes on him, My monotonous existence suddenly became a brand new life. Trey was back.

"You jackass don't scare me like that!" I said jumping into his arms

"My bad." He laughed lifting me in the air and squeezing me tight.

"Oh I missed you!"

"I missed you too."

Uninhibited by the fact that we were in public in full view of people with camera phones and digital cameras I met his face with mine and kissed him. He returned the kiss full force backing me against the wall next to the door both of his hands gripped my bottom, both my legs wrapped around his waist as he pressed against me. Every nerve in my body was on fire. It was only when I tried to lock my right foot with my left that I pulled away hissing in pain.

"You ok?"

"Yea, it's my ankle." I said unwrapping my legs from around him and putting them back on solid ground. He looked down at the brace on my left foot and jumped back.

"What did you do to yourself?" He asked.

"I'm surprised you didn't hear about it."

"Nah. Baby Daddy do this to you?"

"No..it's a long story I don't want to go there." Thinking about it made me panic and uneasy.

"What are you doing here?" I asked "You with some people?"

"Nah, I came here for you. I told you I'd find you when I got out." He smiled. "I came by yesterday and they said you'd be here today."

I fought back a smile and, instead, narrowed my eyes at him and scowled.

"You got out in May. It's October." I folded my arms across my chest.

He laughed at my fake indignity.

"I know, my bad." he said grabbing me by my hips and pulling me against him. "I had to get some stuff situated first, and you weren't even here in May."

"Are you here to stay now?"

"I'm going where you goin." He said looking down at me. His eyes wandered all over my face and my neck to my breasts back up to my face.

"What you doing the rest of the day?" I asked.

"Whatever you want to do." He said. I lost my breath with him that close to me, my heart raced and my bones ached.

"Wanna go back to the house?" I asked.

"Let's go." he said. He picked my cane up off of the ground where I dropped it and let me lead the way to my car.

Like James and Ruby and Monroe and DeVon and Anthony, Trey was excited and impressed by my dark gold Audi convertible with black leather interior.

"Oh hell yea!!!" he shouted. "You gotta let me drive!"

"I what?" I laughed.

"Baby, please? C'mon," he pleaded.

I rolled my eyes and smirked in amusement. I held the keys out to him and he snatched them excitedly and thanked me with a kiss.

"You're the best." He opened the passenger door and helped me in, then closed it before jogging over to the drivers side. I'd removed my work shirt to reveal the black tank top underneath.

"This is sexy." He growled as the engine came to life. "How much this set you back?"

"Nothin' It was a gift."

"From who?!"

"The makers of Audi, I'm their spokeswoman."

"Word?"

"Yep. My first commercial ad airs tomorrow during the premiere of season two."

"Doin' big things now. huh?"

"Yep," He glanced at me eyeing me from head to toe, I played with the collar of my shirt to draw his attention to my exposed cleavage. He smiled and looked away back to the road ahead of us. The car lurched forward at an accelerated speed. Someone was in a hurry to get back to the house.

We didn't stop to greet anybody, and Trey didn't have the patience to wait as I took one step at a time, he picked me up and carried me over his shoulder to the only room with a door.

I closed the blinds so that it was dark inside, I was still very insecure about my scar and I didn't want him to see it.

"No, let some light in here." he said "I wanna see you."

"I want to keep it dark." I said "I don't want you to see where they cut me."

He walked over to me and slowly slid my shirt off and gently pulled my jeans and panties down and then he opened the blinds and let the light in. I covered my stomach. He grabbed my wrists and then looked me in the eye.

"There is nothing about you that's ugly or unattractive." He assured me "Let me see you." I hesitated but I allowed him to remove my hands and see my body in all it's scarred glory and rather than flinch away like I did every time I saw it, he kissed it.

Trey and I had been waiting for this moment for two years almost since the minute we met. Being with him was everything. I finally understood what sex was about. Everything I felt for him and he felt for me combined and created this feeling of ecstasy as it poured out of us and into each other. I'd never felt anything like this my entire life. I don't mean just physically, I mean emotionally and mentally. We went upstairs when it was daylight, 3 o'clock in the afternoon, but we didn't stop until it was dark. We'd fallen asleep a couple of times woke up and had sex again until we ran out of condoms and energy. After that last time we slumped down on the floor next to the window we'd opened to let air in. I leaned my head against his shoulder too weak to get up. We sat there in silence for a minute.

"I love you," he said breaking the silence. I waited for a laugh, I searched his face for a smile. "I mean that," he said searching my expression.

"For real?" I smiled.

"Hell yeah!"

"I love you too."

He smiled like it was the best news he'd heard all day and kissed me. I was ready to go again and kinda leaned over but he pulled away

"Baby, I'm hungry and we don't have any more condoms."

I laughed. "Yea I'm hungry too."

"Come on let's go." He said but neither of us made a move to leave. "You didn't move," he laughed.

"I don't want to go downstairs," I whined.

"Why?"

"Because I'm in a happy bubble right and the minute we go downstairs, we gotta face the outside world."

"I got you though."

"What happens when you go away again?" I said "I just want to live in this space with you for as long as I have you."

"Ok." he said moving to stand up and face me. "First of all, I already told you, I'm not going anywhere." he held his hand out to help me up. It was difficult coming up off of the floor on one foot but I managed. "Second of all, I love you so there's no way I'm ever leaving you again."

"Pinky promise?" I asked holding up my pinky to him. He smiled his leading man smile and locked his pinky finger with mine.

"Come on, let's go eat."

After I changed clothes and fixed the frizz the friction created in my hair, Trey and I headed out to TGI Fridays. That night I finally felt like I was going to be ok, that things were going to be better now that Trey was back. We caught up on everything that happened in our lives since the last time we saw each other. I told him everything, how I felt then, how I felt now, and he didn't judge me for continuing to be intimate with Anthony back then, he understood the emotional need to feel wanted especially when you're at your most vulnerable and insecure. I stopped short of the night I lost her, I didn't want to cry in the restaurant. He could see that it wasn't something I wanted to discuss further so he didn't push it. He apologized for not trying harder to get in contact and for not being there.

"F--k that nigga" He dismissed "You can have my baby if you want." I laughed.

"I'm serious, we can go start right now, let's go." he joked.

"You're stupid," I smiled.

"Ok so what's been up with you? Let's talk about that now."

He told me that he was sentenced to 2 years for 2nd degree aggravated assault, he served less than a year and was on parole for the remainder of his sentence which was only a year considering the time spent on house arrest. He wasn't allowed to leave the country and had to get permission to leave the state. He had gotten a job at a barber/tattoo shop that someone hooked him up with and was trying to save up to get his own place. He had been staying at his older sister, Jen's house, but her baby daddy didn't like him and she kicked him out, his grandmother had no room because his younger sister Keisha, was living there with her two children, and being on parole he couldn't live with his mom because her husband had a criminal record, he also said issues with his mom were too deep to be put aside. He wouldn't elaborate on exactly what the issue was and I could tell it made him uncomfortable so I didn't push.

"So where have you been living?" I asked concerned.

He took a deep breath and exhaled "With this girl...." He said "Who think's she is my girlfriend."

My face turned cold, and the air around me went thin and I started to feel dizzy. The evening started out so full of hope and now that hope came crashing down.

"You have a girlfriend?"

"No, I just let her think that because I don't have anywhere else to go and she's letting me stay."

I couldn't look him in the eye, I didn't want him to see my expression

"I don't care about her. I love you , but what can I do right now?"

I stayed silent, processing the situation.

"Baby, please tell me what you're thinking." He said trying to meet my gaze I looked up at him, trying to decide if I wanted to make this offer or not. I didn't want him to be with me simply because I had my own place and he needed a place.

"How long until you have enough to move out?"

"I don't know, a couple months."

"You can't live in the clubhouse, but I'd been looking into getting my own place for a couple months already and I found out yesterday that I can move in on the first...why don't you stay there until you get on your feet."

"How much a month?"

"Seventeen hundred."

"I can't even afford half of that right now and I don't want to live off of your money. That's all yours."

"Oh you'll be paying the light bill and cable and I'll pay the rent."

He smiled at me. "You'd do that for me?"

"I just want you to be in a place where you're not stressed out, where you don't have to put up with a chick you don't want just so you have a place to stay."

"You are an amazing woman, you know that?"

I smiled "And I don't want you to think that you're obligated to be with me either."

"Obligated? Are you kidding me? I want to be with you."

"Are you sure?"

He paused and his expression changed from happy to curious.

"Why do you do that?"

"Do what?"

"Doubt yourself. You must not see yourself very clearly, any man would be lucky to have you by his side. Stop being so surprised when I tell you that I do."

I tried not to smile, but I felt my cheeks blush. "Ok."

"So the first?"

"Yep."

I had a renewed sense of security in my life. There was nothing that could bring me down off the cloud I was on. In 3 weeks I would finally have him all to myself. Life was a good. He stayed the night with me. There was something to be said about falling asleep in a man's arms. This was the first time in my life that I had. My ex didn't sleep, Anthony jumped up, showered after sex and then went to his bed to sleep. Trey and my breathing synced and our hearts beat to the same rhythm. It was the first peaceful night's sleep I'd had in months.

SAMANTHA SANCHEZ

Sixteen

The next morning he kissed me goodbye and went home to change. I pouted at the thought of him going back to that other girl, whoever she was.

"3 weeks and I won't have to deal with her anymore." He reminded me. "I'll see you tonight." I held up my pinky and he locked it, kissed me again and left to catch the bus. I changed the sheets on the bed in The Boom Boom Room and febreezed and vacuumed the carpet and disinfected every surface, making it fresh and new for the next person who came in here. Then I showered and headed out. I needed to get my hair and my dress ready for tonight. I was so happy, I wasn't even bothered by Anthony's existence at the moment. I wondered if Trey was using me the way he was using this girl he was living with, and then I banished the thought from my head. I've known him for two years and he has never given me any reason to believe that he didn't care about me. He's always treated me with respect and I've never gotten that sense that I was just a game to him. He's always been very genuine with me. Trey said that he loves me and I believed him. I believed him because I was love with him and I would do whatever I could to keep him in my life.

In the end, I decided not to even go to the premiere. I'd take advantage of having the house to myself. I prefered the alone time with my Freakboy anyway. Around 8pm, I put on a tight pair of jeans, a tank top and a zip up hoodie. I let my hair stay down in it's natural wavy curls and headed out to pick up Trey. I was too impatient to see him to let him take the bus back over here so I pulled up at the shop where he worked. It was a barber shop/hair salon with an area for tattoos, next door to Tradewinds Liquor store in Oak Park. Not exactly the safest neighborhood, but I grew up in unsafe neighborhoods, they didn't scare me.

"What's good wit you, ma?" One of the guys said "Can I help you with something?" He looked me up and down. He was brown skinned, of average height with a stocky build and a gold capped teeth.

"Put your eyes back in your head, nigga." Trey laughed scooping me up in his arms and kissing me hello. "Let me finish cleaning up my station and I'll be ready."

"Ok." I replied.

"My bad, T, I didn't know that was you." The guy with the gold capped teeth revealed.

"Yea that's all me." He laughed.

"Hello. I'm Dante" His friend introduced. There were 3 other people in the shop. A dark skinned dude with baby dreads whose name was Kevin. The white girl with muddy brown hair and flower patterned nails was Trina. The short stocky dude with a du-rag was named Omar.

"I'm Lyric, nice to meet you."

"Didn't I see you on TV?" Omar asked.

"Yea." I said nodding and sitting down on the sofa against the window. "Probably."

"That's right, you on that show... Breakfast Club right?" Trina asked adjusting her station.

"You are correct."

"So we finna be on TV right now?" Dante asked as the cameras came in behind me.

"Shout out to mama, and all the homies in SouthEast daygo. My grandmama all my aunties and my cousins "

"You're not supposed to talk to the camera, nigga" Trey laughed. "Pretend they aren't there."

"Oh my bad."

"Hey, but that show is crazy from what I've seen. I haven't really kept up with it. Is all that real? Or is it a set up?" Trina asked.

"No, that stuff actually happened." I said.

"When do the next episode come on?" Kev asked "Now that I know you, I'ma start paying attention."

"Wednesday night at 8 I think. They'll have a marathon of the first season all weekend if you need to catch up. I don't really watch it myself."

"Cuz you lived it," Omar said.

"Exactly."

"I feel it."

"So how's the baby?" Trina asked. She must not have heard. A lot of people hadn't if they didn't keep up with the show. "Was it a boy or a girl?"

"You ready to go, babe?" Trey asked saving me from having to talk about it anymore.

"Hey hold up let me get a picture. If that's cool." Dante asked

"Why you asking me?" Trey laughed.

Dante turned to me. "Do you mind? It's not everyday somebody famous comes through."

"Sure." I said standing up.

Dante handed Trey his camera and suddenly everyone flocked around me to be in the picture. I threw up the peace sign and smiled while the guys threw up whatever hand signs they were throwing up and Trina made a kissy face.

"Do me a favor, take a pic of me and Trey." I asked Dante handing him my phone cued up for a pic "Come on babe."

Trey smiled and wrapped his arms around me from behind and I stuck my hands in my sweatshirt pocket, the top of my head touched the bottom of his chin. Dante snapped the pic.

"Aww ain't that cute!" he teased.

"Shut up!" Trey laughed.

"Thank you." I said taking my phone back "Hey if you guys aren't doing anything for Halloween, We're having a party at On Broadway that night. It's a $20 cover charge but If you guys want to come I can put your name on the list and you can get in for free."

"Hella!" Kev said "I'm down."

"I might could make that," Dante said.

"Sounds cool." Trina answered.

"Aiight, I'm out." Trey said slappin' hands with the guys and waving giving Trina a side hug.

"It was nice meeting you." I shouted back as Trey ushered me out the door.

"Can I drive again?" Trey asked. I sighed again and handed over the keys to my Audi.

We stopped at the grocery store and using his EBT card we got food to cook and went back to the house. He insisted that I not pay for the groceries.

"Ya'll look nice." Trey said as the roommates piled through the living room dressed for a night out. "Where's everybody going?"

"It's the premiere for season 2 at Decos tonight."

"Oh word? Why ain't we going babe?"

"Because last semester isn't something I think back on fondly." I said

"Why? We had some good times," Anthony said.

"You would say that," I snarked.

"Ay, blood. How's that jaw?" Trey asked. "Heard you begged like a b---h for it to stop." I laughed a little. The rest of the house looked from Trey to Anthony to see who would say what next.

"Man, whatever, enjoy my leftovers." He nodded toward me

"The f--k did you just say?" I asked. my hand gripped the knife I was holding to cut the onions. I imagined tossing it and landing it in one of his eyes.

"He can have you. You're my gift to him."

"Your gift?" Trey said "Blood, You really gon stand there and act like it's

PRODIGAL   136 not killin to you to see her with me?" Trey moved behind me and wrapped me tight in his arms, taunting Anthony with his presence and smoothly removed the knife from my hand and lay it on the counter away from me.

"I don't care."

"Is that why you look like a lost puppy every time she's in the room, blood?"

"A lost puppy? Never."

"Hey you did say you missed her, Ant." DeVon announced

"And you said were mad that you guys never had a 4 hour sex marathon," Monroe added.

"No, I didn't." Anthony defended, embarrassed that he had been called out Trey laughed "Nigga mad cuz he can't hit it right. Blood get the f--k outta here you makin my girl sick at the sight of you."

"Man whatever," Anthony pouted.

"B---h ass nigga. Talkin bout a gift. Like you wasn't always gonna be mine no matter what position he held." Trey laughed "Yo, disrespect her again, blood, and you gon have more than a few broken bones and stitches to worry about."

I laughed. I loved hearing Trey speak up for me, I loved hearing him call me his. It made me tingle all over. Eventually, the housemates left and Trey and I were alone in the house. No camera crew, no security. We ate and talked about what we both wanted for our future and ended up making love in the jacuzzi and again in The Boom Boom Room upstairs.

"What are you doing next weekend?" I asked him as we lay on our sides staring into each other's eyes.

"You tell me." he said moving a piece of hair from my cheek and tucking it behind my ear.

"Well it's my birthday and my cousins are taking me to Vegas."

"For real? It's your birthday? How old are you going to be?"

"Twenty-Three. You want to go?"

"To Vegas? Hell yea! What day we taking off?"

"Next Friday and coming back Sunday night."

"Sounds fun. I gotta check with my P.O. though. See if I can get a pass."

"When are you gonna ask?"

"I gotta meet with him Monday morning, I'll see what's up then."

"I love you," I said.

"I love you too." he replied smiling. From the way he was looking at me you would think I was the most precious thing in the world to him.

"MiMi, Come on!" James called as I walked out of my room ready for some CQT the next night. James was my heart. He'd called me every day last summer after I lost the baby to check on me. He didn't care that I didn't want to see anybody. He wouldn't let me wallow. On the days I didn't answer, the days I just wanted to die from the pain of the loss and humiliation, James came over, picked me up and took me to the waters at Mission Bay. He helped me know that life would go on. That it's ok to hurt but I can't let the hurt kill me. James was the only one I was ok with crying around. He was against me coming back for the third season, but supported my decision and he and his girlfriend Jaycee, were my favorite people on my mom's side of the family. We came up with Cousin Quality Time so that through all the chaos of school and football and filming, we made sure to have time for each other. We'd do something I wanted to do and the next time we'd do something he wanted to do. He came up with the idea but I enforced it. Tonight we were going to see Romeo and Juliet on stage

"My name is Lyric!" I corrected walking down the stairs one step at a time, careful not to put too much pressure on my left foot.

"Your name is Naomi Marie Reyes." He said "No-No or MiMi for short."

"I changed it!" My voice still playfully yelling at him.

"I don't care!"

I laughed when I got down to him "Hi my heart."

"What's up, Noe?" he pulled me into a hug and squeezed me affectionately.

"You ready?"

"Yea. let's go."

"Bye ya'll." James said waving politely to everyone else scattered around the living room kitchen and backyard. Anthony hid in his room. We stopped for dinner at Los Pancho's downtown before heading to the show. James, like Trey wouldn't allow me to drive my own car when he was with me. They were in love with the way they looked behind the wheel.

"So how you doin' MiMi?" James asked eating the complimentary chips that were placed on the table for us and pushing the basket toward me. He wanted to make sure I ate. I had developed a habit of not eating all the time. It wasn't a conscious decision. I didn't have an eating disorder. I just wasn't hungry and I didn't want to eat. I'd go a whole day without eating anything except maybe a cracker but then get hungry around midnight and then go get something from the taco shop.

"I'm alright I guess." I said "I try to stay out of the house as much as I can. Keep myself occupied. Now that I'm not hanging out with Ruby anymore, I'm usually by myself."

"I'm still surprised you didn't beat the hell out of Ruby."

"You and everyone else. I just couldn't there's too much history between us.I don't think she actually realized how f---ed up she was at the time. Like if she knew what was going to happen, I don't think she'd have left me with them."

"I guess, So you ready for your showcase yet?"

"God no." I laughed nibbling on a chip myself.

"Why not?"

"I know the songs. I'm just nervous."

"You'll be alright." He assured me. "You got a beautiful voice. Just picture the auditorium is empty and you're just singing for yourself."

"That might work," I shrugged.

"It's what I do when I play football. I imagine that I'm just on the street playing with my friends and the kids in the neighborhood. It helps take the pressure off."

"So you just tune out the roaring crowds?"

"I pray before I get on the field and I ask God for peace and he calms the nerves. I start to feel excited and ready and I go out there and I play and have fun."

"Hmm." I responded. I wasn't really in the mood to talk about God.

"So when are you coming back to church?" Clearly, that didn't matter to James.

"I'm not ready yet." I said as the waitress placed our drinks in front of us. I had a giant strawberry margarita and James was unhappily stuck sipping on a sprite. He would much rather have had a drink but I told him if he was going to drive he wasn't allowed even a sip. I don't care about legal limits, not in my car.

"Why not?" he asked.

I shrugged "I'm just not. I'm still too pissed off."

"That's why you need to come to church." He laughed "Are you reading your bible?"

"I didn't bring my bible to the clubhouse."

"Why not? I bet you brought the entire Twilight series with you."

"I actually read Twilight," I pointed out.

"You need to be reading the bible."

I rolled my eyes playfully, but deep down I knew. I should have turned to God with my pain but I didn't believe I could be healed from something like this. More to the point, I didn't believe I should be. I needed the pain as a reminder to never have sympathy for a guy like Anthony ever again. All the good men were either taken, gay or in my family. Except for Trey. I

139   SAMANTHA SANCHEZ

doubted Trey would have put me through so much if I'd been pregnant with his baby and so far he's proved to be most attentive.

Seeing Romeo and Juliet for the first time on stage was nice. Not much different from the movie. Which is probably why Franco Zeffereli's version was hailed as THE movie adaptation over Baz Luhrman's with Leonardo Dicaprio. I couldn't wait for the day that I was up on a stage performing. It's the only thing I looked forward to in the future. The only thing I KNEW I could make happen if I worked hard enough. If given the opportunity I'd like to play the nurse in Romeo and Juliet : she's the only one who had any sense.

"I couldn't understand a thing they were saying, could you?" James asked on the way out the theater.

"I got some of it. I translated one of Juliet's monologues last year so I could understand how to perform it better. It's just bigger words used to say something more poetically than you would in regular conversation."

"You're really into all this stuff huh?"

"Yep. Well theater not Romeo and Juliet specifically."

"What's wrong with R&J?"

"Nothing is wrong with it. I just don't believe it. According to 'Shakespeare in Love' Romeo and Juliet was supposed to display 'the very truth and nature of love' but to me all it displayed was a couple of whiny teenagers."

James laughed as we climbed into my car. "I mean they met, married and killed themselves over each other in a week. How do we know that they would have still loved each other after a month or even a year? They didn't even give themselves a chance to get to know each other. They killed themselves over what could have been a summer romance."

"True."

"They were teenagers. Everything seems life and death when you're in your teens. In this case, Romeo and Juliet just made it literal. Which is completely ridiculous if you ask me. I wish my daughter would..." I cut off once we got to the car.

The analytical and playful atmosphere that had just been, vanished. I found myself thinking about Tiana. I tried so hard not to sometimes because it hurt too much. I thought about the life she and I would have had. Me as a mother to a child with so much ahead of her. My eyes started to burn with tears and I had no alcohol to help wash them away.

"You ok?" James asked.

"Will it ever stop hurting?" I asked him in a moment of allowed vulnerability.

"I don't know Meems." He said putting his arm around me and I leaned my head on his shoulder "I think it will get easier to bare over time, you just need to pray."

I sniffed and he wiped the tear from my cheek. We sat there in silence for a minute, my cousin just held me. He knew I couldn't be preached to right now. So he was just there.

"So, you excited for your birthday?" he asked starting the car after I lifted my head up.

"Yea," I said trying to keep my tone light.

"Anyone of The BFC coming?" he asked.

"The producers want everyone to go. To see how everyone gets along in Sin City. They're paying for most of it so I agreed. Though, I drew the line with Anthony." I answered suddenly remembering Trey "Oh! and I got one more person possibly coming."

"Who?"

"Trey."

"Who is Trey?!" He asked his voice rising as the protective side of him took over.

"He's my.......... boyfriend," I laughed.

"Boyfriend?" he asked in mock outrage. "Since when? How long have you known him? Does your mama know?"

"It's a recent development but one that's been coming for a long while."

"Well I want to meet him." He said suspiciously. I just laughed and smiled the whole way home.

James and I argued over the musical selection for the ride. I despised hip hop most of the time, that's all the boys and Ruby ever listened to in the house. I preferred Goth Rock or Heavy Metal. I found that the music had a numbing effect on my spirit. James didn't like any of that. He called it, and me, evil. He said Marilyn Manson was the devil and Disturbed lived up to its name. As a compromise we listened to Soul. Soul I could deal with. Jill Scott, Erykah Badu and 90's R&B, I could listen and sing along to without any annoyance. We sang along to The Fugees "Killing me softly."

"You gonna be ok, Naomi." James said as we parked in the gated driveway in front of the house I just nodded in response. "I know. It's gonna take time." I repeated that mantra to myself over and over for the past five months.

"You gotta remember to pray, girl." He said enthusiastically, trying to lift my mood. I managed a small smile as we climbed out the car. He walked around to my side and handed me the keys, pulled me to him and squeezed me rocking me side to side.

"I love you cuz"

"Me too." I said.

He let go of me, kissed me on the top of my head. "I'll see you Friday." I thank God for my cousin. I don't know what I'd do without him.

Walking into the house, I thought I had walked back into season one because all I heard was DeVon yelling at Athena. It'd been clear since day one of this semester that DeVon wasn't over Athena or maybe wasn't ready to let her go. He threw other women in her face to try and get a reaction out of her. The exact same thing that Anthony would do to me except, unlike me, Athena would keep her composure about it. If she did care then nobody would know. She told me that she didn't think they had a future together right now. That she felt he still had a lot more growing up to do. I guess DeVon just wouldn't accept that. He expected her to sit back and pine over him.

"See?! I told you she's a whore!" DeVon shouted as I walked into the house. "Call me what you want." Athena said walking away. I walked over to the breakfast bar and to my happy surprise Trey was standing there next to Monroe and his girlfriend, Heather.

"Hey." I said hugging Trey "What's going on here?"

"I don't know" he shrugged." I just got here two minutes ago.

"Roe." I said "What's up?" I nodded toward the fight. DeVon was the only one shouting.

Athena was clearly trying to get away from the situation but DeVon kept following her in and out of her room.

"Athena got a new man. She brought him to the premiere last night and DeVon been mad about it ever since"

"Uh-Oh."

"Yea, he's the neighbor guy that Von was trippin on before they broke up."

"She says she hasn't had sex with him yet. That they're waiting." Heather explained "But DeVon says she's lying."

"Wow."

"Was they poss to get back together?" Trey asked.

"I don't know." I shrugged "Not that I know of."

"Maybe he should have thought of that before he put his hands on her." Monroe said.

"Word?" Trey asked

"He what?!" Heather asked outraged.

"According to DeVon, he 'Chris Browned' her." Monroe explained.

"For real?" Trey asked.

I shook my head "Exaggeration." I said watching the chaos in front of me. I wondered if this what I looked like last semester when I was yelling at Anthony all the time.

"He didn't beat her to hell but he pushed her and held her down on the bed. Her hookah fell over and she got burned by the coal but he still wouldn't let her up."

"Oh My God!" Heather said outraged.

"Hold up, isn't it the female who usually exaggerates the situation?" Trey asked.

"DeVon is dramatic. He exaggerates everything good or bad," Monroe explained.

"But even if he didn't do what Chris Brown did to Rihanna, that still had to be scary for her." Heather sympathized

"Yea." I agreed.

"I BET YOUR WHITE BOY GOT A SMALL...." DeVon shouted kicking the bathroom door. I wondered what he was more mad about, that Athena's new man was white or that she had a new man at all. I mean if it was that he was white, then he certainly didn't have any room to talk because he likes to have sex with white girls so what's the difference? I hate double standards.

Athena and DeVon were an odd pairing from the start.

"I thought I had anger issues," I commented pouring myself a glass of orange juice.

"You do!" Monroe insisted "You busted a half full glass forty over Anthony head last semester. And you snatched the chick he was smashing and dragged her across the floor."

Heather's mouth fell open and Trey looked amused and impressed

Poor white girl from La Jolla. Monroe joked on screen I brought her to a house full of crazy niggas from the hood. We are such stereotypes sometimes. He shook his head.

"Hormones." I shrugged turning to add vodka to the orange juice "I was pregnant and pissed off."

"When did you turn into a gangsta though?" Trey asked.

"When my tolerance level got to zero and never went up."

"You have a baby?" Heather asked. "Aww how old?"

"I don't have a baby," I corrected.

"But you just said...." Monroe caught the evil expression on my face when I looked up at him.

"Babe." Monroe said shaking his head to silence his girlfriend.

"Ohh." Heather said. Realization clicking in her brain. "I'm so sorry."

"Don't worry about it." I said drinking some more

"What'd he do? Why'd you hit him with the bottle" Heather asked. Trey was amused by my craziness.

"He was being himself" I said drinking big gulps from my cup. Trying not to remember the night that cost me the life of my child.

"He got caught smashin' a chick in her bed," Monroe revealed.

"What's wrong?" Trey asked as I quickly poured another cup.

"Nothin." I said not looking at him while raising my cup to take another drink. "She would have be going on six months." I said answering Heather's earlier question. With one last curse and kick at the door DeVon gave up yelling for the moment.

"You comin' Ant?" He asked storming by. I didn't even notice Anthony was sitting on the couch the whole time. Strangely, watching me more than the argument because he was jerked back to attention when DeVon said his name. DeVon rushed passed everyone in the kitchen and out the door. Anthony tagging along behind him like a puppy.

"Glad that's over." Heather said. "You ready to go?" She asked Monroe

"Yea. C'mon." He said. "Later Lyric." He waved "Alright then Trey." They slapped hands and Monroe was gone.

"What are you doing here, by the way?" I asked.

"I couldn't stand being in that house with her anymore." He said wrapping his arms around me. "Is it cool if I stay here with you again?"

"I don't mind." I said leaning up to kiss him. "Let me go check on Athena first and I'll meet you upstairs in my room."

"Ok." With another kiss, I slid past him and he smacked my butt again before I could get out of reach. I knocked on the bathroom door "Thee, you alright?"

"I'm good," she said lightly. "Did you have fun with your cousin?"

"Yea. It was cool. You gonna stay in there all night?"

"No. Just a little while longer. I'm trying to finish up some homework and I don't feel like moving."

"You want to talk about it?"

"Not right now. Maybe later."

"Ok. I'm gonna be upstairs with Trey then."

"Ok, have fun girly."

Upstairs I found Trey waiting for me on my bed with his hands tucked behind his head with his eyes closed. I snuck up on him straddled him and kissed him softly on the mouth. He smiled beneath my kiss and wrapped his arms around me, rolling me over on my side so we were facing each other. He pulled my left leg over his hip so it'd be elevated.

"Hi." I smiled.

"What's up?" he asked and gave me another kiss. "How was the play?"

"Eh. Everyone died at the end."

He laughed "That sucks."

"Aren't y'all cute?" Ruby laughed from inside the bathroom where she was putting the finishing touches on her make up. My smile faltered into an annoyed eye roll and Trey laughed. Ruby had been trying to make up all week but I was still upset with her. I didn't feel like letting go of anything, I just put on like I was over it.

"Alright. I'm going to go downstairs and wait for Gunnar, I'll give you two some privacy. Have they stopped yelling?"

"DeVon is gone."

"Oh Lord, he'll be back. I hope Gunnar show up before he come back and start again."

"Bye." I said, hoping she'd stop talking.

"Bye." she said, a little taken aback by my shortness.

She walked out.

"Who's Gunnar?" Trey asked.

"Her dude."

"I thought she was f---ing DeVon"

"She's seeing a few guys" I explained

"That's bomedy." he laughed "So how long you going to be mad at her?" Trey asked.

"She seems like she's sorry."

I just shrugged "Why do you care so much about her? You wanna smash her too?" I pulled away from him a couple inches.

"Don't be like that." He laughed pulling me back.

"So does this girlfriend of yours know you're here?" I asked still in a bad mood.

"She's not my girlfriend." He corrected, flipping me over onto my back and pinning me to the bed. "And I don't care what she knows. I talked to my grandma and she's going to let me crash on her couch until the first so I don't have to be in that ugly b----'s house."

"Eww she's ugly?" I laughed. My mood lifted just like that.

"And short, nasty as hell."

"Eww, the things niggas do when they desperate."

"Do I need to point out who you did when you was desperate?" he joked.

"Touché," I laughed.

"I'm glad you're getting away from her, and I'm glad you're here."

"You ok?" he asked.

"Mmm-hmm why?"

"Downstairs when the white girl..."

"Heather."

"Heather," he corrected "mentioned the baby, you kinda had a look."

"The baby is something I don't like talking about or having brought up," I explained.

"Why not?"

"It hurts too much and I don't want to feel it." I said quickly looking to change the subject. "So if you can go to Vegas are you going to be cool with meeting my family?" I asked.

"I want to meet everyone in your life," he said kissing me.

"Be prepared my cousins are going to ask you all kinds of questions."

"Like what?"

"Like who you are, how we met, what the nature of our relationship is...."

"The nature of our relationship?" he laughed.

"Yep."

"So what should I say?" He asked caressing my cheek moving my hair behind my ear.

"Well I told my cousin James that you were my boyfriend so if you could go along with that, that'd be nice."

He laughed "Aren't I though?"

"I mean I guess you are." I mused " Technically you didn't even ask, you just assumed..."

"Naomi?"

"Yes Trey?"

"Will you be my girlfriend?"

"Yes. I will" I laughed "And my name is Lyric."

"Your name is Rose because no matter what you say your name is, you're still the same person to me. 'A rose by any other name would still smell as sweet.'"

"Whatever." I smiled rolling my eyes "and that's Juliet's line."

"It's my line now."

PRODIGAL

SEVENTEEN

The plan for Vegas was simple. It was supposed to be James, Jaycee, Aisha, Aisha's boyfriend, Trey and The BFC (minus Anthony). It was intentional, not inviting Anthony, and I was very vocal in my reasons why. But it seemed even my birthday wasn't a good enough reason to stop DeVon from creating drama. Whether it was for the show or for his own personal entertainment. No one ever knew.

"No!" I exclaimed in the van on the way to L.A. We had an interview on Lopez Tonight to promote season 2, (Christopher was meeting us there) and after that we were going to drive to Vegas from there.

"Lyric don't be like that," DeVon laughed.

"How are you going to invite someone on her trip? After you know she don't want him there?" Ruby asked "And there's no room anyway."

Ruby and I had made up earlier in the week. I was so excited about Trey finally asking me to be his girl that I had to tell her. She's the only one who would understand and would listen to the complication of our situation without judgement.

That's my girl. I said on green screen *No matter what we go through, we go back almost to birth. You can't throw away a friendship that deep. I'll never go out to club alone with her again though.*

"It'll be fun," DeVon said.

"Anthony is not invited to my birthday weekend."

"There's extra space now cuz Athena's not going."

Athena said that she couldn't go after all, because she had a test on Monday and would rather stay home and study.

"You was wrong not to invite him anyway."

"It's HER birthday!" Ruby defended "If she don't want him to go then she don't want him to go."

"He can stay in the room with me and Monroe."

"No he can't." Monroe said. His hatred for Anthony was almost as strong as mine but his tolerance for him was higher.

"You can't leave the dude out."

"Man, I don't care." Anthony said "I don't even wanna go. She trippin.'"

"Who gave you permission to speak?!" I snapped at Anthony.

"Who do you think you're talking to?" he asked annoyed.

"You! What you gonna do about it?"

"Stop." Monroe interjected "If ya'll aint fighting, it's the other two." Everyone just shut the hell up til we get out the car."

"You tryin to be bold cuz your jump off is here." Anthony mumbled under his breath trying to pay heed to Monroe's demand.

"Man." I corrected. I didn't give a crap what Monroe said. I was on one and couldn't stop. "He's my man . Somethin' you have no clue how to even start being!"

"Whatever."

"And he don't need to be here to do nothin' I can handle a b---- myself." DeVon, Ruby, and Monroe cracked up "ooh-ing and Ahh-ing" Athena just shook her head with a smirk. Trey laughed quietly but proud that his woman was a fighter.

"Baby, chill," Trey said softly, squeezing my knee. "It's gonna be ok."

"Yea, chill," Anthony said.

I opened my mouth to reply but Monroe covered it quickly with his hand before one sound could come out. "Enough." he laughed

"DeVon, it's Lyrics birthday you know it's messed up to invite Anthony when she doesn't want him there." Athena said.

"It's foul to leave him behind."

"If you so concerned about him stay here and keep him company then," Trey offered.

"No." He and Athena said at the same time.

Take him please, let me get some peace for once. Athena pleaded on her green screen

"It's funny how you always claiming not to care about her and yet you always trying to be around her when you know she can't stand you," Trey directed toward Anthony.

"I'm not going for her, I'm going cuz it's Vegas," He laughed.

"Then you and ya boy can go next weekend why go this weekend?"

"Cuz this is the weekend that everyone is going."

"This is the weekend Lyric is going." Ruby pointed out "That's what you mean."

"No," Anthony denied.

I peeled Monroe's hand from over my mouth finally able to talk calmly.

"Whatever , you two need figure it out then, cuz Anthony's not invited."

"I invited him," Devon argued.

"Von," Monroe reprimanded shaking his head.

"What? It's not that big a deal."

Like everything I said about Anthony and what I wanted, it fell on DeVon's deaf ears.

Nothing I said mattered and he was constantly disregarding my feelings.

"Don't let him ruin anything." Ruby said when we were all safe inside my dressing room at the studio. "It's going to be alright."

"I hate him" I said walking up to her so she could zip up my dress for the interview. "I hate him with a passion. DeVon knows this and he still keeps trying to orchestrate situations. It's all a big joke to him."

Barefoot, I impatiently walked over to the vanity and poured myself a glass of the complimentary champagne and drank it down. My ankle was much better when I had alcohol in my system. I could walk and stand on it normally but not for too long and not in heels.

"Baby, you givin' blood what he want. He tryna piss you off why you lettin him get to you?"

"Because I don't get it!" I shouted "Is it just for TV? Why?! He knows what I went through, he saw it! He was there! He and Monroe tried to beat the hell out of Anthony last reunion so why is he suddenly........." I threw my hands up, careful not to spill a drop from the raised glass. I felt tears coming and I was so tired of crying. I drained the glass and poured another.

"Hey come here." Trey said coming up to my side. I wouldn't look at him and tried to pull away, but he was stronger than me and managed to hold me to him.

"Take a deep breath."

"I just..."

"TAKE.... a deep breath." he reiterated forcefully. I did as he said. I loved it when he was commanding. "Relax it's not worth it. We'll figure something out, maybe we can cancel the reservation and move to another hotel."

"Are you more mad about Anthony going, or that DeVon invited him?" Ruby asked from the couch.

"All of it." I said "But I don't even know why I'm surprised." I tried to push away from Trey and drink my frustrations away. I wasn't about to cry and show weakness not on camera not in front of Trey. "Their favorite thing to do is piss me off. My life is a freakin' game for them to play with."

"So don't let 'em then." Ruby said "Don't let them know they're getting to you."

"I'm just pissed that I can't control things in my own life anymore. I can't control people. I can't control Karma." After everything that happened he seems to get away scott free. Both of them. It's just not fair. Yea he got his ass beat but physical wounds heal."

"You wanna just go?" Ruby offered "Forget this and let's just go to the airport and fly there instead of driving with them lames."

I considered it for a moment. I didn't feel calm enough to be around them and not go off.

"Yea lets go."

"For real?" Trey asked "You can do that?"

"Yes."

"She not getting paid to be here." Ruby said grabbing her purse "Let's go."

"That's boo then. Let's bounce."

It's true. I wasn't getting paid to be here. I was here to promote the show, I did sign a contract that I would do all I could to promote it so hopefully me walking out won't get me in too much trouble. Maybe my walking out would create some buzz about why and what's going on, causing people to want to tune in and see the, apparently, real life drama that is The BFC. I wrote a hasty apology note to George. I called him Mr. Lopez to gain affection and to be respectful and cute.Then the three of us bailed.

We had just pulled up at LAX when I got a phone call. "Hey Lyric, it's George."

"Hi, Mr. Lopez how are you?" I asked surprised. Trey and Ruby climbed out of the back seat both quietly laughing.

"I'm good. I'm good. Listen, I'm on stage with The BFC, and you're missing. Why'd you leave?"

"I just....I...I had to go."

"But why? Monroe here says you're pissed about somethin'." The cab driver opened the trunk and Trey grabbed our bags and Ruby grabbed hers.

"She's throwin a freakin tantrum over nothin'. I'm tellin you." Anthony remarked.

"You really need to keep my name out yo' f---in mouth, Anthony," I said.

"I didn't even say your name."

"Don't even reference me!"

"What?! You're trippin you need to relax"

"And you need to go f--- yourself."

"Woah easy easy." George laughed "This is prime time."

"I'm sorry." I said in a nicer tone. " and I'm sorry for leaving, Mr. Lopez I just....I couldn't be there right now." I said walking through the airport looking for the place to buy a ticket and trying to keep calm. The camera crew wasn't with us. We had bodyguards but not the whole entourage. They were waiting for us in Las Vegas.

"Well, why not?"

"I'll make it up to you I promise."

"Ok, but you didn't answer my question."

I sighed, and sat down in the closest chair I could find, trying to think of a way to talk around it. There wasn't one, so I decided to tell him what I really felt. I switched to Spanish so that The BFC wouldn't interrupt.

"Because the guys are inconsiderate SOB's and I'm so pissed off and I can't just sit up on stage and smile like everything is good with them when I really want to beat them across the face with my six inch stilettos." I tried not to laugh at Trey's confused and comical expression.

"All of the guys?" George asked in Spanish.

"No, Christopher and Monroe are good but the other two are inconsiderate a-----cs."

"What the *hell* did she just say?" DeVon asked.

"He's the biggest mother f---er of the two," I said in Spanish.

"Damn, what did you guys do to piss her off? She has kind of a temper huh?" George asked the cast in English.

"Yea she definitely does," Athena said.

"But you'll see what happened."

"In season 3," Monroe added.

"But it started in season 2 which is what we are here to talk about right?" Athena laughed.

"Alright, Well Lyric I'm going to call you later and maybe we can reschedule with just you by yourself so you don't have to hit anybody with your shoe."

"Ok yea definitely that works."

"Alright well I will definitely do that then."

"Ok. bye bye." I laughed and hung up.

"Damn girl, you think they're going to bleep out the cuss words even though they're in Spanish?"

"Probably."

"I've never heard you speak Spanish like that," Trey said. "That was sexy. What did you say though?" I just laughed.

The flight to Vegas was short and easy. I still wasn't completely calm, I didn't have to drive with the rest of the house but they would be here eventually and I'd have to see them all weekend. Maybe being around James would cheer me up. He usually does the trick. Aisha, James, Jaycee and Aisha's bf were already at the hotel when I arrived along with a surprise guest, My cousin Kendrick. Kendrick had rented his own room at the Motel

Six. When Trey told them why I was pissed Kendrick was ready to fight. He'd been dying to get his hands on Anthony since the night I lost the baby. He agreed with Trey that Anthony was a chump. Aisha and Jaycee were annoyed almost as much as I was. Not because he was coming but because it was rude on both his and DeVon's part.

"How does he invite someone else on *your* trip?" Aisha asked as we walked through the casino to the elevators.

"I don't want to be in the same suite with them. I don't even want to see them this whole weekend."

"Don't worry about it, Meems," Jaycee said. "Ken can stay in the penthouse with us and those guys can just share the room Ken got. It's at the Motel Six so they won't even be in the same hotel."

Kick them BOTH out the room? I LOVE that idea.

Eighteen

The penthouse upstairs at MGM came with its own pool, and jacuzzi which was ideal so we didn't disturb the other patrons in the hotel with the entourage of bodyguards and camera men that followed us where we went. It was also a relief not to have curious gawking crowds. I wasn't used to being stared at but I guess it comes with the the territory of being a TV star. I had a feeling it was only going to get worse from here. The living room had a HUGE flat screen TV with various video game consoles, a stereo, a bar, a kitchen, and next to the glass door that led out to the pool was a billiards table. It was two stories and three bedrooms and a pull out couch. I was in the room at the top of the stairs, with just one bed since it was my birthday. I had a king sized bed. The other 2 rooms had 2 two queen sized beds each. Trey and I were in my room, James, Jaycee, Aisha and her boyfriend shared one room, Monroe and Ruby shared the other. Ken would sleep on the pull out couch . It was originally expected that Monroe and Athena would share the room and Ruby and DeVon would share the sofa bed but obviously sleeping arrangements had to be changed.

The rest of the afternoon was spent floating around in the pool with the girls, except Ruby, who wanted to take a nap, while the guys got to know Trey a little bit better. They were very curious about my friend turned boyfriend.

"You're boyfriend is cute," Aisha said.

"He looks a little like Trey Songz," Jaycee speculated.

"I think he looks like Chris Brown," I offered.

"How did you guys meet?" Jaycee asked.

"At the church a couple years ago."

"He goes to our church?" Aisha asked.

"No. He was visiting for Easter Sunday with his friend and we all ended up sitting together in the back row of the balcony. We couldn't do much talking because church was going on but I liked him right away. We managed to hold hands without anyone seeing but then I had to leave early so I didn't get a chance to give him my number. He came back the next week for the Youth Extravaganza and we did more talking and flirting. We exchanged numbers and he walked me home, since I lived across the street. We've been in contact off and on ever since and now...."

"Well he seems like a nice guy."

"He is."

"Do you love him?"

I smiled trying not to answer but my blush and my smile answered for me.

"Oh My God! Really?!" Aisha squealed in excitement.

I just laughed.

"Does he know?" Jaycee asked.

"He knows and he reciprocates."

"Who said it first?" Aisha asked.

"He did."

"Awww."

I looked over and smiled at him and waved. He nodded his head "what's up" to me in return and smiled back.

When the boys of The Breakfast Club arrived that evening, Kendrick, James, Trey and Aisha's boyfriend met them in the lobby and told them of the new sleeping arrangements. I had Trey put me on speaker so I could hear the exchange.

"What up Monroe?" James and Kendrick greeted and then introduced him to Aisha's boyfriend.

"Hey whats good, ya'll?" DeVon asked "Lyric calm down yet?"

"Naomi is fine." James answered correcting my name. "Roe, you cool. You can go up but ya'll two... there's been a change of plans."

"What you mean?" Anthony asked. Even over the phone he sounded as confused, stupid and terrified as he did in person. I laughed picturing the scrunched up look on his face.

"Well first of all you weren't invited, so I don't know why you thought it'd be cool for you to bring yourself here unless you trying to start somethin'."

"Nah, man." DeVon said. He sounded a bit shocked by the hard tone of Kendrick's authority. Kendrick was tall and heavy set and tough. The only real gangster there with any kind of respect from ANY set. Even though he stopped hanging out in the streets and was trying to get his life right, he still could turn on the intimidation at the drop of a dime. He was like Ice Cube in Boyz in the Hood meets Martin Lawrence, in any comedy starring Martin Lawrence. He could alternate between the two depending on his mood.

"We just came to have fun," DeVon said.

"Good. So then we don't need to see you the rest of the weekend. Here's your room key ya'll not staying with us."

"You got us a different room?" Anthony asked.

"Nah see I'm finna take ya'll place in the penthouse and ya'll can have my room at the Motel Six by the airport."

"It's one bed though, so one of you is gonna have to sleep on the floor or take turns," James said. "Or hey, if ya'll get down like that you can sleep together."

"That's messed up," Anthony protested.

"Later!" Monroe cackled.

"Yo that's messed up, Roe," DeVon commented.

I feel kinda sorry for DeVon but not really. Monroe confessed *He shouldn't have pissed Lyric off, it's her birthday and Anthony should have stayed his hairy ass at home. I wouldn't be surprised if he caught a beat down from her people by the end of the weekend.*

"Like I said we don't need to see you the rest of the weekend, you have fun and stay away from my cousin and won't be no problem. Feel me, blood?" Kendrick said. I could imagine him looking Anthony up and down in disgust. I laughed and hung up the phone. I took a deep breath and sighed. I wasn't going to be bullied or disregarded this weekend, not while my family had my back.

Same as always, crowds of people followed us wherever we went. Some knew the show and others were just curious about what was happening. Some girls shouted Monroe's name, begging him to lift up his shirt and show his abs. I don't know what it was about this little dark chocolate bag of bones but the longer the show went on the more women loved him.

My group was on the dance floor of the 2nd club of the night. Monroe was grinding against a couple Asain girls, who couldn't dance, Ruby was breaking dudes left and right. I couldn't dance either not like Jaycee and Aisha. I'd look ridiculous trying to get low like they did with my heavy behind. I had packed a couple pair of heels to at least try to look good for my man and to keep up with the rest of the girls in the group. I blamed the alcohol and my bad ankle for my wobble on the dance floor, so I wore fashionable flats.

"Here. Stay still." Trey said. He put his hands on my hips and stood behind me. "You live here. It's just like we havin sex, your body and mine are in sync with each other and the music." He started rollin' his pelvis and moving my hips at the same time. I felt so embarrassed that I had to be taught to dance that I stopped. I was not Julia Stiles and this was not Save The Last Dance.

"I want another drink," I shouted over the music dragging him to the bar.

"Why you stop dancing?"

"Cuz I wanted another drink," I laughed.

"You're not that bad." he said "You just need to loosen up more. Be more in your body and less in your head."

"I don't know what you're talking about," I lied.

"Ok." He chuckled "I don't know why you gotta be embarrassed, it's just me."

Yea you and millions of people who'll be watching at home. I thought.

I knew once we kicked DeVon and Anthony out the hotel, it wouldn't be the last we'd see of them before we went home. The producers wouldn't allow it, they wanted to create as much drama as they could get on film. I stood at the bar waiting on my drink when the crowd parted, watching, as a couple more cameras made their way thru, following and leading DeVon and Anthony to the dance floor.

"Don't worry about them," Trey said.

"Let's just go," I said. Trey led me back to the dance floor where I found the rest of our group. I told them I wanted to go. Monroe chose to stay there with his new groupies, But the rest of us moved on to the next club. I didn't want a ghetto club confrontation. I was in too good a mood and I wasn't going to let them affect me tonight. Kendrick clearly warned them not to come anywhere near us the whole weekend and this was a direct challenge to his threat. They wanted a fight, the producers probably did too, for ratings.

Vegas drinks were strong and some of them could be big depending on how much you paid. One of the cups looked like a fish bowl with a wine glass base, I wanted to keep it and James had to stop me from putting the empty glass in my purse to take home.

"That is NOT a souvenir cup," he pointed out.

"But I want it." I pouted.

"Naomi, you're drunk," he laughed. "Put it back."

My ankle was throbbing by the time we got back to the hotel and I couldn't walk on it anymore. Trey carried me over his shoulder, like Tarzan, through the hotel lobby because I refused to let them get me a wheelchair. I was amazed at how strong he was, how easily he carried me. Kendrick carried my bag and high heels and walked ahead talking with Ruby next to James who was supporting a drunk Jaycee. Monroe never met back up with us so he must still be with the girls we left him with or with DeVon and Anthony. Aisha and her boyfriend walked hand and hand.

It was almost sunrise when we got back upstairs. I was ready to pass out and go to sleep in my clothes. Trey was the one who reminded me I needed to ice my ankle or I was going to hurt tomorrow.

"Can you get it for me?" I asked smiling sweetly.

"Why can't you get it?"

"Cuz my foot hurts," I pouted and whined dramatically.

"You lucky, it's your birthday."

"Thank you, Baby," I smiled. "I love you."

What seemed like an hour was really only a couple of minutes. I hadn't even realized I had fallen asleep until Trey woke me up by pulling me out of my jeans.

"Nooo, I'm tired," I whined.

"I'm not trying to do THAT," he laughed.

"Ow!" I winced as he lifted my ankle to pull them all the way off.

"Sorry." he said resting it down more gently "Here." He placed a gel ice pack over my ankle. I don't know where he got it and I didn't ask.

"It's cold!" I complained.

"You are such a baby," he teased.

I laughed at his true assessment of me. He took his shirt and pants off climbed into bed next to me. I shifted a little so I could rest my head on his chest, he wrapped his arm around my shoulders , our breathing became synced with one another and pretty soon we were asleep. I didn't wake up until one o'clock in the afternoon and that was only because of the beat that was being banged out on my door like drums in church. On the other side Kendrick, James, Jaycee, Aisha were serenading me with Happy Birthday in three part harmony. I opened the door at the very last line. I laughed and applauded. It's never been like this with us before. I mean I expect it from James but not Aisha. I always felt like an afterthought to Aisha and now she was talking to me and laughing with me, wanting to go places with me like we were best friends. A part of me believed that since we were adults now that she had learned to appreciate family. The other part suspected that it could be because of the cameras, because now that I was a little famous she wanted to be linked to me. I pushed that suspicion away as paranoia, she'd never asked me for anything.

"Happy Birthday!" they all shouted in unison.

"Thank you!" I beamed drinking in all the attention.

"We didn't interrupt anything did we?" Aisha asked taking in my attire. I'd awoken a couple hours before and slipped on one of Trey's wife beater shirts that reached down just to my thighs.

"Oh!" I said pulling the shirt down lower to cover my underwear "No," I laughed. "We were just sleeping."

"Aww man!" Kendrick whined. "What you been doin to my cousin, homie?" He reminded me of Martin Lawrence in this instance.

"Stop it!" Jaycee reprimanded.

"What?" he asked feigning innocence

"Anyway," Aisha interjected. "We were going to head out and do stuff. We just wanted wish you a happy birthday before we left."

"Aww thank you," I smiled. "Where you guys going?"

"Gambling a little, you wanna go?" James offered.

"You don't have plans with your friends?" Aisha asked.

"Nothing planned but you guys go ahead, I'll see whats up. If anything, I'll see you guys at dinner tonight."

"Alright, Happy Birthday."

I closed the door as they left and climbed back into bed with Trey who was checking his phone.

He lay it on the nightstand next to the bed and pulled me against his chest.

"Your fam seems cool," he says.

"Yea, they're awesome sometimes. I'm glad we're finally connecting."

"Ya'll ain't always been close?"

"Me and J have but Aisha and I are a recent development. We lived in two different worlds for a while and she never understood me, but I think now she's starting to and I'm starting to see that we're not so different after all."

His phone beeped and he ignored it which I thought was unusual. "Everything good?"

"Yea it's just....her. She's mad that I moved out."

"Let her be mad then. Change your number."

"She'll give up eventually."

"Whatever," I said and pulled away.

"What? Where'd you go?"

"Nothing, I'm just gonna go take a shower." I slid out of bed, my happiness washed away by the reality of having to share the man I love with another woman. I walked--well limped because my ankle was still stiff from the night before--out the room with him calling after me. I passed Ruby who greeted me with "Happy Birthday"

"Thanks," I said brusquely. "You aiight, mama?" she called through the door.

"Yea," I said back,

"What'd you do?" Ruby asked Trey.

"I don't know." he claimed "Baby?" He knocked on the door.

I ignored him and stepped into the shower. I get his situation, He did what he had to do to survive but I hate that he ever had to stay with her at all. I hate that she's on him, calling him, checking up on him like he's hers. I hate that his sister has no sense of family that she would let her baby daddy put her own brother out on the street. What kind of family does that? Am I an idiot? He's using her, how do I know he's not using me for the same thing and more? Does he see me as a way to get on TV? To make money? To be taken care of by me? He says he loves me but maybe he said the same to her, why else would she be so convinced that she was his girl? I don't even know her but what if she's prettier than me? What if she's thinner than me? Is he still having sex with her? He moved out, he's living on his grandma's couch rather than be with her is she not getting the hint? Or is he telling me and her 2 different stories?

As much weight as I had lost one hotel towel still didn't fit all the way around me I had to hold on to the towel as I walked. Trey was sitting at the breakfast bar talking to Monroe, who was still dressed in last night's clothes. Trey met my eyes when I came out the bathroom and followed me into the room before I could shut him out again.

"What you mad for?" He asked closing our bedroom door.

"I don't like feeling like your side chick, I don't like sharing." I said sitting on the floor with my left leg outstretched. It would hurt to cross it with my right or bend it in at all.

"Baby, you not a side chick you the only one I'm even thinking about."

"Why did she think you were even together in the first place?" I pulled my suitcase out and began searching for my for my brace "Did you say that you loved her too?"

"I don't love her, I never said that I did."

"Are you f---ing her?" I finally ask.

"No, not since me and you and not like me and you," he grabbed my brace from under the bed knelt down beside me.

"So in like a week. And what's the difference?"

"The difference is I don't care about her, and it was for a different reason than it is when I'm with you. Do you really want to argue about this on your birthday? I moved out of her place and I'm staying on my grandma's couch, and you and I are moving in together in a couple weeks. What are you worried about?"

"I'm worried that you could be using me, the same way that you used her, what makes me any different?"

"Baby, how many times do I need to tell you that I love you before you believe it? Even if I wasn't in this situation, I would want to be with you."

"How do I know that I'm not just like her?"

"You're not her. At all. She's so negative all the time, I never actually liked her, she's disgusting and annoying. You are the one I can see spending my life with one day, having a family, white picket fence and all that s--t. You are my peace of mind in this bull going on around me." He looked me in the eye and there was no trace of lie or doubt. No shiftiness, no laugh only sincerity.

"Will you change your phone number please?" I pouted looking at him with playfully, wide eyes.

He cracked a smile and laughed "Alright, if it makes you feel better, I will change my number today." He stood up and held his hand out to me

"Thank you," I smiled widely and allowed him to pull me up. I kissed him sweetly on the mouth and turned to go search the clothes I'd hung up in the closet, for something to wear for today. He spun me back around and kissed me again. I playfully resisted. I didn't kiss back right away. His kiss became more insistent as if he could wipe my worries away with the brush of his lips against mine. I allowed him to lay me on the bed but I still remained unresponsive while he kissed any and everywhere he could to get a reaction. I held in my laughs at the tickles his caresses created. Finally, he stopped and looked at me "I love you and I promise you," He said boring his eyes into mine, begging me to believe him "You ain't never got nothin' to worry about from no other female. You all I need, babe." I considered his words for a minute before accepting them as truth.

Nineteen

Before heading out to another night of club hopping and drinking, everyone met up for dinner at the top of the Eiffel tower inside Paris. I was in such a good mood that even Anthony and DeVon's surprise appearance at the table didn't bother me.........much.

"What are they doing here?" I asked Monroe, calmly and quietly.

"I didn't tell them to come." He swore.

Monroe had spent the day with the boys of The BFC. Trey, Ruby and I hung out on the strip, along with Gunnar, who showed up to keep Ruby company. He got his own room so it wouldn't be an imposition on my party. I was fine with it. Gunnar was cool he even brought me a bottle of Bacardi 151 as a birthday present. We rode the roller coaster at New York New York, took gondola rides at the Venetian. I didn't like gambling. I liked my money way too much to risk losing it, but Trey begged me to let him roll the dice just once. So I spotted him a hundred, he swore win or lose that he'd pay me back. He had an appointment to do a chest piece on Monday that he was going to be paid $250 for so he would definitely have it. I didn't have to wait that long. He turned that hundred into a hundred grand, cashed out and gave me my money back right away. I liked that whenever he won a game and re-bet he didn't put it all back in. He kept most of it and only put a little back in case he lost. Most people don't have the restraint.

Trey was happy to finally be the one to spend money for a change. Not that he let me do much spending when we were together. He told me that since it was my birthday, I wasn't allowed to spend anymore money. He bought himself a nice black and red three piece suit and shoes to go with it. He bought me a tight strapless red dress. He wanted me to wear something else other than black. The dress hugged my hips and flared out at the knee. If I bent over you would see my entire behind. He wanted me to try and wear heels with them but I couldn't walk right in them yet. Not with my ankle being sore still. He bought them anyway for me to wear next time and also bought me some matching red ballet flats.

Sometime during the day we lost Ruby and Gunnar, though I knew where they went and why. With my hair flattened and then loosely curled into spirals and having applied my signature smokey eye with clear gloss on my lips, I felt truly beautiful for the first time since my senior prom. Feeling beautiful is different from feeling sexy. To me sexy is for the benefit of men, knowing I had something they wanted and could use it to get the attention I wanted. Only it was often meaningless. Beautiful was different, it's not about getting attention from anyone, it's about looking in the mirror or at a picture of yourself and liking what you see. Feeling happy in your own self and appearance. Not necessarily because of what are you wearing or because you have make -up on, but because you feel good about yourself as you are.

"I thought I told ya'll we ain't want to see you the rest of the weekend." Kendrick said.

"What you wanna do MiMi, you want to go?" Aisha asked.

"No don't leave, man, we family this thing needs to be squashed already," DeVon pleaded. "We both want to be here and celebrate your birthday."

"No, we're not going to leave." I decided "but let's be clear." I said to DeVon " He is not my family. He killed my family," I was referring to Anthony who's eyes were stuck on me.

"You starin kinda hard at my girl, blood." Trey pointed out as he pulled my chair out for me at the other end of our table.

"My bad. You look nice, Lyric" Anthony offered.

"Ain't she tell you to keep her name out yo mouth?" Kendrick asked.

"I just said she looked nice." Anthony defended.

I bet dude kickin himself for lettin her go right about now. Ruby laughed on screen *Is that drool on your chin, homie?*

Ant, starin at Ric like he's 'can't get -right.' and she's the white girl from the movie LIFE with Eddie Murphy and Martin Lawrence. DeVon observed humorously. Everything was a movie to DeVon especially when it came to me and Anthony.

"Can we not right now?" Aisha asked trying to nip the verbal hostility in the bud.

"Yes, let's be adults about this," Jaycee agreed.

"Lyric, ain't even her real name anyway," DeVon insisted.

"It is to ya'll," I corrected.

"Blood, you still starin," Trey remarked to Anthony. "You high or somethin?"

"Oh. Uh Nah... I was just thinkin bout somethin, sorry."

"Oh yeah? bout what, man?" DeVon asked. Let the instigation begin.

"It doesn't matter," I said. I admit that I liked how Anthony couldn't take his eyes off me.

Not that I want him or his attention but it's validating to know that he

FINALLY sees me. His expression confused me though. It's not the usual nervous, faux calm, jealousy that he normally gives when Trey's around. The looks that Trey brushes off and sometimes provokes just for a laugh. Tonight, though, Anthony looked at me with longing. A mixture of sadness and lust that I've never seen on his face. I tried my best to ignore Anthony and DeVon throughout the dinner. Most of my attention was paid to everyone else, barely acknowledging them even when spoken to by them. It clicked that this was a set up by the producers to create drama. They wanted to see if I would get ghetto and yell and scream at them in public for being here, but I wasn't going to. I was going to keep my composure no matter how I was provoked.

"It's nice to see you happy Ric," DeVon said.

"It is new huh?" Anthony agreed. I rolled my eyes and ignored them both.

"Not new, just rare," DeVon countered.

"True. I have something for you by the way," Anthony announced to get my attention.

The table went silent at this revelation. The chatter stopped, the clinking of plates from people cutting into their dinners ceased and everyone sent their attention in the direction of me and Anthony.

"Why?" I asked.

"It's your birthday."

"You've never cared about my birthday, why now?"

"Just open it." He said smiling passing the gift to DeVon who passed it to Monroe who passed it to Jaycee who passed it to James who put it on the table in front of me. I stared at it like it was a foreign object.

"What is it?" DeVon asked excited by this twist. Though of course he knew this was coming. There was nothing Anthony did that DeVon didn't know about. I looked toward Trey to see what he thought. His expression said he was bothered that my ex has suddenly decided to give me a present but curious about what it was. He shrugged his shoulders.

"Open it." he said. I pulled the wrapped box to me and calmly ripped the paper off. No way did he wrap this himself.

"The lady at the store wrapped it for me." Anthony said confirming my suspicion. Underneath the wrapping was a smooth white box. I took off the lid and inside was a fancy eight by ten picture frame wrapped in white tissue paper.

"A picture frame." I said politely "Thanks," I moved to lay it back down and put the lid back on the box.

"Wait, look at the picture," He said.

163   SAMANTHA SANCHEZ

I picked up the tissue wrapped frame back out of the box, ripped the paper down revealing a beautiful solid silver frame. I froze, staring at the image in front of me.

"I know you didn't like how you looked when you were pregnant, but I thought you looked nice and thought you might like the picture." I didn't even realize my eyes had watered until a tear fell on the image. The one thing I didn't want to think about this weekend was the baby and yet here was a giant reminder of the life that never got to be. It was a black and white still image, a profile shot of me and Anthony with him on his knees and his cheek to my giant belly. It was one of the pictures of us taken at our season two photo shoot. In the photo I smirked looking down at Anthony and rested my hands at the top of his head while he rested his cheek against my pregnant belly and holding onto my thighs. Underneath the picture on the bottom of the frame were the words "Tiana and Mommy and Daddy- April 2009" engraved in fancy script. This was taken a week before Easter.

"I was going to give it to you at the baby shower, I thought we would still be doing us and we could put it in her nursery, but things change you know? So yea happy birthday."

I felt a familiar hitch in my throat. The aching dryness that comes from trying to suppress a sob. "But things change, you know?" He said it so casually. Like I simply just changed my mind about having a baby shower. Because babies suffocate inside the womb so frequently that it's no big deal right? It's not like I was attached to my child or anything.

"You f---in dumbass," Monroe commented shaking his head.

"MiMi, are you alright?" Jaycee asked.

"Hey homie you need to leave," James said.

"What? Why?" Anthony asked "It's a peace offering."

"You thought...this…" I said calmly "would bring peace?"

"Yea," He said honestly.

"You thought reminding me of the life that you stole from me…." I gripped my steak knife.

"I stole from you?" Anthony asked.

"With your indifference, your selfishness, your inconsideration, your games, your inability to man the F--K up, Would bring peace?"

"You blame me?"

"Yes I blame you!" I shouted I lifted my hand to throw the knife but Trey caught my wrist and pinned it down onto the table.

"Calm down." He whispered "Not on camera. This ain't the place."

"DeVon please take Anthony and leave. Both of you." Jaycee ordered "Neither of you are welcome among us."

"What did I do?" DeVon asked.

"You brought him here." Aisha answered "It's my cousin's birthday and she made it clear that she didn't want this nigga here this weekend and you ignored her. It is disrespectful."

"How is it disrespectful, it shouldn't be that big a deal."

"But it is!" Ruby insisted "Clearly! You stay defending this piece of s--t."

"Piece of s--t?" Anthony asked.

"Yes a piece of s--t. That's what you are."

DeVon and Anthony didn't make any moves to leave and I couldn't stand being in the same place with them anymore. I stood up "Let's just go," I announced. "They're not going to leave," I walked away not spending another minute in there.

"MiMi, wait," Aisha called.

"I got her." Trey said He opened his wallet and dropped a 50 dollar bill to pay for his dinner and mine and grabbed my arm.

"Hey slow down." He said and pulled me into a hug. I started to cry.

"I'm sorry I'm such a mess." I whined. He led me to the elevator, away from the others.

"You don't have to apologize. You been through some s--t, you're allowed to hurt," I started crying a little harder.

"You gonna be alright." He assured me. "I got you."

Ruby came up to us, "You ok, boo?" she asked.

"Yea," I said sniffing.

"I just need a really big drink," I chuckled.

"Come on, let's go fix your make up," Trey handed me off to her.

"I'll get you that drink." he said as Ruby and I walked into the restroom next to the elevator. I continued to cry. Seeing that picture was like peeling a scab off of a fresh wound. I had been avoiding seeing myself pregnant this semester so I could attempt to move past it. Nobody was even allowed to talk to me about it. My family who watched the show weren't allowed to ask me and Trey told the people at the shop that they weren't allowed to bring it up either.

"Naomi?" Aisha asked coming into the bathroom. "Are you ok?"

"Umm yea." I said sniffing and wiping tears from my eyes "I'll be out in a minute."

"You want to talk about it?" Jaycee asked.

"I don't know what to say, It just hurts," I offered. "I felt her move inside me, I heard her heartbeat. That picture he gave me, was taken a week

165   SAMANTHA SANCHEZ

before I lost her."

"It's always going to hurt, but eventually you'll be able to think about her and look at pictures of yourself without collapsing. It's just going to take time," she said pulling eyeliner and concealer out of my purse.

"Why did you even come back this season? It was too soon." Aisha asked "It's not a healthy environment for you." Aisha used a paper towel to clean the splotches off my face.

"I needed the money," I said. Which was true but only part of the reason.

"But is the money worth it?"

"I thought it was. I mean I couldn't really go back to working a dead end job after this. It's too humiliating."

" You know, if you want and when you're ready you can have another baby right?" Jaycee said applying the concealer.

"Yea, but it's still not going to replace her."

"It won't but I'm saying that it's not the end."

"Anthony knows how to push your buttons," Aisha said. "Do you think he does it on purpose or that he really doesn't know what's going on?"

"It's both. What pisses me off though is the fake concern. He puts on a show to get some sympathy, when he really doesn't give a s--t. He did everything he could last year to upset me and now she's gone and suddenly he cares?"

"He's jealous." Aisha said "That's all that is. Plain and simple. He thought he'd broken you and had you locked in and now he's mad that you're putting yourself back together and chose up," she grabbed my chin and spread lipstick across my lips.

"And girl did you choose up." Ruby said. I laughed a little at her admiration for my man's incomparable good looks.

"Trey really does make it all a little bit easier to bear, I feel safe when he's around."

"Good. He's supposed to. He seems really nice too. Like he has a really good heart. He really cares about you," Jaycee said. "Close your eyes."

"He really does," I agreed, closing my eyes to allow Jaycee to draw lines on my eyelids.

"Boo, you good?" Trey asked pushing the door open.

"Oooh Speak of the devil and he shall appear," Aisha joked.

"Dude!" Jaycee scolded. "This is the ladies room!"

"And?" he laughed. "I ain't all the way in."

"I'm good." I said. My tears had dried all the way up from the mention of Trey's name. I couldn't help but smile when I thought of him.

"Here's your drink." Trey said handing me a big blue drink.

"Can you hold it for a minute?" I said "We're almost done."

"And we're all done." Jaycee said putting my eyeliner away. I looked in the mirror. Most of the black eyeshadow I'd had on had been dabbed away and what was left had been finessed with the addition of black eyeliner that swooped up at the corners, my eyes really popped. I took the drink from Trey, thanking him for it and took a nice long sip.

When we got outside the casino, Anthony and DeVon were waiting for us.

"Ey, can I talk to you for a minute?" Anthony asked as the group walked passed them.

Trey had his arm around my neck and mine was around his waist. It was kinda windy so Trey put his suit jacket around me.

"No," Trey answered for me.

"Man, I wasn't talkin to you," Anthony said.

"What?!" Trey asked quickly removing his hand and sliding me behind him "You want to get bold, blood?"

"No disrespect,nigga." DeVon interjected "But this ain't got nothin to do with you, this is between Lyric and Anthony."

" Ey just come here." Anthony reached around Trey pulling on my arm.

"Let go of me!" I said snatching away. Trey stepped up.

"You touchin my girl, blood?" he asked.

A crowd had already gathered because of the cameras and lights surrounding our group.

Now people had their cameras out, ready to snap pictures or capture video of a fight that I felt was coming

"Trey, you can't get arrested," I reminded him. I wasn't sure if he heard me.

"What is your problem, man?"Anthony asked

"You, blood." Trey responded "And you lucky these cameras here."

"Talk to the dude, Ric, come on," DeVon said.

"What part of 'no' don't y'all get?" Trey asked.

"Lyric, c'mon." Anthony said trying to sidestep Trey. I backed away and Trey blocked Anthony's way. James and Kendrick flanked Trey's sides blocking me from reach on all sides.

"Man, move!" Anthony ordered.

"Make me, blood," Trey responded staring down at him menacingly with his fists balled at his side ready to swing at any moment.

"Let's just keep walking," Monroe suggested.

"Roe, for real they need to talk," DeVon said.

"Just leave it alone." Monroe told DeVon "Stay out of it."

"Come on." I said grabbing Trey's hand. "Let's just go. You're on parole," I said quietly. "I can't have you going back to prison over this nigga." Trey allowed me to lead him away kissing me on the head for good measure before wrapping his arm around me again, his fists stilled balled and ready. Kendrick and James brought up the rear in case Anthony and DeVon were punk enough to try something while our backs were turned. I turned my mind off of the drama for now. It was my birthday and I just wanted to have fun. Which is exactly what I did. I drank and danced and celebrated in VIP areas everywhere and since it was my birthday I didn't pay for any drinks. First my group bought me a round of drinks each and then randoms in the clubs who found out it was my birthday would buy me shots. I was sleep on the way back to the hotel. Kendrick carried me this time through the hotel while Trey held my bag and shoes. In the end despite all the drama, it was a good birthday.

TWENTY

Trey, Ruby and I arrived in San Diego hours before the boys of The BFC. We rode with Gunnar leaving earlier in the morning than the rest of the group who preferred to stay and gamble. Trey and I reluctantly said goodbye when I dropped him off at his grandmother's house. We'd spent the entire weekend engrossed in each other and as much as I wanted to, we couldn't monopolize each other 24 hours a day 7 days a week. His younger sister Keisha who was 19 with a 3 year old and a one year old, ran out to meet me. She was a really big fan of the show and of me. Trey told me that she was the one who brought my letter to the hospital, even though I wasn't receiving visitors, and made sure that the nurse got it to me. I thanked her and told her to get my number from her brother and we could go hang out some time and get to know each other. I kissed Trey goodbye one last time and left. I missed him right away but refrained from texting him to say as much. Although he didn't.

I already miss you, I'm gonna come see you tomorrow when I get off work He texted.

I smiled walking into the clubhouse texting back.

I miss you too. I hate having to leave you. I can't wait for the 1st

"What are you all smiley about?" Athena asked.

"Trey," I said.

"So you guys had a good weekend?"

"Yea. For the most part. There was this one thing at dinner."

"Uh Oh, What did the boys do?"

I told her about the entire weekend. From my cousins kicking Anthony and DeVon out of the hotel to the confrontation at and after dinner.

"Maybe the picture was his way of saying sorry." Athena offered "I honestly think that he did care about you and the baby but it scared him so he ran from it."

"I used to think that too, until I realized he got pleasure from messing with me."

"Who ya'll talkin' bout?"

"Dumbass," I answered.

"That dude is immature and young actin'. He don't know what to do with feelings, you should have seen the way he was looking at her at dinner."

"Did he jizz in his pants?" Athena joked.

"I think he just might have," Ruby laughed.

Ruby was energized and decided to call her baby daddy, who was in town for a week to come get her so she could see her son. I decided to take a nap before unpacking. I was wiped out. When I woke up, Ruby was back and the boys were home. I came downstairs to get some water and everyone was standing around Anthony who had taken his shirt off and stood there in his jeans and his wife beater.

"When did you get this?" Ruby asked.

"Last night, after dinner. It still hurts," Anthony answered rubbing the side of his arm.

"It's a tattoo homie it's going to hurt and itch like hell for while."

"Has Lyric seen this?" Athena asked.

"Have I seen what?" I asked.

The sound of my voice made everyone jump. No one said anything. Even DeVon was quiet. Anthony looked scared. I walked from the kitchen to the living room praying that the tattoo wasn't my name or anything referring to me. It was a crown. On the base of the crown, however there was a name: "Tiana." The letters "R.I.P" were in the tips of the spokes and in the gaps between the three front facing spokes were the words "Daddy's Princess Always". The heat and pain began to slowly boil inside me.

"No." I said simply.

"No?" Anthony asked.

"NO!" I shouted raking my nails across the fresh tattoo.

"AHHH! you b----!" Anthony said covering up the pain with his palm and checking for Blood. "No! How dare you?!" I shouted slapping him across the face "You have no right!"

"Stop!" Anthony shouted.

"No! you don't get to mourn her like you gave a s-- about her!"

"She was my baby too!" He shouted.

"No!" I yelled again slapping, punching, scratching. Two security guards on set approached. One pulled me back away from Anthony by my waist the other pushed Anthony back "You didn't give a f--- about her! You didn't even want her! SHE'S DEAD BECAUSE OF YOU!!!" I started crying, fighting and kicking as the guard pulled me away to keep me from hitting Anthony "You never gave a f--k about her" I sobbed.

"I'M SORRY!" Anthony yelled taking everyone by surprise "Alright?! I'm sorry. I f----ed up! I didn't know..."

"You didn't care!" I corrected.

"I was scared! ok? I'm sorry. That's what I wanted to tell you last night."

"No! It's not ok!" I sobbed swinging myself out of Security's grasp I walked away up the stairs. I was shaking with rage and tears as I climbed the stairs. I couldn't stay in this house. I paced my bedroom floor trying to get a grip on my breathing. The whole house was full of my enemies. DeVon, Monroe, Athena, all of them. For the simple fact that they tolerate his existence, that they could so easily stand in the same room with him, talk to him, laugh with him. Like he didn't do everything he could to ensure that the life I was carrying, the life he helped create was ripped from my body. The pacing wasn't working, and I wanted to calm down. I couldn't stay in this house another minute. I hadn't unpacked my suitcase from the weekend yet and I threw a bunch of stuff into a 2nd suitcase and my purse and I left. I'll ask Ruby to bring me the stuff I missed tomorrow. I quit. I'm done. I couldn't stay in that house anymore or I would have killed him in his sleep.

"Lyric. Don't leave." DeVon insisted as I came down the stairs dragging my suitcases down the stairs. "Over a tattoo? C'mon man" I ignored him and walked outside not bothering to close the door behind me. "Anthony go stop her, dude." I heard DeVon say.

"Why me?"

"Cuz you the one that did it."

"I don't think anyone should go out there. Just leave her alone. let her go," Monroe said.

"Yea, if you send Anthony she might run him over," Athena said.

I tossed everything in the trunk, started the car and drove away. I called Trey while I was at the stoplight to let him know what happened but he didn't answer, I texted him but I got no reply. He was probably busy with his family.

The lights were on when I pulled into the driveway in front of my mom's house. I could see my mother through the window washing the dishes. She saw me and smiled and met me at the door but her smile turned into a confused frown as she took in my face.

"Mimi, what's wrong?" she asked. I threw myself into her arms and finally sobbed. Away from the cameras away from the judgements.

"I wanna kill him, Mama" I said through the tears. "I want to see him dead."

"Who? What happened?"

I just cried until I couldn't anymore. When the sobs dissipated my mother wiped my tears and sat me down and I explained everything that happened. How he intruded on my Vegas trip, how he showed up at my dinner and the picture he gave me, and the tattoo on his arm.

"What is wrong with him?!" My mother asked.

"He doesn't get to do that. He doesn't get to be sorry! He doesn't get to suddenly care and be forgiven!"

"Well that's not true, honey, you know that."

"No! He's a jerk!"

"Still, you have to forgive him."

"Mama!"

"Naomi, listen, I know you're angry and you have every right to be, but you have to forgive him."

"It's not that easy!" I snapped "He's not just some ex boyfriend that mistreated me! If only it was that simple.."

"I know but still.....holding on to this rage is only hurting you, not him. You need to let it go, honey. So you can move past this."

"How do you move past this?! How can someone move past losing their baby?!" my voice broke "He took my child, Mama! She died inside of me because of him."

"You can move past it. You have to let God comfort you and lead you, that is the only way, otherwise the pain and the anger and the hate will eat at your heart and it will kill you."

"I don't know how to do that," I wailed.

"Just Forgive him. Get on your hands and knees and pray and ask God to help you."

Forgive him? How?

"Why? He doesn't deserve it. He hasn't earned it. I doubt his apology was even sincere. He loves to lie and play and bounce back and forth. He's sorry today and maybe he'll be sorry tomorrow but the next day? He can apologize all wants, but at the end of the day, he never wanted her, he never loved her and if he says he did it's bull."

"You don't know that."

"Yes I do," I said. "He doesn't get to get off that easy."

"Then I don't know what else to tell you, MiMi." she sighed. I got up from the table and retired to my room. I hated that I was crying I hated crying. I lay silently on my bed staring out at nothing, listening to the pressing silence ringing in my ear. I hated Anthony so much and I refused to excuse him. I refused to hear him out when DeVon blew up my cell phone with texts begging me to talk to Anthony and just hear him out. Ruby text me and asked me if I was coming back. I told her that I didn't know. I passed out with my phone in my hand waiting for a reply from Trey that never came. The next morning, Uncle Ivan, told me that I couldn't quit the show. It'd be bad for future business if I walked out on my contract. I was given two weeks off and promised to be back for the Halloween Party. It was another promotional event for the show. They rented out our favorite night club, On Broadway. At least I wouldn't be alone with anyone there.

I'll have crowds of people to separate me from the rest of the club and even if that's not enough, I gave comp tickets to the party to my cousins, they'll keep Anthony away from me for sure.

After two days of not hearing from Trey, I decided to pull up on him at his job. I took my mustang I wanted to be a bit inconspicuous. The Audi drew more attention and if he was doing something that he shouldn't, he wouldn't see me coming in the mustang. I was pissed as hell that he wasn't answering and I wanted to know why. I'd hoped there was a good reason, I don't think I could handle any more hurt. He was standing outside with Dante smoking a cigarette when I pulled up. He wasn't holding on to any female, he wasn't talking too long to any female. He said hey to them as they walked in. Their glances lingered but his didn't. When I was satisfied that he didn't have any other girls with him, I pulled up and made my presence known.

"Before you get mad...." Trey said as I walked up "My nephew threw my phone into the toilet and I haven't been able to get a new one yet. I went to the clubhouse on Monday like I said I would and they told me you quit."

"Why didn't you have one of them call me."

"Only one there was DeVon and you didn't answer." Sounded about right. "Fine."

"You cool now?"

"I guess." My anger toward him had diminished but my anger over all was ever present.

"Good. Cuz I missed you." He pulled me into a hug and a kiss "Why'd you quit? DeVon said something about a tattoo."

"Did you see the Tat?"

"Nah he wasn't there. It was just DeVon."

I explained the look of the tattoo and how angry it made me.

"That's messed up but you can't quit over that."

"I can't not be mad. I'm so mad all the time. Not just at him. At the entire situation, at God, at the world. I don't know what I'm going to do. I can't quit, my manager won't let me because I signed a contract. I have to go back for the Halloween Party and I have to do season 4 and I don't know how I'm going to get through it without busting another bottle over someone's head or stabbing someone."

"We just need to find an outlet for your anger."

"Like what?"

"You ever taken boxing?"

"My dad used to teach me when I was a kid but that's it."

"Alright so how bout we try that. Why don't you just chill here til after my next appointment? My uncle works at City boxing, I'll see if he can hook us up."

I fake pouted.

"What?" he laughed "You still mad?"

"I thought you left me again," I said looking up at him.

"I'm sorry." he said softly lowering his head to kiss me.

"Don't do it again," I said against his lips.

"I won't." he chuckled. He pulled me to him and I couldn't keep up the fake pout. My face broke into a huge smile. God, I love this man. I can't stay mad at him, not with that face. That giant smile and those deep dimples have captured me since the moment we met and now I have captured him. I don't know how or why he loves me but I'm not going to question it. I'm just going to live in this reality for as long as I can. He makes everything so much easier to deal with.

"And when did you get 2 cars?"

"I bought this one last year and the audi was an endorsement," I explained.

"Where you been hiding this one?"

"At home with my mom."

It was cool hanging out at the shop. We were there longer than I expected because after his 2 hour appointment was done he had a couple walk -in's. I wasn't one to get in the way of my man making his money so I hung out. Got to know some people, laughed at some of their jokes. I felt like I belonged there, the negativity that I felt in the clubhouse didn't follow me here. I gained everyone's favor by going to get a New York Giant Pizza, a couple bottles of Henny and coke. It was Wednesday and the show was on, so going on that errand for the forty five minutes that the show was on didn't bother me at all. When I came back I told them that they could only have food and drink if they kept from asking me any questions about the episode. I didn't want to know, I didn't want to watch.

The female patrons asked for pictures but still flirted with Trey who rebuffed them at every opportunity. I didn't have to intervene or say anything, Trey shut them down every time. And the ones who weren't accepting his words, he would make a show for. He'd come over and pull me to him, grabbing on my booty and kissing me deeply, and then tell me he loves me. When his last tat was done, Trey and I left. Even my mustang he wanted to drive. It was safer that way anyway. I'd been drinking and he hadn't. I obviously couldn't bring Trey home to my mother's house, nor could he bring me to his grandmother's house, so using some of the money he had earned that day, he rented us a room for a couple nights at The Travel Lodge. He took me to City Boxing downtown the next morning and introduced me to his uncle who set me up with a membership and gave me my first actual boxing lesson. It actually was really cathartic, an excellent outlet for my anger. I went every day for the next two weeks. I worked on my straight punches so I didn't hurt my wrist when I punch somebody like I did when I punched Anthony at the Reunion.

Trey came over and helped me pack up my room, because it was almost time to move into our apartment downtown. My mother knew that I was moving into my own place. She didn't agree or approve of me being so close to the clubs and away from the protective shelter of her roof where she can pray over me every night, but she accepted it. I knew she knew that Trey was going to move in with me, though neither of us acknowledged it to the other. She used to like Trey at one point. He was always polite and respectful to her and she was very much in favor of him being in my life. Until he actually became a part of my life. Ever since she's been suspicious of him, she says I didn't need to be around him because he'd been in prison. It didn't matter to me, my mom never liked any of the guys I liked. They had to be "good ol church boys" who came every Sunday, bible in hand and a dress shirt on his back. Bible thumpers and nerds were her pick for me because they were "safe." I loved my mom and I understood her need to protect me, but I needed and wanted to be with Trey more than I wanted anything in my life. Her opinion didn't factor much in my decision making process.

Halloween was a packed house, there was barely any room to breathe. Every member of the breakfast club took turns doing something. Monroe was one of the D.J.'s of course who was again dressed as a vampire but this time he was the black vampire from Twilight, Laurent. Complete with dreads and the red contacts and the coat.

Athena, who was Magenta from Rocky Horror, stamped the hands at the door and handed out the VIP wristbands to the ones on the list. Ruby and I made a show as bartenders downstairs. She was a slutty nurse and I was finally able to pull off my dark fairy with red fishnets, fluffy punk rock skirt a black corset that showed more cleavage than I was used to and flexible red lace wings and all. We flirted and laughed and poured drinks. Our bar was packed with men, black, white, mexican, and all of them were pervs. Ruby would tell the guys we were secret girlfriends just to get a reaction from them. It didn't take long for all of them to offer ten dollars extra in tips to see us kiss.

I looked to Trey for his opinion and he just laughed and signaled me for me to go for it if I wanted to.

"Money first!" Ruby announced. They all dug in their pockets and held bills up high in the air. I had one of the bar backs empty the ice bucket and go around and collect the money. Upon seeing the overflowing container of dollar bills. I took a double shot of tequila and Ruby and I gave them a show. It was different kissing a girl, but not something I could make a habit of doing. The drunken hoard roared with cheer and laughter. When we pulled away from each other laughing there were even a few who were drooling and I wouldn't have been surprised if a couple of them let it go in their pants. Trey's jaw had dropped, surprised I actually did it. I told him not to get any ideas.

It was like Vegas all over again, except with costumes. My family was there and Trey was there and we were our own little bubble most of the time. Gratefully, Anthony was preoccupied with his own set of groupies to try and speak to me. He was dressed as a basketball star showing off his tattoo.

The boxing lessons were already working because two weeks ago I'd have been pissed as hell about Anthony using my daughter's death to get sympathy nookie from groupies, but that night I couldn't be bothered.

Karma is a bigger b---h than me, so Dumbass gon get his. Sooner or later.

DeVon, who got on stage upstairs and performed a couple songs with his wanna be G-Unit or D12 rap group, was dressed as Spider-Man. The rest of the group were dressed as the other members of The Avengers. We had The Hulk and Iron-Man, and Black Thor. The music wasn't that bad actually. I mean the crowd seemed to like it, I guess I just wasn't into Rap enough to tell if anyone had any unique talent. Most of it sounded the same to me. I finally met Athena's boyfriend who was so laid back, he didn't feel the need to dress for Halloween. He was very mature and I really did enjoy talking to him. He was smart and silly and fun to be around. I see why Athena liked him so much; he was the complete opposite of DeVon. Even though they lived in the same building, next door in fact, He didn't crowd her and she actually WANTED him to be around.

"It's new," she laughed. "refreshing actually."

As the night went on, drama seemed to erupt on all fronts for the Breakfast Club. Ruby was fighting with her baby daddy over her "friendship" with Gunnar who inserted himself into the situation in her defense. When trying to make her jealous of a bunch of groupies wasn't working, DeVon picked a fight with Athena's boyfriend. Monroe's girlfriend was yelling at him about flirting with other girls. They broke up and Monroe ended the night in the Guest Room with another groupie, who was in love with his abs. Anthony was in his own personal heaven. Every time I saw him he was surrounded by women, the types of women he always said he wanted; video hoes, strippers, regular hoes and some of them were actually quite attractive for a change. A couple even fought over him.

Trey was giving me another dance lesson on the main floor when she approached. He saw her before I did.

"Oh s--t," he breathed.

"What?" I asked.

"She's here."

"Who's here?"

He nodded toward the short fluffy black girl dressed as a cat. I didn't recognize who she was at first. My only thought at the moment was that she really shouldn't be wearing clothes that tight, she was too big for all that, seeing all her jelly rolls was NOT cute. Until she got closer and then I realized it was Kyanna and she looked pissed.

"Really Trey?" She asked coming up. "This where you been? This why you changed your number?"

"Man, go home Kyanna." Trey said wrapping his arms tighter around me I hadn't seen Kyanna since Easter Sunday at church. She looked at me funny and I had always intended on seeing what her problem was with me. I just hadn't gotten around to it.

"What's going on?" I asked looking between Kyanna and Trey.

"Remember that girl I told you I had been staying with?" Trey asked.

"You were talking about Kyanna?" I asked. I would have never guessed that of all the women in San Diego that Trey was staying with, it would be Kyanna. I knew she harbored some kind of crush on him but he never showed any interest in her besides friendship. She was his homeboy's little sister. I immediately felt even worse for the way he played her. I'd buried down the guilt for a random stranger but for someone who was at one point my friend? I became furious with Trey for not telling me that she was the one he had been complaining about. The other part of me however, scoffed at the side of me that felt bad.

That's what I was worried about? I asked in my confessional *No wonder Trey wasn't claiming her. I'm ten times better than she she is. This little butterball ain't even on my level. Never has been. I was amused that she had deluded herself into thinking she was ever anything more than a slide because it's always been clear that she was into Trey but he wasn't into her. There was no contest or competition.* I started to laugh

"Yea, that's my man," Kyanna said.

"I was never your man," Trey said.

"That wasn't what you was sayin before."

"It's what he's sayin now though," I told her, wrapping Trey's arms tighter around me.

"MiMi, we live together."

"First of all, my name is Lyric so if you're going to speak to me get my name right. Second of all you LIVED together, he moved out weeks ago. He lives with me now."

"Then why his s--t still at my house?"

"Because you let it become a storage unit?" I asked.

"I'll be by in the morning to pick up what's left," Trey declared.

"It's like that now?" she asked Trey.

Trey just smiled and licked his lip, like LL Cool J, trying not to laugh. He tilted his head in confirmation, letting her know that where I am, that's where he is going to be.

"Come on, babe." I said holding on to the hands around my waist and starting to walk away with him still holding on to me

"MiMi…"

"My name is Lyric." I repeated "Don't make me say it again," I laughed continuing to walk away.

"Did he tell you that I'm pregnant?" she asked stopping me in my tracks.

"She lying!" Trey said immediately. "Don't listen to her, keep walking babe."

I ignored him and turned back around back to Kyanna.

"Don't be one of them chicks, Yanna." I urged "Take the loss. He doesn't want you. He never did. Walk away. Move on."

"You know he only want you for the money right? If you didn't have that, you wouldn't have him."

"You simple b---h," I laughed. "You really don't get that he never wanted you, It's always been me over you. You were just a thirst bucket he gave a few drops to. Stay on your level."

"My level? You think you better than me? But you so stupid."

"I'm stupid? but you the illiterate ho, who couldn't even get into a community college cuz you failed high school right? Did you even pass 8th grade? Can you even spell stupid Kyanna? Is that too hard for you? Do you spell it with a U or two O's?"

She spit on me, and before I even wiped it off of my face, my fist flew across her face in perfect form and we were fighting. Hair was pulled, punches were thrown, faces were scratched. I was still trying to stomp on her when security pulled me off of her with pieces of her weave stuck in between my fingers and her blood was smeared across my wrist.

"Somebody call the zoo and tell them they're missing a baby elephant," I shouted. All I could do was laugh as they carried me out of the club and sat me outside. They couldn't kick me out altogether, it was technically my party, but Kyanna had to go.

"Are you aiight?" Trey laughed. "Lemme see," he took my chin between his thumb and forefinger and turned my face from side to side. "You barely got a scratch on you." He was impressed.

"Is she tellin' the truth?" I asked with no trace of humor in my tone.

"Who?" He asked surveying my body for any cuts or traces of my own blood.

"Kyanna!" I shouted "Is she pregnant?!"

"She says so."

"Is it yours?"

"She says so."

"But you don't believe her?"

"Nope. I mean it's a possibility but I doubt it."

"How do you know?"

"Cuz I strap up. Everytime. I didn't trust her about no birth control s--t"

"Alright, but if I find out you the one that's lying..."

"You saying you don't trust me then?"

"You know condoms aren't 100% effective right?"

"I know, but I still don't think it's mine."

"You told me you weren't f---in her."

"I said I hadn't since you and I linked up. But before then I smashed a couple times I didn't even want to, she was just there."

"I am so sick of hearing that s--t. That's all I f---in heard last year."

"Don't compare me to that b----h ass nigga you was f---in, I ain't nothing like him."

"Why didn't you tell me it was Kyanna?"

"Don't feel bad for her, all she ever do is talk s--t about you. I didn't tell you cuz I didn't want the drama."

"How'd you even link up with her?"

"She wrote to me while I was locked up."

"Oh so she had your address but I didn't."

"It's not even like that, she's friends with my sister Jen. You know Jen and her cousin used to be a thing back in the day. Jen gave her my address, not me. I even asked her for your phone number in a letter and she said she didn't have it."

Now it was clear. That look Kyanna gave me on easter? She was in contact with Trey the whole time, knowing that I wanted to get in touch, that he wanted to get in touch. She was laughing at me because she knew she had something that I wanted, something she thought she could keep from me. Now I wanted to stomp on her again

"Look, it don't even matter." Trey said "I'm with you now. We here, We good. It's me and you from now on."

"And what if the baby is yours?"

"It's not cuz I'm not the only one she been f---in, she got some other nigga is Chula Vista she was f---in too, and I guarantee she was doing him raw cuz she always begged me not to use a condom."

"But what if it is?"

"I don't know, we'll handle it."

Truth was I still loved him, we were still moving in together and I wasn't going to let some thirsty troll get in the way of my happiness.

My mood the next morning was much more pleasant than the night before. A relaxing shower and being with the man I loved would do that for me. I decided that Kyanna was lying about being pregnant. And if she wasn't lying about that then she was lying about the paternity. Trey decided that he and I didn't need to go over there to get anything. It was only a few things anyway, and none of it was important. A couple pairs of jeans some old tennis shoes. Maybe some shirts...all of his important papers and most of his clothes were at his grandmother's.

"Lyric! You have a guest!" DeVon shouted from downstairs. I put on my shower robe, wrapped up my wet hair and went downstairs followed by a shirtless Trey in basketball shorts. It was probably my cousin Hector who was helping me move today. When I came downstairs I saw a trash bag, Kyanna with swollen bottom lip and the start of bruising on her cheek, standing next to it with something in her hand.

OH! Round two! Anthony laughed on screen.

The boys encircled us loosely like children in a school yard wanting to get the best view. Athena sat atop the counter eating an apple barely interested but still somewhat curious about what would happen next.

"What's the hungry hippo doing here?" Ruby asked coming down the stairs behind me and Trey, Gunnar in tow.

"B---h, you don't know me," Kyanna retorted.

"Who would want to, thirsty ass groupie."

"Ruby." I said shaking my head at her. I didn't see the need to insult her. The pain was already evident on her face when she saw Trey and I emerge together, both fresh from the shower. Part of me pained for her, my old friend, who probably loved Trey like I did.

"What are you doing here?" Trey asked bored with the sight of her.

"I'm just bringing you the rest of your stuff, I don't want you anywhere near my house."

"Cool. Thanks. Bye," he hinted.

"And I brought this for you." She said and handed me an envelope. I took it and opened it. It was a print out of a positive pregnancy test from planned parenthood, she was 6 weeks along.

"Congratulations," I said. "What you giving me this for? It doesn't mean anything."

"It means I'm having his baby."

"It means you havin somebody's baby not mine." Trey said "You been f---in a couple niggas but I wrapped up. Everytime."

"It's yours nigga stop tryin to front cuz you got yourself a new bank account," she said referring to me.

"Right, cuz money is all I have on you." I said sarcastically, the momentary sympathy now gone. "Even if it is his baby, that don't make you shit but a baby mama."

"You would be the expert about not being s--t huh? Maybe that's why your baby died cuz it knew you weren't s--t and didn't…"

I didn't let her finish her sentence. I flew at her faster than security could move. I hadn't even realized I was choking her until my fingers were being pulled from around her neck I hadn't felt her hitting my face or my hands or my arms. I vaguely remember biting her fingers when they slipped into my mouth while she was pushing my face away from her. They finally got her out from underneath me while I still reached and kicked for her. A gasping and choking Kyanna was taken outside of the house by way of the front door.

"I'm good! Let go!" I said snatching away. I picked up the towel that had come off of my hair and wiped away the little bit of blood that was coming out of my mouth. DeVon came over with his hand held up expecting a high five.

"I knew you were crazy," he laughed but I just looked at him with an evil glare. He high fived himself and moved on.

Kyanna had caught her breath and drank some water and was shouting threats at me and Trey. She told me to wait until the cameras and crew weren't around she was going to f--k me up. She told Trey to watch his back cuz her brother was gonna f--k him up. I tried to rush her again but Trey picked me up with one arm and held me back.

"You got hella anger issues," Anthony said.

"Shut the f--k up" I snapped still amped from the fight with Kyanna. I was still itching to hit somebody and I wouldn't mind pounding Anthony's face in.

"As many times as she took off on you last year? And you just now figuring this out?" Monroe asked.

"She didn't take off on me." Anthony argued.

I grabbed a bottle of rum off the counter, Anthony flinched away, to everyone else's amusement but mine, and I walked up the stairs.

"Man! She beat that b---h ass like that b---h was Anthony," Monroe said.

"What did you expect?" Ruby asked "She shouldn't have mentioned the baby."

"She was trying to kill her," Anthony said.

"Nah, Naomi ain't capable of murder," Ruby disagreed.

"Lyric might be," DeVon offered. "Did you see your girl choking her out?"

"Let's not forget she almost killed Anthony last semester," Athena said.

"Now that was funny," DeVon laughed.

"You gonna go check on her?" Monroe asked Trey.

"I'm gonna give her a few minutes to cool down first," Trey answered.

I turned on my Queen of the Damned soundtrack to tune out the rest of the conversation. I let it play loud to signal that I wasn't to be bothered for a while. I was angry while dressing for the day. Angry and scared. Not of the threats that Kyanna made, she'd come at me twice and twice ended up on the ground, but of losing Trey. If the baby was his, what made her so different from me? I'll never have him to myself now. Moving in together won't change anything. How can he be there for the baby and not be there for her? Especially now while she's still pregnant. It's the same thing I went through with Anthony but instead of many chicks in her way there was just me. What kind of woman would I be if I asked him not to be there for her? What kind of man would he be if he listened?

With the help of Bacardi Gold and Queen of the Damned, I was able to numb and zone out the situation. I had just finished flattening the last piece of hair when Trey came in carrying an ice pack and turned off my radio in the middle of an other worldly vocalization of "Forsaken."

"You summoning the devil in here?" he asked.

"It's the Queen of the Damned soundtrack. It calms me."

"How?"

"By speaking out loud about everything I'm feeling inside."

"You kinda scary you know that?"

"Yep." I said with a smile.

"How's the jaw feeling?"

"I'm not feeling much of anything right now." I said taking another swig of Bacardi straight from the bottle.

"Baby it's not even noon," He laughed.

"It is somewhere."

"Put this on your cheek." he said handing me the ice pack "It'll keep the swelling from getting too bad."

"I'm good though," I said.

"Please? It'll hurt later."

"Did she even hit me that hard I didn't feel s--t."

"You weren't yourself but you'll probably feel sore eventually."

"Ugh fine." I rolled my eyes took the pack and placed it on my cheek and sat on the bed.

He looked worried. "So I guess she's not faking huh?" he said.

"I guess not." I said irritation rising up in me.

"You know this doesn't change anything right? We can still do us. I mean I highly doubt that it's mine. If it is then she turkey basted like the desperate ho that she is."

"What happens if you get the DNA test and it is yours? You'll have an obligation to her, how is that not going to affect us?"

"It won't because it's not mine. She's just jealous and trying to f--k things up with us."

"Maybe but what if…"

"Man, f--k the what if's." He said sternly "I'm telling you, you gon be the one to have my baby not no gutter bucket like Kyanna."

"You used to call her your little sister. Now she's a gutter bucket?"

"She used to be your friend, now she's all the stuff you called her?"

"How could you not tell me it was her?"

"Because I didn't want to risk losing you because it was her. I love you."

"Whatever, man." I said.

"Just don't worry about it." He said "Nothin' gon change with me and you, I'm gonna marry you someday and then me and you are going to have a family."

I smiled at the idea. Me and Trey and a little boy that looks just like him. Not today and Not tomorrow, but someday was a nice thought. It was an idea that I toyed with in my mind since the day I met him.

"You can really see yourself married to me?" I asked.

"Hell yea. I mean life won't be perfect but all I really need is you and all you really need is me and we can work it out together."

"Ok." I laughed.

"What you laughing for?"

"We sound so silly, like a freakin soap opera. Let's go move into our apartment." I said tossing the ice pack at him and grabbing the bottle.

"You know you're not driving now right?"

"Like you ever let me drive my own car anyway." I said and headed downstairs I wouldn't believe Trey was the father of Kyanna's baby until the DNA test come back. I knew her, she had always been more insecure than me when it comes to guys and as such more sexually open, thinking that would keep them interested in her. I realized that every time in the last two years when Kyanna said Trey could never be serious about me, how he's a playboy and I deserve better, just so she could keep us separated because she wanted him. I wouldn't put it past her to try and push a baby on him to try and keep him close to her and further from me. I knew Trey wouldn't allow that to happen and neither would I.

TWENTY ONE

I loved our new apartment. It was Trey's first time seeing it, so he was way more excited than me. It was luxury one bedroom in Little Italy 650 square feet and we were on a high enough floor that we could look out from the living room window and see the San Diego Harbor. Moving in was easy. All we had right now was a bed, my flat screen TVs and DVD collection. I brought my TV from the clubhouse and put it in our bedroom, once we got a wall mount or a dresser we'd be able to hang it. We put the big TV from my room at my mom's house into the living room. We didn't have any furniture or dishes yet, just ourselves our clothes and a bed but that's all we needed to start. That was a lot more than most people had. I stared out at the sun over the water and completely lost myself in thought.

"What's wrong?" Trey asked.

"Hmm?" I asked snapping back into reality.

"You have a weird look on your face, you ok?"

"Yea I'm just tired. It's been a long couple of days. I could use a nap."

"Well you're home now." He smiled "Take a nap, I'll lay down with you."

"Yea...that's a good idea." I said calmly walking into the bedroom.

The bedframe hadn't been setup yet so we just layed on a bare mattress with a light blanket and spooned.

"So are you going to be able to live here with me while you're filming?"

"Thanksgiving week probably, but the show is set up so that I have to be in the house until around Christmas. After winter break, we're filming spring semester in Mexico."

"Mexico? For how long?"

"From March until June"

"That's a long time."

"It's ninety five grand an episode," I said.

"Damn!" he laughed.

"I'm thinking of quitting after that." I finally admitted.

"Why?"

"I came back for season 3 because I felt like I had something to prove to the world. The comments about me were so mean, they talked about my weight, all of first season, and I'm scared to look at the second season because I'm even bigger in that one."

"Baby, you were pregnant, you're supposed to be big. You were still beautiful. I been watching it at the shop."

"I was crying all the time I felt like I wanted to prove to people that there's more to me than a complainer, that I wasn't stuck on my baby daddy like he and a lot of other people believed. I wanted to prove that I was sexy and desirable."

"You are!" Trey insisted.

"But I didn't feel that way!" I said "I felt like the lowest most repulsive female in the world last year and the negative comments didn't help."

"I'm sure there were more than just the negative."

"But the negative stood out more."

"Why do you care so much about what people think though?"

"You wouldn't understand."

"Try me."

"I've never been seen or accepted by the people I thought mattered in my world. Aside from my parents, I really didn't have anybody. I was alone all the time. My cousins didn't want to be around me and when they were there it's like they didn't see me. Nobody saw me. I came on this show because I wanted to be seen. I wanted to be liked and now I feel like all it's doing is driving me closer to insanity than I've ever been. It's a lot of pressure to not be seen as weak."

"OK so you were lonely and wanted people to like you so you went on TV and now that you're on TV not enough people like you to make you want to stay on TV?"

"I guess that sums it up."

"Alright well first, not everyone is going to like you and f--k them if they don't. You don't need them. Are they paying your bills? Are they living your life? No so f--k them hater ass mother f---ers. Second of all you are anything but weak I don't know who told you were or what makes you think you are but you are a strong woman. You had every right to feel the way you did last year, you were dealing with a lot of changes and you had no support from that punk ass mother f---er that put you in that situation. What happened to you, losing your child like that, would have broken most women but you are holding yourself together, smiling. Every time I see you, you smiling."

"I'm smiling because you're there," I clarified.

"Well I'm happy I can make you smile. Look, You are allowed to feel what you feel, f--k what all them niggas in the house say, they stupid as hell."

"I don't like how I feel around them, I don't feel like myself."

"Wasn't that the point though? Ain't that why you make people call you Lyric? New name, new you?"

"Lyric was just supposed to be a character at first, tough, aggressive, no nonsense, don't play type of girl. Now I feel like the character is kind of taking over me. Do you know I didn't even realize I was choking Kyanna today until I was being pulled off of her." I confessed looking at the scratch marks reddening on the back of my hands. Trey chuckled a little "Yea, your eyes were a little different but she provoked you, she shouldn't have said what she said."

"She's pregnant, and she was hurting. That's why she said it. Last semester I felt like a part of me had left my body when I smashed the bottle across Anthony's head, I could have killed him. I think and say really mean things and I'm starting not to recognize myself."

"That's why I love you because even when people are dirty toward you, you're still concerned for them but Kyanna is gonna be alright, I'll talk to her brother. He knows how she is. As far as Anthony is concerned, I've been watching the show, everybody in the shop who watch the show are ready to beat his ass and it's only been 4 episodes, he deserved it and if you hadn't done something to show that you wasn't one to play with, he would have still been laughing at you, thinking he got you in his pocket."

"But maybe my baby would be here," I thought aloud.

"Maybe, but maybe not."

"I feel like the tougher I try to be, the weaker I feel."

"Baby, trust me, *nobody* sees you as weak. Mother f--kers is scared of you, Anthony is in love with you and he's still scared of you."

"Anthony is not in love with me." I scoffed "He's just mad because I don't want him and he thinks I should."

"That dude get's a chubby damn near every time you walk in the room. He's scared and turned on at the same time, he don't even know what to do with himself. He can't keep his eyes off you."

"Eww." I laughed.

"Exactly. Look, if you want to quit that's fine, but think about it first. It's not even the money, it's the opportunity you have by being on the show. Take advantage of it while you can, ride that s--t through the doors that lead to your singing and acting gigs, to that real money that will make ninety five grand look like 95 cents. Build a brand for yourself first and then quit. Otherwise what are you going to do with yourself?"

"I don't know." I shrugged.

"You're not alone anymore, if you start to feel weak just tag me in, I'm in your corner. I got you."

"Me and you against the world?" I mused.

"Hella"

"Pinky promise?"

"Double pinky promise," we locked both pinkies and just like that my mood lightened.

"Now, roll back over so I can go to sleep." he ordered "I'm tired."

I giggled and complied. I thought about what he said and it made sense. I needed to go forward not backward. I couldn't let this bull make me quit on a dream I'd had since I was nine years old. I had a chance not many aspiring actresses had and I would take it. Starting with this showcase for my musical audition course. I was still terrified of singing in front of an audience but if this is what I wanted to do in life I would have to.

The news of the fight at On Broadway had reached the internet and entertainment channels quicker than I had anticipated.

It was a Lyrical Brawl Halloween Night inside On Broadway nightclub. As anyone who watches The reality show The Breakfast Club knows, Lyric isn't one to take things lightly. However usually her temper and outbursts are reserved for her ex boyfriend as well as co star Anthony Smith. However, this time she came to blows with another young woman over claims to new boyfriend Trey Lovell. Witnesses say it seemed like it was going to stop with words but things escalated when the woman spit in the stars face. Security intervened shortly after and Lyric was seen to be laughing as they pulled her away from the altercation. It is still unknown who the young woman is or what connection she has to the star and her new boo (though I'm sure we can guess). Whatever it was she didn't seem phased by it continuing the night in high spirits as if the whole thing didn't happen. Watch a video of the altercation below.

Sure enough there was a video of the night's events. You couldn't hear what was being said over the music and it was from a little bit of a distance but you see me walking away with Trey and then turning back to Kyanna saying a few things, then she spits and I give her a straight punch to the face and continue punching as she tries to punch and block at the same time. People around us moved out of the way to not get hit and Security scrambles to get through to stop it and pull me off of her laughing like it was the funniest thing in the world.

I laughed while watching it and so did Trey.

"You were a beast, babe," he said.

"Would you believe that was the first fight I'd ever been in?" I asked.

"For real?" Trey asked.

"Yep. My cousin Kendrick taught me some stuff after I got jumped in 7th grade but this was the first one where I was actually fighting."

"Don't look like it," he laughed.

You would think that I had committed some kind of crime from the way my phone blew up all day. My Uncle Ivan and Aunt Yvette, my mom, my other aunts, my cousins, various church members, my grandmother. Nanny left a very long voicemail chastising me for fighting over a man. Something I "know better" than to do. My cousins who were there didn't bother. They saw everything that happened and were shocked and probably a little scared. They'd never seen me so angry before. I wasn't the cry baby cousin they grew up with anymore and they weren't sure which version they preferred. My dad called, asked me if I was ok and then told me to be careful getting in fights in the club and not to get arrested. He accepted the fact that I was an an adult and was going to do what I wanted to do. He also said that it was a "good punch."

Radio interviews were part of the promotion obligation for the show so unfortunately I wasn't able to spend Trey's and my first Thanksgiving as a couple together.I had to go to New York and make my rounds to different radio stations with The BFC. The fight on Halloween was brought up a lot and I was asked the usual questions about my relationship status with Anthony, and what my major was, my aspirations. A couple of them even asked me to sing right there in the station and I told them they would have to wait and if they wanted to hear me sing they could come out to the showcase in a couple weeks

"What song are you going to be singing?" I was asked.

"I'm actually really torn between two, Home from the Wiz or I Dreamed a Dream from Les Mis."

"Why are you torn between those two?"

"Because Home I can sing really pretty but I don't know if I can really relate to it enough to act it out. I Dreamed a Dream is really powerful and I can relate to it but I'm still having trouble holding the note. I keep running out of breath." I laughed "I'm still working on it. Everyone in the house hates it. I practice it so much, I get told to shut up a lot."

"Well I can't wait to hear which one you choose, I'm definitely going to be there," one of the radio hosts said.

In the end I chose to do the song from Les Miserables. I figured out that if I paused for a beat and took in air before the climb then I wouldn't run out of breath. I was happy and excited and very pleased with myself. The director and accompanist loved the pause it added an element of anticipation but as the night of the performance came. I was suddenly petrified to go on stage.

"Picture everyone naked," Trey said.

"That's gross."

"Ok don't do that then. Uhh... ooh! Just imagine you're by yourself at home in the shower or doing your hair."

"Close your eyes if you have to," my mom said.

Technically you weren't supposed to close your eyes when you sing in theater but I would need to. I was so scared. When it came my turn I eyed James in the front seat who gave me a thumbs up and my entire family smiling in encouragement. I started off bad at first my voice cracked in the nerves and I asked to start over. Nanny signaled for me to breathe and I cleared my throat exhaled and started again, perfectly, as rehearsed. Then I got to the line that I had been working on for weeks "But the tigers come at night, with their voices soft as thunder...as they tear your hope apart and they turn your dreams to" I paused. I closed my eyes, took in air and continued climbing higher and higher and more intense "shame". It was a perfect delivery and the rest of the song wasn't as bad for me. I just had to focus on acting it out from that point. The character was hurting, the song was about a girl who fell in love with a man and had such high hopes for the relationship only to give herself to him and then have him leave. She's bitter about it but yet still wished for him to come back but knows that he won't. She has this child that she can't support and she's been doing everything she can but it's not enough, and she feels dead inside, everything she had planned, that she had been promised was gone. In my mind I substituted the man for Tiana and the child she's trying to support for the pain I was trying to move on from. When I was finished, I had tears in my eyes and I received a standing ovation. After the showcase I came outside to greet my family and I was swooped up and spun around by James.

"I knew you could do it!" he said. "I'm so proud of you!" He pushed my face against his chest and squeezed me affectionately.

"James, I need to breathe," I choked out.

"Oh my bad."

He released me and passed me to my dad who handed me a bouquet of roses. "I didn't know you could sing like that " my dad admitted "I'm proud of you baby, you might actually be able to make your dream come true. Keep practicing." That meant a lot coming from my dad because he never actually believed that acting was something that I could really succeed at doing. Not because he didn't believe in me but because he didn't think it was a realistic and practical goal. There were no guarantees and he just wanted me to be able to support myself and get by in life.

"You started off a little shaky." Nanny said "But you found your footing and you blew everyone away! I'm so proud of you." She said hugging me "I knew you could do it."

Trey smirked at me with his face glowing in pride and his eyes lit up in excitement. "You did that." He said "I told you." All of my aunts and uncles and cousins passed me around hugging me, telling me what a good job I did, how proud of me they were and handing me bouquets of flowers.

"We gotta get you to come sing at the church one sunday." My grandfather said in his sweet raspy voice. He didn't go to the big church like the rest of us he had his own small church that only a couple of my mom's siblings were members of.

"Haha maybe." I laughed. I didn't plan on singing at a church at all but I wouldn't tell my grandfather that. He would start preaching and praying right there on the spot if I did.

The third season wrapped after finals as usual, and the next day Uncle Ivan called me and Trey to his office said there was some news he wanted to talk to us about. I couldn't figure out for the life of me what my agent would need to talk to both me AND Trey about.

"The network called me this morning," Uncle Ivan said once we were seated on his couch. "According to the polls you, Miss, are the breakout star of The Breakfast Club and after seeing some of the footage of season three, the network wants to offer you your own show."

"My own show?" That sounded so ridiculous. "About what?"

"About you two" he said "Your relationship, your life as you struggle to become a Broadway star. They want to call it Lyrical Chaos."

"Wow," Trey laughed.

"Think about it, a rising star in love with her average joe boyfriend, and the drama that surrounds your relationship, and how you guys make it work. The test audience loves your storyline.

"How much?" Trey asked.

"They're offering twenty thousand an episode for you and a hundred and fifty thousand for Lyric since she's an established star and the show is centered primarily around her."

"How many episodes?"

"Ten to start off and if it does well they'll order a second season of thirteen."

"What else?" I asked.

"What do you mean?"

"They want me to let cameras invade my life outside of the clubhouse they gotta come better than that."

"Well I could negotiate for more."

"Tell the network I want 250 and I want Trey to get 100 since he is the primary person in my life. I want producer credit, a say in the editing of the episodes and 10% of all merchandising from The Breakfast Club and Lyrical Chaos."

"Can you do that?" Trey asked.

"They're coming to me about this. I'm really not interested in it so it needs to be worth my while."

Two days later during my photo shoot for Audi, Uncle Ivan called with the networks counter offer: Two fifty per episode for Lyrical Chaos if I agree to do the 5th and 6th season of The Breakfast Club which I still hadn't signed on for. They would give Trey sixty five an episode and I would get producer credit a say in what gets filmed but not the editing. Also only 7% of merchandising, not 10."

"Sixty Five G's is better than twenty." Trey said "I'm in."

"MiMi?" Uncle Ivan asked.

I rolled my eyes I hated the idea of another season with The Breakfast Club but remembering what Trey said about making it work for me. I reluctantly agreed. "Ugh! fine when does it start?" Trey was so excited he picked me up and spun me around rubbing off the body paint on his white tee.

"In June. A month after you come back from Mexico, until the beginning of August before the fifth season begins filming."

I sighed and shrugged and went back to my photo shoot. At least I was becoming rich off all these annoyances.

TWENTY TWO

I dreaded doing the season two reunion show after New Years. It had been such a peaceful 2 weeks away from them. I dreaded DeVon almost as much as Anthony. My annoyance level went from zero to sixty just seeing either of them. You couldn't find one without the other. The eighty thousand dollar check for being here made it easier though.

Aisha helped me pick out a gorgeous red sleeveless cocktail dress that ruffled at the shoulders and hugged my hips and fell below my knee. I wore the matching red pumps that Trey bought for me in Vegas. My eyeshadow was blended in shades of gray and matte red lipstick.

The show started like it did last time, the cast was introduced to applause and cheers Anthony's cheers were mixed with booing from a lot of the women in the audience, which confused Anthony but made me laugh.

"Alright, let's get right to it." The hostess asked "What is the status of everyone's romantic relationship as it stands now? Athena and DeVon, how are things with you, it seemed to be a bit touch and go there at the end of the season."

"We are no longer in a relationship," Athena said.

"No longer in a relationship? What happened? Did it at least end amicably?"

"I can't be in a relationship with a female that I can't trust." DeVon said "She was way too cool with too many dudes, parading herself around in booty shorts for attention. She'd be next door chillin with a bunch of dudes while I was in her spot waiting for her. I just can't be with a chick like that."

"Wow ok. That's so not what happened," Athena laughed.

"So you're not dating that dude now?" DeVon asked.

"Yea, I am but he has nothing to do with why we broke up."

"Well why do you think you guys broke up?" the hostess asked.

"To avoid an endless argument, let's just say that our differences became a major issue in our relationship and we're just not mentally compatible."

That was Athena's way of saying DeVon was immature and irresponsible and needed to grow up.

"Mentally compatible? What does that mean?" the hostess asked.

"It means DeVon is immature and insecure who thought of Athena as his possession not his girlfriend and would never give her any space to breathe," I chimed in.

"Man, shut the f--k up, you the one who's insecure!" DeVon retorted.

"Von, you flipped out every time a dude looked at Athena. She couldn't have a casual conversation with a classmate without you thinking that she wanted to f--k them."

"Pretty much. What she said," Athena agreed.

"You flipped out every time I talked to another female." Anthony defended to me. "We weren't even dating."

"That was different," I said.

"How?"

"I didn't flip out when you talked to a chick. I just didn't want to see or hear about it and you would go out of your way to throw it in my face. What pissed me off was when you cared more about a female you trying to smash than your child."

"What?!"

"Hold that thought guys, we'll get to you." The hostess said "First I want Athena to explain what she meant."

"It's pretty much what Ric said. DeVon isn't at a level of maturity that I would prefer in someone I date. He was jealous and was smothering. I couldn't have any time to do anything without him being right there. He would show up at my house without warning, and stay all night."

"You just wanted a little breathing room," the hostess said.

"So you go and chill with a house full of dudes while I sit at your house."

"So you get mad and decide to put your hands on her?" I asked.

The crowd gasped.

"It was an accident," he laughed.

"Holding someone down while they're screaming in pain because they're being burned is an accident?" Athena asked.

"Wait so he held you down and burned you?"

"No, this is what happened." DeVon said "When I grabbed her and held her by her shoulders on the bed, the hookah got knocked over and the coal was burning her leg and I didn't know."

"But she was screaming?"

"I was too busy yelling at her to hear her."

"Wow, Athena you're ok now though right?"

"Yea I'm fine."

"Well I'm glad to hear it. So is it safe to say there's no chance reconciliation for you two?"

"No," Athena said.

"What about as friends?"

"That'd be kind of awkward."

"DeVon?"

"It's whatever, man. I really don't care."

She cut to commercial and when we came back she talked to Monroe about his storyline. He was The Ladies man and he had gotten caught up last year when one of his girls caught him out with another one of his girls and they fought over him. Monroe just laughed and said "Pimpin ain't easy." But he did say he had put all of that aside and was, for the time being, a one woman man.

Finally they came to the biggest storyline of season two: Me, Anthony and the baby. I had purposely not watched the second season. I didn't want to relive what I already played in my head every day since. I didn't need to be reminded of what I would never forget, yet here it was on screen in front of me and I couldn't look away. My eyes watered at some of the clips, I looked away at the last scene of me collapsing in pain on the bedroom floor, and turned to Trey who was sitting in the audience with his sister Keisha, Aisha, James, and Jaycee. He mouthed that he loved me and nodded toward the side of the stage asking if I needed a break. I nodded yes and when the clip was done I asked for a minute. The hostess called a commercial break when she saw the redness of my eyes and allowed me time to regroup.

I walked back stage where Trey curled me in his arms as I sobbed at the newly tapped ache in my soul. He rocked me side to side and kissed my head. He didn't need to say anything he just stood there and held me. I managed to dry my tears and the makeup team fixed my face in time to head back on stage and finish the show.

"Let's start with you Anthony." The hostess asked "You and Lyric had some ups and downs this season and for a minute there it looked like things were going to stay up....what happened?"

"I don't know," he said. "Things just got out of hand and took too far and she over reacted as usual."

"Over reacted?!" I interjected. "You had a b---h in my bed!!! Literally a b---h! A female dog how did you expect me to react?"

"I don't know....I expected you to yell at me of course but then I thought you'd go somewhere and cry like you always do. It was your fault she was there anyway if you hadn't have went crazy on me at the first reunion I wouldn't have had to put you in your place."

"In my place? The f--k you mean in my place?"

"I had to let you know that you were replaceable. If you wasn't going to act right you'd get replaced."

"Do you really think.....that just...do you have any idea how stupid you sound when you talk? Seriously. And don't think just because I'm in a dress and heels that I won't come over there and bust you in the mouth. Say somethin' else disrespectful, nigga get put in *your* place b----ass" The audience roared with applause.

"Whatever. You're not gonna do nothin'," he said trying to front.

"Oh yes she will." Monroe laughed "You got that scar on the side of your head cuz you didn't think she'd do nothin'" The audience laughed and ooh'd at the blast.

"The thing you always got f---ed up was that you thought everything i did or said was about me and you, and it wasn't I couldn't give two s--ts about whether or not you wanted to be in a relationship with me, it was always about the baby."

"But the baby wasn't even here yet."

"She was inside of me! I needed your support, I needed to know that I could count on you."

"I'm confused about something." The hostess said "Anthony you were adamant for 2 seasons that Lyric wasn't your girlfriend, that you didn't want to be in a relationship with her and yet on Valentine's day, you made this grand gesture of wanting to be with her. You brought her roses and chocolates, a teddy bear, you even said that you might be in love with her…. and then you go and say and do things that are very disrespectful."

"Ok, the Valentines thing….she was planning on keeping my baby from me so I did and said what I thought she wanted so that I could be there for my child."

"I never wanted you!!!" I said. "I wanted your consideration, your respect, your f---in support, I wanted to know that I could f---in depend on you to show up and be there for your daughter! Instead what do you do? You laugh at me when I'm upset, you show up at my house on New Years and you won't leave, talkin about how you missed me…and in the same breath tell me about a b----h you f---d earlier that day to prove you weren't gay!"

He opened his mouth to respond but I cut him off "And if you say I can't get mad because I wasn't your girlfriend, I promise you, I'm comin across this damn stage to bust you in yo muthaf---in mouth!" I took off my heels and handed them to Monroe to pass to Trey so I wouldn't fall over them.

He laughed and I knew he was about to say it, even DeVon knew he was about to say it. He stood up and moved off the stage so he wouldn't get hit. "You can't though because you weren't" The crowd roared with shock as I ran across the stage, ducking underneath one guard's raised arm, and got inches from Anthony's face before another pulled me back. "How many doctors appointments did you go to?! How many times did you hear her heartbeat?! You didn't give two shits about the child whose life you claimed to want to be involved in! but you can f--k a random b---h to prove what?! That you were a man? That we weren't in a relationship?!"

"Lyric sit down," the guard said.

"F--k you!" I said. "Get off me!"

"Not until you sit down."

"Let her go. I got her." Trey said to the guard. Trey sat down on the arm of the couch and held me against him.

"It's alright, calm down," he whispered in my ear.

"I don't get why she's so upset though," Anthony said.

I looked to the audience. "Anyone in here had a baby? Raise your hand." About half the women in the crowd raised their hands.

"When you were pregnant, were you more emotional than normal?"

"Yes!" they shouted in agreement.

"Did you need help and reassurance that things were going to be ok?"

"Yes!"

"Isn't the baby's health and well being dependent on you staying relaxed and stress free?"

"Yes!"

I held my hand out to the audience "This is why I'm mad. You got your arm tatted 'Daddy's Princess' you sit there and talk about how you were trying to be in your child's life and all that bull but you didn't care enough about your 'princess' to make sure that I was ok. That I felt secure enough in you as a man, to believe that you were going to be a dependable partner when it came to raising my daughter, instead you cared more about yourself, and pullin' females, and what them bum ass niggas you call your "family" said to your puppet ass…"

"Puppet?" he asked confused.

"Yes a puppet, you let muthaf----s pull your strings tell you what to do and how to act. You let DeVon do it, you let your uncles do it you let your cousins do it. It's your fault my child is gone!" I jerked toward him again but Trey pulled me back and kissed my temple trying to soothe me.

"So you blame him?" the hostess asked.

"Yes because I feel like if he hadn't gone out of his way to upset me at any and every opportunity, to test me and see if I cared about him just so he can say that he didn't care about me, then I wouldn't have been so stressed out and my daughter would be alive today."

"I don't think he did it on purpose," DeVon defended. "Anthony is just stupid that way."

"No I'm not."

197   SAMANTHA SANCHEZ

"Yes you are." DeVon, Monroe and Athena said in unison. The entire audience laughed.

"So it's safe to say that you guys will not be able to put your differences aside and remain friends."

"We were never friends."

"Aww come on 'Ric, you know you had some kind of love for the nigga." DeVon laughed "You ain't the only one that lost the baby yo, Anthony been through it too."

"Anthony didn't lose shit but face when I went upside his head. You know what? I can't" I said unhooking the mic from my dress. "I'm done with these niggas. F---in monkey see monkey do mutha f----s. F----n' dumb and dumber ass niggas." I tossed the mic onto the couch and walked away. I wasn't about to repeat myself to dudes with the bodies of an adult and the mind of a kindergartner. Everyone else understood me, I said what I needed to say and I was done. I didn't wanna see any of them until Mexico.

The break was longer this time to prepare for our trip to Mexico. I spent most of the break, improving my necessary skills, dancing classes like Ballet, tap and jazz, and vocal lessons. I took some head shots and did a couple of other photoshoots, went on some auditions. I worked out twice a day. I switched from boxing lessons to MMA lessons in the mornings, Trey thought that was hot and would spar with me sometimes which led to sex every time, and then I had cardio and weights at night. I was losing weight and getting in shape. I was determined to look good in a bikini for Mexico. Best of all though was the event hostings. I hosted events at clubs all over California at $10,000 a pop. I brought Trey along with me when he could go. We used the money to decorate the house with furniture and shelves and knick knacks and put pictures on the wall. I found out that tattooing wasn't Trey's only source of income. He sold weed and a lot of it. He and his cousin Patrick grew it and sold it. He didn't give me complete details of how and where they grew it in case I was ever questioned by police, I wouldn't have to lie and that was fine with me. His share of the bills were being paid and that's all I needed to know. As long as it was JUST weed and not in my house, I was ok with him selling it. I smoked with him and his friends sometimes. I'd get high and start singing along to whatever song was playing if I knew it. I got laughed at and praised for my vocals at the same time. His cousin wanted to put me on his track because, of course, he was a "rapper" too. Trey told his brother he couldn't afford to have me on his track.

"Ain't nothin' free." Trey laughed. "Not even for family."

Our place had become a somewhat kick back pad, when Trey wasn't working at the shop. He would invite a couple of his friends that he trusted and his cousin over to play video games, smoke, drink and just kick it. I heard "blood" so many times I started incorporating it into my vocabulary just for a laugh. I drew the line when it came to females though. There would be no non biologically related females in my house, ever. Ruby, of course didn't count. I knew her so she came over with her little sister Tanya who was about 18 and we would talk about our childhoods and laugh and catch up. It was no surprise that Ruby ended up adding Trey's brother, Patrick, to her galley of suitors. Gunnar had gone back to Texas for a while to see about something with his family. I wasn't sure, however, if it was Ruby who added Trey's cousin to her team or if was it was him, that added her to his team. All I know is it wasn't happening in my house, she could take that to a hotel or to his car for all I cared no one was doin NOTHIN in my house but me.

I was confident and secure in my standing. I was a celebrity to them. They wanted to take pictures with me as proof of affiliation. I found it easier to get along with guys than with females. It was nice and while I enjoyed finally feeling like I belonged somewhere and I could relax, I wasn't a maid and I wasn't anybody's mama. Though I had the money I wasn't paying out of MY pocket to feed a house full of men with the munchies. If they wanted to eat they needed to put in for delivery or groceries or go find their girlfriends, baby mamas or their side chicks to get food. If they tried to complain Trey told them to stop being beggars.

On Valentine's day, Trey gave me an elaborate tattoo on my lower stomach to cover up my C-section scar. It was a beautiful black and white with shades of grey, intertwining thorny branches going from hip to hip with a couple of roses in various stages of bloom scattered throughout. It signified that I was tough, and beautiful and that no matter where I was in life I still had more growing (blossoming) to do. I always said I would never get a man's name tattooed on me, but in the center right over my scar the branches formed the letter T. It was subtle but it was there. Apparently Trey was the exception to all my rules. He got a kiss mark tattoo of my actual lips and my signature in the middle of it, on the side of his neck. It wasn't your typical kiss mark either it was one where the bottom lip was dripping with blood. We had branded ourselves as belonging to the other. I had the best 3 months of my life that break, the best part being when Kyanna chose to abort her baby rather than get a DNA test to verify paternity. It was proof positive to me that she was lying and caught. She told Trey that she had a miscarriage and I felt bad for her, until I was told by Tanya, Ruby's little

199   SAMANTHA SANCHEZ

sister, who worked at the Planned Parenthood, as part of a work study for her nursing degree, that Kyanna came in and had an abortion, I couldn't stop myself from revelling at the fact that she was caught in a lie. Trey and I chose not confront her about the lie, it was over and we were free of her and that was that.

By March I had lost another 10 pounds. I just worked out my stomach had gotten flatter and abs had started to form. I was down to a size 9 and it was time for bikinis in Mexico. I bought a black one, of course because I always had to wear black, and I got a purple one. I got a white one piece with holes in the side that had one strip of material connecting to the cups that covered my boobs and tied around my neck with red Hibiscus Flowers covering my boobs. It was still new to me that anyone would need more than one bathing suit but Aisha and Jaycee insisted that it was necessary. The bottoms were cut low enough on me so that you could see my tattoo. I packed sun dresses and skirts and shorts and hiking boots and club outfits as well. I really didn't want to go and leave the happy bubble I was in with Trey but I reminded myself that I had to, I told myself it would be fun. There was family in Mexico that I hadn't seen in years and others I'd never met at all, and they were as excited to see me as I was them. It would have been an even more exciting trip if I wasn't going to be with Anthony and DeVon, and if Trey were going with me.

My grandfather was stepping down as head of his church and asked my uncle, James' father, my mother's brother in law, to take over as Pastor. My mom left our church and again became a member of my grandfather's church. As a favor to my mother and in support of my uncle and grandfather, I went to the retirement/ascension service and I made Trey go with me. I'd grown up in my grandfather's church. I hadn't actually been there since I hit puberty and my mom decided to go to a different church. Coming back this time, I thought the church was laughable compared to what I was used to. It didn't really have much structure at all and the choir, I wouldn't have even called a choir. There was one "tenor" who kept singing too high and I couldn't differentiate between the soprano's and alto's, the lead singer giggled in the middle of her song....that would never have flown in the choir I was apart of for eight years. But if anyone can sort things out it would be my Uncle Jim. He had a background in music and studied under the pastor at our old church, so I was sure things would get better.

In the middle of the service my grandfather called me up to the altar. I tried not to laugh as the gasps and whispers of recognition waved its way through the small sanctuary. "This is my granddaughter." Poppy introduced "She on her way to Mexico tomorrow for 3 months to film her TV show."

If people didn't know me before then they do now especially the younger members. "Can we all stand and reach our hands out? We gon pray a hedge of protection around her." Everyone followed and my mom put her hands on my shoulder and Nanny did the same on the other side of me.

As he'd done so many times before, my grandfather rubbed oil on my forehead and took hold. He prayed loud and hard. He was an old school preacher who growled and shouted at the drop of a dime. I tried not to laugh while he pushed and pulled my head. When we were little this was James and my favorite thing, to go up and let Poppy pray for us so we could pretend we were falling out in church. I peeked over at Trey who was standing in the front row with the rest of my family, he was fighting back laughter as well.

I spent the rest of the day with Trey and we said our goodbyes. My mom wanted me to spend the night with her. She was nervous about me going to another country for three months so I humored her and agreed. Trey wasn't allowed to cross the border into Tijuana to take me to the airport so my mom would do that. I parked my Audi in her garage and left the mustang for Trey to get back and forth with.

"I'm coming to see you the day after I get off parole." He told me as I pouted. He'd come to the house the next morning to say one more goodbye. "I already got my ticket."

"Ok."

"I'm gonna miss you."

"Me too."

"I'm gonna Skype with you every night And I have aim on my phone so we can chat throughout the day."

"I know."

"You know that nigga is gonna get out of pocket and try and piss you off. Don't let him upset you. Try and keep your cool."

"I'll try," I said.

"And if he try to push up on you and touch you or anything like that, let me know right away and when ya'll get back I'll handle it."

"Yes babe." I laughed "And you: no females in my house, no females in my car. Family only. I trust you but I'll be damned if I trust a female around you."

"You ain't got nothin to worry about," he chuckled.

"Neither do you," I said.

Having the entire congregation pray for me wasn't enough, my mom asked the breakfast club and their parents to join hands and pray again in the middle of the airport. She asked Monroe, whom she knew was my only

SAMANTHA SANCHEZ

true male friend in the house to look after me for her and not to let me kill Anthony and end up in a Mexican jail. Anthony, was all alone in the airport. There was no family there to see him off, no friends, except DeVon, those people he tried so hard to impress were nowhere to be seen.

TWENTY THREE

O ur hacienda in Mexico was beautiful. Something straight out of the Zorro movies, right on the beach. Inside was a study and a huge living room with period furniture, a beautiful kitchen that was bright with sunlight and had an adjoining grand dining room. The roof covered everything except the foyer, where there was a stone water fountain attached to the wall complete with fish. The balcony that overlooked the living room wrapped around the room in a square, with a terrace overlooking the beach Three sides of the square led to a bedroom the fourth one led to a bathroom. The second bathroom was downstairs just underneath it. The only drawback to this otherwise majestic home, was it was only two bedrooms for the six of us. The rooms were huge but aside from the walk in closets there was no privacy but half the house couldn't stand the other half of the house which would make the living arrangements difficult.

Athena and Monroe didn't like Ruby and didn't want to share a room with her Monroe and I hated Anthony and both refused to live with him. Athena and I both weren't too fond of DeVon but Athena was indifferent when it came to living with him, whereas I would rather not be near him if I could help it. I spent the entire plane ride next to him telling me about the show he and Monroe were going to be doing. It would run back to back with the airing of the third season when we got home. "DeRoe TV" an after hours talk show with the breakfast club as guests answering audience questions about the nights episode. It wasn't set to air until June once we got back from Mexico. Our show had been such a hit out the gate that the network decided to try and franchise it and see if the magic could be recreated in another city with another group of twenty something's. Their first season was set to air from February to the end of May with our first episode premiering the following week.

While Monroe and I were arguing about who would get stuck with Anthony. DeVon decided for us. He didn't want to be in a room with me because I didn't want to be in a room with him, so he put Anthony in my room and of course Anthony didn't argue.

You say you don't want any drama you say you don't want me wildin' out on you but you know that I can't stand you and I don't want you anywhere near me so why are you letting DeVon put you in my room. You better not say nothin to me this whole trip. I said in my narrative

It was easier to ignore Anthony than I thought it would be. He was scared of me so he tried not to speak to me unless absolutely necessary like "pass the hot sauce please" which I ignored and someone else would pass it to him. If he asked a question like where someone was I wouldn't answer. He knew not to even attempt being friendly with me. Every time I saw that tattoo on his arm, I hated him and wanted to peel it from his flesh with my bare hands.

Our antics as a group were the same as in Cali only in Spanish with Tequila and margaritas. Once, when we were at the beach, DeVon, who had been fascinated by Ruby's sudden growth in cup size, decided he wanted to see if he could really tell the difference between implants and real boobs. He put one hand on Rubys boobs and the other on mine gripped and jiggled trying to see if it moved the same. I hated DeVon 80% of the time in the house but for the other 20% he was like an annoying little brother that you care about but still can't stand. DeVon touching my breast wasn't a big deal, He invited Monroe to feel and see if he could tell the difference. That wasn't a big deal either, he was like the favorite little brother that got into trouble when paired with the annoying brother but on his own, he was solid. Ruby and I both drew the line at Anthony. No way was Anthony ever going to touch either of us. I could tell that he wanted to though. He told me that I looked nice, which since I wasn't speaking to him, I didn't respond to, but I admit that it was a nice vanity boost to be lusted after by a guy who at one point in time made you feel like the least sexiest woman in the world. I guess I finally met the visual/physical qualities of his dream girl but it didn't change anything. I still hated him, as exhausting as it was to do so.

DeVon and Ruby started "seeing" each other again a couple weeks into the trip. As much crap as DeVon talked about her, he was all over her and she reveled in his attentions. It was a complicated situation and I just stayed out of it as best I could. Whenever Anthony brought someone home to smash, I excused myself into the study and read a book or skyped with Trey or exchanged dirty messages with him on AIM until I fell asleep on the couch.

Sometimes Ruby and I would go out and walk along the shore behind the house. I wouldn't go out to a club alone with her anymore, not after what happened in September but I wasn't shutting her out anymore. She'd walk along and talk and wait until we thought they were done. Which, from experience, wasn't long, but we were generous with the time we stayed out the house. I counted down the weeks until Trey was supposed to come to Mexico, eleven weeks from the day we landed.

On the one year anniversary of Tiana's birth and death, I spent most of the day alone at the beach. There was no sobbing. I wasn't angry. I was sad but I found myself praying at the shore, the first time in a long time. I prayed for peace of heart and mind. I asked God to help me understand why. I also asked him to take away the hate I felt for Anthony. To help me let go and that was all it took. I wasn't devastated anymore. Losing my child will be a painful part of my life for as long as I lived but I knew that she was in The Father's arms. He was loving her more than I ever could and who knows maybe she was growing up in paradise instead of staying a baby forever. I was silly enough to even think that maybe she could be an angel surrounded by other angels. Who knew? Maybe she could be, no one knows what happens in heaven except those in heaven. For the first time I was at peace with the loss.

"Are you ok?" Anthony asked coming down the stairs that led to the water cautiously. I felt too much peace to be annoyed by his voice.

"Yea, I'm ok." I said pleasantly. Speaking to him for the first time in a month.

"Just checking," he said and began to walk away.

"Do you think she's an angel?" I asked. "Laughing and smiling, happy while she learns to flap her little wings." I looked up at the sky shielding my eyes from the sun.

"It's possible. I mean, I like that idea." He said halting in his tracks. He must have been thinking about her too because he didn't even need to ask who I was talking about. He was silent for a few seconds I thought he'd gone until he spoke again. "I know you don't believe it, but I loved her too."

"I don't want to talk about it." I said. I was in a good place at the moment and I didn't want to get worked up.

"Just hear me out. Don't wild out on me ok?"

I sighed, unsure I wanted to hear what he had to say but curious none the less and something inside me quelled the fire that threatened to rise.

"Fine."

"Thank you. You want to come sit down?" He motioned to the rocks on the side of the stairs that led down to the shore. I hesitated, but sat on the edge of the the stone at the bottom step and he sat on the one across from me.

"First of all I'm sorry. After you said what you said at the reunion a couple months ago, I went back and watched the first two seasons and I was really f---ed up last year. I get why you hate me and blame me for everything."

I remained silent.

"I shoulda looked out for you, I shoulda taken care of you and I didn't, but it's not that I didn't love the baby."

"You just didn't care about me. " I said. This wasn't news. We'd been over this a thousand times last year. "Yea, I know. It was your mantra all last year."

"No I did." He insisted "I mean, I didn't at first. I felt forced to be with you by DeVon because you were pregnant."

"I never..." I started to argue.

"I know. You told me you wasn't tryna make me be with you. You only wanted me to be around for the baby. I was scared of that, though. See, you, you would have been a good mom. You have a good mom but I didn't know anything about being a dad because I didn't have one. And then the fact that you didn't want to be wit me, even though I didn't really care bout you, made me start to care bout you and the more time I spent wit you, the more I thought bout what it would be like to actually be wit you. You know, like one on one. I mean you were nice to me, you know how to treat a nigga, until I pissed you off, and I did start to want you." This I hadn't heard before but why was he telling me now?

"Honestly, I still kinda do," he continued. "I mean you look hella good. You was always cute but you different now."

"Oh wow," I rolled my eyes unreceptive to his sideways compliment.

"I acted like I didn't care because you kept shutting me down every time I tried to start somethin' and then when I found out that the baby was a girl, I got excited. I stopped being scared and all I wanted to do was protect her and take care of you. I didn't want anyone to ever hurt her or do her the way I was doing you so I started acting right because you were going to keep her from me if I didn't and I didn't want to miss out. Everything was good until the first reunion. I was drunk and I was mad at you and I said things that were out of pocket and I'm sorry."

"Mad at me for what?"

"I thought you and Monroe were f---ing when no one else was around."

"But you said you didn't care about me then so why would that make you mad?"

"Cuz I did sorta care then too. You was my baby mama, you wasn't pos' to f--k anybody but me or else you was a ho."

I opened my mouth to respond but he cut me off.

"No no." He said "Calm down. I'm not callin' you a ho I know you wasn't f---in Monroe, DeVon told me, that's why I ended up over at your house on New Years."

"You just said that at the reunion you were mad because you thought I was f---in him. That was months after New Years.

"Well seeing the footage again, made me think that DeVon was lying to me and that you were. Until Monroe and the producers and everyone else said that you weren't but by then it was too late."

"Get to the point Anthony," I said. I didn't need a complete play by play of his perspective on the entire year.

"That night...." I knew what night he was talking about "I did it to get back at you I was mad at you and my cousins and uncles were sayin' that I was whipped and being punked by my baby mama....and that chick was just there and I didn't even really want to. My cousins actually made me kinda" He added as an afterthought "But anyway when DeVon told me the baby died....." he paused to compose himself "You not the only one who lost her. I didn't grow her inside me like you did, but she was my baby too. DeVon took me to Miami to help get my mind off things but it really didn't help. I didn't call to check on you because I didn't think you wanted to talk to me ."

"I didn't. but you still could have tried." I said "at least I'd have known you gave a s--t."

"See? I didn't know that. But I just wanted you to know that I did care about both of you and I'm sorry."

"Ok." Was all I could say.

"Can I get a hug or somethin?" he smiled standing up, arms wide open walking toward me.

"Uh No." I laughed pushing him away. "We're still not friends."

"But..."

"I hear what you're saying and I'm willing to believe you did care about the baby and maybe even about me at one point, but nothing has changed. You're still the same disrespecting nigga that took pleasure in causing me pain and for what? Because I pissed you off? Because you thought I was having sex with another man when you spent every day telling me I could if I wanted to? I don't want to be friends with a person like that. All I can do is forgive you and move on and leave it at that. And that's what I'm going to do." I walked away from him and dived into the waves trying to remain at peace.

As the weeks progressed, Anthony didn't seem to understand, what "not friends" meant, or maybe he thought I would change my mind. He started being nicer than usual to me, sometimes even flirty. He complimented me on my body, which despite my previous satisfaction at his unspoken lust, made me uncomfortable, he complimented me on my voice when he caught me singing to myself. I tried to ignore him, because I didn't want to give him any ideas that there was anything to be had between us, beyond a peaceful co-existence. He and DeVon even tried to tag team me about a song they were working on and needed some female vocals for. They'd been in the study for days mixing stuff on a studio program Anthony downloaded on his lap top. I declined to participate.

The Saturday before Trey was due to visit, along with Athena's boyfriend, he messaged me on AIM to tell me that his grandmother had passed. I skyped him immediately.

"I'm so sorry babe, what happened?" I asked when he answered. His eyes were red with pain and grief.

"She had a stroke in the middle of the kitchen, Keashon found her."

"The baby? Oh my God that must have been scary for him."

"Yea, he was pretty freaked out."

"Are you ok?"

"No." He said honestly "I'm gonna be alright there's just a lot of s--t that needs to be done, so I'm not going to be able to come see you next week."

"Of course, yeah, be with your family. Do you want me to come home early? Can I do anything to help?"

"Nah, you don't have to do that."

"Baby, if you need me to be there with you, I'll come home. F--k the show."

I could see the heartbreak all over his face. I wanted to reach through the screen and pull him into a hug, tell him that it was going to be ok .

"Baby, you don't have to do that." I could tell he wanted me to though. Trey and his grandmother were close. He didn't like to talk about his childhood except that his grandmother raised him, his brother and his sister Keisha, because his mother couldn't. His sister Jennifer was already 18 and living with her older boyfriend and first child's father. The relationship between Trey's mother and her children had always been tense as far as I could tell. So much that Trey didn't really talk to her, he didn't visit her, I'd never met her or her husband, whom Trey had always made clear was not his father. From age eleven until now it's only and always been his grandma, he described her as the blessing that kept their family together.

Grandma Dorothy, Dotty or Dot to her friends, had a party where I'd met almost all of Trey's family. Grandma Dotty told me that she was happy that I was in Trey's life, how pretty I was, that I had been a good influence and kept him off the streets and out of trouble and that she could see why he loved me. She even said she hoped I would lock him down for good, meaning marriage, and help him be the man she knew he could be. I didn't know her very well, only that Trey loved her deeply, and I felt her loss through him.

"No, I want to." I said " I'm going to try and leave tomorrow morning."
He chuckled "You are amazing."

I smiled at his assessment of me "I'll message you in a little bit with the details as soon as I get them."

"I love you," he declared.

"I love you too."

I wished I could leave right away, but my family had planned a party for me while I was there and, by association, the rest of the BFC, to celebrate my finally coming to Mexico. It was that night and I couldn't bail on them after they'd spent so much time and effort and money for me.

There was good food, beer, tequila, dancing and karaoke. I may not be able to get convincingly nasty in the clubs back in Cali but I could do a pretty good Cumbia and I also could keep up with Mi Pobre Corazon which is really a spanish version of My Achy Breaky Heart. It was like a party at my dad's house only more spanish was spoken. Ruby and I often had to bridge the gap between the languages. Athena was really good at holding her own she payed attention in class this semester. DeVon made a joke out of it and just completely messed up the language but my family were good sports about it.

When everyone was sufficiently buzzed or drunk enough, it was time for karaoke. The selection my cousins had was very broad; mexican musicians, old school American musicians, new school American musicians. My uncles sang something in spanish, my aunts sang something in english, my cousins sang something in English. I sang a Selena song in spanish solo and then Athena, Ruby, two cousins, and I got up to sing "Wanna Be" by The Spice Girls. Athena hated The Spice Girls but she sang along anyway just for the fun of it.

Monroe, DeVon and Anthony got up to do a song. "This is somethin I been working on for about a week or so." Anthony said plugging his Mp3 player into the speaker. The Jackson Five's "I Want You Back" began playing over the speaker I thought it was strange that Anthony was on lead as Michael until...

"Lyric, pay attention. This is for you." He winked and smiled at me.

"Oh No." I lowered and shook my head . My family whooped and awed at the dedication.

They knew nothing of our history so to them it was sweet but to me it was just.....wow. I looked pleadingly at Monroe and he just laughed, I couldn't help but chuckle a little myself "No more alcohol for this nigga... Oh God."

He started "When I had you to myself I didn't want you around, those pretty faces always made you stand out in a crowd" but instead of singing, he remixed the song into a rap but still sort of sang the original hook with DeVon and Monroe singing back up. DeVon did Jermaine's part "Oh just one more chance to show you that I love you." Monroe did Jackie's part.

"Forget what happened then."

The entire performance I kept my cool. I sang along to the classic, how can you not sing along to this song, and acted as if I wasn't bothered. I would not embarrass my father by acting up around his family. Anthony tried to raise me up out of my seat to get me to participate but I snatched away. My cousin sitting next to me shrugged me and urged me to go. I laughed it off and shook my head. I was amused by his ridiculousness and the fact that it knows no bounds but that was it. I wasn't touched by his musical declaration. It was very creative, but no unresolved feelings were stirred. I didn't even plan on acknowledging the performance once we left. I knew I would be asked about it but my answer would simply be "it was just karaoke, and he's drunk." Nothing more. That was my plan, until Anthony went one step too far and tried to kiss me. I turned my face just in time but he wasn't giving up. I clapped my hand over his mouth.

"No." I said fiercely, looking him in the eyes then I pushed him away from me.

What on earth got this nigga thinking he could kiss me? I asked on green screen *This is why I'm always "mean to him" like people say. Because everytime I start to just be cool and co-exist. He takes it to a whole other level. He's disrespectful. I have a man and clearly he doesn't respect my relationship which meant that he doesn't respect me. Which, honestly, shouldn't be a surprise. It was Anthony after all.*

I'd never seen Anthony so drunk before. He was goofy to everyone else but overly amorous with me. I don't know how many times I told him to stop touching me and to shut up in the cab on the way back to the villa.

"No!" I shouted walking in the front doors followed closely by a slurring Anthony.

"Why not?" he asked.

"Because I don't want you." I stormed into the kitchen and opened the refrigerator.

"Yes you do," he said pushing up against me from behind.

"No, I don't," I said pushing him away. "Here. Drink this," I held out a bottle of water to him.

"Why?" he asked looking at it confused.

"So you don't wake up with a hangover."

"See? you DO care!"

"I'm just trying to be nice." I rolled my eyes and walked past him back into the courtyard. The BFC was lined against the banister upstairs trying to watch what was going on.

"That's how I know you love me because you're trying to take care of me like you used to."

"I don't love you, Anthony," I said walking up the stairs. "I just don't feel like being a b---h and you're annoying so the sooner you drink that and go to sleep the better."

"No. you love me."

"In case you forgot I got a man," I said.

"What that skinny a-- pretty boy? You don't love him like you love me."

"I don't love you," I repeated walking into my room.

"Yes you do that's why you always wild out on me all the time about everything. I wouldn't piss you off so much if you didn't care."

"I pop off at DeVon and Monroe too."

"Not the way you do at me," he said.

"That's hatred not love. Lay down," I said pointing to his bed.

"Ooh you gon ride it?" he asked excited sitting down.

"Gross. No." I said.

"What you mean gross? You liked it before... I miss it." he argued reaching and rubbing up my thigh "You the best I ever had." he laughed singing the line from the Drake song. I heard DeVon and Monroe laughing too. I pushed his hand away and backed further away from him.

"I'm trying not to be mean to you. Stop talking and go to sleep."

"Lay down with him, Lyric," DeVon instigated.

"No."

"Come on you know you want to," Anthony said pulling my hand. I snatched away. The time for nice was over.

"Don't touch me. I said no," I said walking back out of the room.

"Why not?" Anthony asked following me out.

"Because I know what sex is supposed to feel like now," I said storming down the stairs just to get away. "Why are you following me?"

"Because I love you."

"Oops," I heard Monroe scream in laughter.

"Finally he says it," Ruby said.

"I told you!" DeVon crowed.

And there it was. The thing I suspected and everyone kept sayin' for

211   SAMANTHA SANCHEZ

over a year now. He finally said it. But it didn't mean anything to me and he was going take it back once he sobers up anyway.

"You're drunk and full of s---t."

"No I mean it." He grabbed my arm and turned me around "I love you, you should marry me. I don't have a ring right now but I can get you one when we get back home if you want."

"That's no way to propose, nigga! You gotta get down on one knee and do it right."

DeVon laughed. I glared at DeVon, again wishing I had the power to cause pain with a single concentrated stare. Anthony followed DeVon's advice and with a grip on my hand lowered himself on one knee.

"Lyric....hold up, wait, what's your real name again?"

"Anthony get up!" I growled.

"It's Naomi!" Monroe shouted answering Anthony's question. I shot him a traitorous glare. He just laughed and shrugged. He was enjoying the show. Everyone was, even Athena was laughing. Ruby and DeVon had their cameras out recording the interaction. Traitors, all of them.

"Thank you." Anthony said to Monroe before turning back to me. "Naomi...."

"No," I said.

"I love you."

"No."

"Marry me."

"No."

"And let's have another baby together."

"F--- NO!!!" I snatched my hand away.

"Why not?" he asked standing up.

"Because I don't want to be with you!!!"

"Why do you keep saying that?" he laughed "It's a lie. You're still mad about before but I'll do better this time. It'll be different you can love me now and I won't push you away."

"Anthony shut up!" I snapped "You're not hearing me. I don't want to be with you. I don't want to marry you. I can barely stand being in the same house as you. I get sick just looking at you. Get it thru your head. I don't love you. I never did."

"Yes you did. You wanted to be with me so much you were crying about it."

"I was hormonal!!!" I shouted "I wanted SOMEONE to care about me and I focused on you because you were there! It was your baby."

"I'll care about you this time. I won't be a a-----e anymore."

"No."

"Boo just think about it."

"I'm not your boo."

"You love me."

"Nigga your own mama didn't even love you! she did crack the entire time she was pregnant with you! Your foster mom didn't love you, she told you didn't matter because you weren't really apart of the family. Your aunt keeps throwin you out cuz she don't love you either. You are a weak, stupid, little d---k, boring f--k, B---H ASS NIGGA with no talent. I never loved you because There's NOTHIN about you worth loving!"

That wiped the smile and laugh off his face and I could see that my words hurt him. Part of me regretted having said them telling me "I took it too far" The other part of me just shrugged and said "I tried to be nice and he wasn't getting it."

SAMANTHA SANCHEZ

TWENTY FOUR

I decided I wasn't going to tell Trey about Anthony's proposal right away. I didn't think it was the right time he was already upset about losing Grandma Dotty, and I didn't want to upset him more. I felt guilty about what I said to Anthony, using the stuff he told me in confidence as a weapon against him. I kept thinking about the look on his face, like he was 5 years old and someone had killed his puppy and he was told that crying wasn't allowed. Trey noticed it on my face and asked me what happened.

"It's a long story, don't worry about it."

"I'm gonna worry about it unless you tell me."

"Baby, you got a lot on your mind already."

"What did he do?" Trey asked angrily "I know he did something and then you retaliated which I already told you not to do."

"No, I kept my calm the whole time. I ignored him and he stayed away from me for the most part. I already told you that."

"So what's with the look on your face then?" I sighed.

"Baby, tell me!"

" So I told you he and I had that talk on the beach and I decided to forgive him and let go for my sake."

"Yea and then what?"

"Last night at the party my family threw for me everyone was doing karaoke, and so Anthony decided that it was a good idea to do a song and dedicated to me. Then tried to kiss me."

"He tried to kiss you? Or he kissed you?"

"He tried. I moved my face and then blocked my mouth cuz he wouldn't stop trying."

"What else? I know there's more."

"When we got back to the house, Anthony proposed to me and I said some really mean things back to him."

"What the f--k?!" He asked pulling the car over "Why the f--k would he propose?!" I had never seen Trey this angry before. I knew I should have waited til his emotions weren't so high.

"Cuz he's an idiot who's convinced himself that I love him and that 'No' is just the start of a game that eventually leads to yes the more he pushes."

"What'd you say?"

"I said no, obviously!" I defended "What else would I say?"

He laughed at the misunderstanding and softened his tone. "No, I mean, what mean things did you say back?"

"I basically called him a crack baby who wasn't worth loving."

Trey couldn't contain his laughter. "Damn. That's fucked up. Is it true though?"

"He told me that privately and I shouldn't have announced it to the world like that and his face was….well I finally got him to stop laughing so that's a plus, but still."

"I told you that dude was in love with you."

"Yea you and the rest of the world."

"Wait til I see blood…"

"Let's not worry about that right now. Have you guys made any funeral plans?"

His mood changed as he turned and faced forward again.

"I think my aunts and uncles are still trying to figure out what she wanted, going through her papers and stuff." He pulled back into traffic and continued driving home.

"Tell them we'll help in any way we can."

"I appreciate that babe, but I'm not going to tell them that. They'll ask you for money so they don't have to pay for it."

"Well if it's for your grandmother."

"Nah, thank you though. I don't want anyone trying to use you as a come up. That's your money. My aunts and uncles can handle it. Grandma would say the same thing."

"Have you talked to your mom? How's she doing?"

"Nah, I haven't talked to her. But hey, if it's cool with you, I wanted to let Keisha and the kids come stay with us for a bit. Get them away from the drama at my grandma's with my aunts and sister coming at her."

"Coming at her for what?"

"They think it's her fault Grandma was so stressed out all the time and they blaming her.

Plus since Keashon, was the one with Grandma in the kitchen when she…." He couldn't even say the word.

"He was with her? I thought he just found her?"

"I thought so too, but he was with her."

I rubbed his back in comfort. "It's fine. I'm cool with it. That's what the sofa bed is for right?"

"It's only for a little bit, until we figure out what's going to happen with the house."

"It's fine," I repeated. "I don't mind."

SAMANTHA SANCHEZ

"Thank you."

When we got home Trey didn't want to talk or even think about his grandma. I think he was trying to hold it in because he thought he had to be strong, be a man, be macho, but in the middle of the night I woke up to find him in the kitchen crying over a sandwich. I walked up next to him and rubbed his back and he turned and embraced me. He buried himself into the gap between my neck and shoulder and sobbed. I just held him and rubbed his back and silently prayed for his strength. When he was done, he thanked me for coming back early.

"I know I said you didn't need to but I really did need you."

"Of course." I said kissed the tracks of his tears and we climbed back into bed and watched the first season of True Blood. He'd bought it for me as a random "I love you" gift. I'd never heard of the show before but he knew I liked vampires and that the violence and gore of stuff like this always made me happy. He found my weirdness endearing and sexy.

The next morning, Keisha and her children, 3 year old Keashon and a now 2 year old Amina came to stay. I knew Trey and my privacy was going to be non-existent but I couldn't let my man's little sister suffer from the guilt of losing her grandmother and being blamed for it. Trey told her that we were too busy to babysit like Grandma Dotty did so she would need to figure that out and take the kids with her whenever she left. Also, the kids father was not allowed in the house. I didn't know him but Trey's insistence on it made me think that he really wasn't a good guy.

The funeral was a tough day for Trey and his family. I prayed again for his strength. The circles around his eyes betrayed his exhaustion, and from the conversations I'd overheard with his mother, his fears about using me for money seemed to be spot on. I heard him say that I wasn't an ATM, that he wasn't going to ask me and a second limo wasn't necessary just so she could ride. I didn't ask what was needed because I would have given it, if it was reasonable but Trey was adamant that I wasn't to spend a dime because once I started they would always have their hands out for more, "they" being his mother and her husband.

The service was lovely, it was held at Bayview Baptist Church, Grandma Dotty's church for 40 years. From what I could tell she was very loved. I sat between Trey and Keisha. I held his hand for comfort and he squeezed when things got too much for him, his eyes red with tears and contained sobs. Keisha didn't contain anything and I held her in one arm rubbing her shoulders. The kids stayed with a friend of hers for the service, Keashon was already traumatized enough from watching his great grandmother collapse and die, he didn't need to see her body again. At the end of the service Trey, two of his uncles and three of his cousins, carried the closed casket outside to the hearse. I held Keisha up as we walked behind them. At the gravesite I stood by Trey's side as he watched his grandmother be lowered into the ground. It was like a part of him was going into the ground with her.

"She saved me." He told me in the car when we were parked for a minute by the gravesite. He wasn't ready to leave yet so we just sat there in my audi with the top up. I didn't respond. I just listened.

"When I was little, she saved me and Patrick, and Keisha from Quentin. He and my mom weren't married then. She married him after he was locked up to keep from testifying against him. We weren't his kids, so he didn't give a f--k about us. He only let my mom keep us when she got pregnant to collect the welfare money, and she only cared about him. She still only cares about him. She let him….she made Jen…" His voice broke. "My grandma was my safe place, she called the police, and got us out of there."

I still didn't respond. This was the first time Trey had let me in this far, to begin to share his pain with me. I didn't know exactly what he was trying to tell me but I could gather enough to figure out why his mom's husband wasn't at the funeral supporting his wife in her grief. I knew now why Trey didn't talk about his mother. She wasn't there for him, she gave him life but didn't care enough to protect it. I hadn't even met her yet and I didn't like her.

"I don't want to be here, can we just go?" he asked.

"Sure, anywhere you want."

"I don't care let's just go."

I didn't know where else to go. He didn't want to go to the repass so I just drove us home. I ordered a pizza and just stayed quiet. I allowed him the space that he needed to grieve, bringing him food and drink as he watched a basketball game. I didn't know what to do, or how to be useful to him anymore so I changed my clothes and went to the gym provided by the building. An hour later Trey came down to find me.

"Hi." I said taking my headphones off.

"I missed you," he said sadly.

"I was on my way back up after this." I said. I grabbed my towel and water bottle and stood up. He grabbed me and held me to him. It was a desperate kind of hug.

"I'm all sweaty babe," I warned him.

"I don't care." I wrapped my arms around him in return. "Promise me you won't ever leave me."

"Leave you? I'm not going anywhere."

He pulled away for a minute and held out his little finger "pinky promise?"

I laughed at the way he copied me and linked his little finger with mine and held up my other pinky "double pinky promise." He smiled and locked his other little finger with mine as well. He picked me up and I wrapped my legs around his waist and he kissed me, harder than he ever had before. It was a desperate and pleading kiss. He carried me into the facility bathroom and I gave into his desire, which was also different than before, like he was trying to escape something and cling to me for safety.

TWENTY FIVE

A week later, camera crews showed up and Lyrical Chaos began it's first day of production. Trey decided that the money he got from Lyrical Chaos should go into a savings account to build for our future together. He wanted to save and open up his own tattoo shop.

" I'm going to call it The Inked Rose," he said.

"I like that, it's different."

"The rose part is inspired by you. Because you're my rose by any other name."

"Aww," I cheesed.

Trey was still grieving his grandmother's death but there were no more tears. Keisha was still staying with us, her and the kids. It was fun having the kids around, Trey was amazing with them. He played,wrestled and raced with them. He was also very firm with them, adding that extra bass to his voice when they weren't being obedient. Keashon took a special shining to me, he liked to cuddle with me which made Trey a little jealous that this little 3 year old was moving in on his territory.

"Excuse me, but that's my woman," he told Keashon playfully.

"Mine," Keashon laughed.

"No, that's your auntie, she's my woman."

"No my woman," Keashon laughed again.

"What?!" Trey said grabbing him and tickling him growling at him like a monster and then putting him on the ground. "Go find your mama, it's time for breakfast." Keashon happily ran out of the room, in search of food and Trey reclaimed his spot in the bed next to me.

"You're good with him," I observed.

"We should have a baby," he said.

"Yea, one day."

"Why one day, what's wrong with now?"

"I'm not getting pregnant again no time soon," I laughed. "I don't want to be a baby mama."

"If I marry you, then will you have my baby?"

"I'd be more inclined to, yes."

"Let's go to Vegas right now," he joked.

I looked at the clock, "Oh, bummer, I can't I gotta meet up with my mom."

"Damn," he whispered. "Tell her I said hi. I know she don't like me but tell her anyway."

"Ok," I laughed.

I missed mother's day while I was in Mexico so I made up for it by taking her to breakfast and shopping, camera crew in tow. She filled me in on what was going on at church, the transformations my uncle was making to my grandfather's church. Aisha was placed as temporary director of the choir and they were actually sounding decent and organized. Even brought in some of her friends to help round the sound out. The service was structured and in only six weeks the attendance had doubled.

"Wow, grandpa must be really happy," I said.

"He's very happy. God is really working."

"Cool," was all I could say. My faith in God had been renewed somewhat but I still wasn't trying to go back to church. Which is what I knew she was working toward. There wasn't anything she could say to convince me. James however, could.

I'd been so preoccupied with Trey and helping him get through the funeral and James had been so busy the last month whenever I tried to call him. I hadn't gotten a chance to congratulate him on becoming the number one NFL draft pick for Baltimore.

"My Heart!" I squealed when he called me. "Mr. First Round Draft Pick Congratulations!!!"

"Thank you," he laughed.

"When do you leave?"

"Next week. Monday, actually."

"So soon?"

"Yup. Gotta start training and practicing with the team."

"Awww. Why couldn't you have chosen San Diego so you could stay with me?"

"Baltimore offered more money."

I laughed, "but you're leaving me."

"You'll be alright. Listen, I need a favor."

"What's up?"

"You comin' to Poppy's church on Sunday?"

"No. why?" I chuckled.

"I'm gonna be delivering the word."

"Your daddy finally got you in the pulpit huh?" James and I both were prophesied to be the next generation of preachers and we both adamantly fought against it. That was our parents deal, that was Poppy's thing. Not ours.

"Nah, it ain't like that." James said "It's a one time thing for an early

Father's day cuz Poppy asked me to."

"Well then I'll definitely come to see you step up to the pulpit and accept your calling," I teased.

"Good then you can sing the sermonic hymn."

"I can what?"

"The Lord told me to tell you that you need to sing. It's time."

"Nah, you heard wrong. The Lord said that Aisha needs to sing not me. She's the one with the church vocals."

The idea of singing in front of an audience still gave me a tugging feeling on the inside of my stomach. Even if I had done it before.

"Aisha, directing the choir. And quit acting like you can't sing. You tore up that song at your showcase."

"That was one time! That doesn't mean I'm not still nervous singing in front of people."

"How you gonna get used to it, if you never do it?"

"I'm not even a member of the church, how am I gonna sing with the choir?"

"It's Poppy's Church, we were born members."

"I'm not singing," I laughed.

"Yes you are."

"Is this the part where you tell me that God gave me a gift and I have to use it?"

"No this is the part where I tell you to do it for me as a going away present," he laughed.

"Nah forget that don't do it for me. Do it for God."

"You don't understand, I can't control my voice. It shakes, it cracks, it even stops sometimes." I explained "that's why I never sang lead before."

"You'll be alright. Just pray."

"It's not that easy, James."

"Sure it is."

"What song would I have to sing?"

"Lord I Surrender." I loved that song. I've always wanted to sing lead on that song...

"You're lucky I love you."

"Uh-huh. Love you too. Rehearsal is tomorrow at 10 am."

"10 am? That's early."

"Bye, Naomi," he laughed and hung up.

I had one camera with me, and two bodyguards, as a I walked into the small storefront church in Ridgecrest. I could hear the choir singing from the parking lot and they weren't all that bad anymore. I got the expected and all too familiar gapes and excitement at my appearance. The disapproving look from the senior members of the church. Some of them I'd known all my life, some I didn't. My picture still hung in the back room along with the rest of my cousins and former childhood members of the church. We were Poppy's pride and joy, his "Sunshine Band", the children's choir. My mother and I moved to a bigger, less old fashioned, more progressive church when I was eleven and I haven't sang here since.

"MiMi, we're ready for you." Aisha said calling me out of my reverie. Jaycee was in the alto section helping them stay on key. A couple other friends of hers were in the alto, tenor and soprano section to help create a fuller sound for such a small choir. My uncle and now Pastor of this church played the drums. I was nervous and my voice was shaky just as I knew it would be once I got up there. I lost my breath a couple of times. I probably should have warmed up first but that was what rehearsal was for. We went over it twice I was only slightly better the second time. I caught a glimpse of a lean bushy eyed boy's disgusted eye roll at me. I don't know who he was but he was really the only male in the choir who hadn't come from the big church. He kept trying to sing soprano but Aisha always checked him, Jace was his name, and told him to stop. Soprano wasn't for him, he couldn't pull it off naturally and it didn't sound nice. There were men who could hit the soprano notes and maybe with some more training he could get there but not right now. He gave her a disrespectful eye roll, exasperated at not being able to do what he wanted.

I prayed out with the rest of the group and took pictures with some of the young teenage fans of the show. They asked me questions about some of the more adult aspects of the show and I chastised them and told them they were too young to be asking about all that. I was on my way out, I had a lot to do that day, it was Trey's birthday in a couple days and I had planned a surprise birthday party that night. He needed a reason to celebrate. I was pressed for time. I needed to get my nails done and see about the details at the club and his birthday present, but my Uncle Jim asked for a moment of my time in his office, along with whomever was in charge of filming that day. He started off by telling me that I sounded good and not to be nervous. "Just relax and let the Lord work through you." Then he asked about the cameras. He was concerned about the distraction the camera crew would be during service tomorrow. My growing celebrity alone was enough to cause a sensation without bringing in a whole camera crew. He would allow the service to be filmed. He looked at it as an opportunity to reach a wider audience but not at the expense and discomfort of the people in the church. The producer and the Director of Photography understood exactly what

Uncle Jim was concerned about. Together they went out into the sanctuary and discussed where they could put the cameras to get the perfect shot of the pulpit to get ample coverage without being in the way. There would be medium sized mounted cameras operated by remote placed around the church, with the monitors and everything set up behind the church so there would be no crew inside the church to distract anyone. All the faces, except the family who'd already signed a waiver, would be blurred out as not to make anyone else uncomfortable. Uncle agreed and everything was set.

Trey knew we were going to the club to celebrate his birthday but he didn't know that I rented out his favorite lounge in the Gaslamp for a private party. The building looked small but in fact it had 3 levels. The street level where you walked in had a bar and a stage, a few tables scattered against the walls and a dance floor in between. Upstairs just above the stage was the third level with a pool table, a couch and some other couchy looking chairs and a table. When you walk in the front door, facing the stage next to the bar was another set of stairs that led to the basement and another bar and dance floor.

Come party time I was dressed in a strapless red faux leather mini dress that Trey had picked out for me. I paired it with white five inch pumps and I let my hair stay in its natural curls instead of flattening it again and I wore my Tiana cross ring-bracelet and matching necklace. My makeup was my signature smokey eye with clear gloss. He wore a fancy red t-shirt with abstract images printed in white, brand new jeans that thankfully didn't hang too low, and white Jordans. His hair was freshly lined and neat and he smelled so good. The party was private and you had to be on the guest list to get in. I invited Ruby and Kendrick and Athena and her boyfriend, a few other of my "friends" though they weren't really friends. Since the show took off most people were quick to claim friendship and association with me. I only invited them to fill the space in the club; it would look better on camera. I invited some of Trey's friends and his family.

Trey was thoroughly surprised at the event and grateful. We partied hard posted most of the time on the third level. We did body shots off each other, though instead of lifting my dress up to slurp the alcohol off my stomach, we tucked the shot glass into my cleavage for him to bury his face into. I had to watch these disrespectful thirsty females around my man. It wasn't anything new. Skanks were always throwing themselves at Trey whether I was there or not. They knew he was my man and it didn't matter to them in any way. Trey was polite and laughed pretended not to know women were flirting with him.

"I love you." He reminded me after the fifth female had come up to him with sex in her eyes.

"This is the best party ever. Thank you." He wrapped his arms around me. I just glared at him.

"Mmm-hmm," I said.

"What?" he laughed. "They're just thirsty, don't even worry about them."

"Uh-huh. Stop being so friendly." I warned. He just laughed and kissed me again.

When the party was at it's climax, I decided it was time to give Trey his birthday present. I know he hated when I spent money on him and he'd probably be slightly upset with me about the splurge but I knew it would make him happy. "Ok excuse me everyone!" I called into the microphone. The music stopped and everyone turned to the stage to see me. "Hi!" I smiled "I hope everyone is having fun but you all could step outside for just a minute. I have another gift I'd like to give to the birthday boy. Baby, if you could come down here please." Curious but excited about a present he rushed down the stairs and headed out the door. A crowd of people made its way outside and just as a black 2009 Rolls Royce Phantom with a red under light and interior light pulled up in front of the club. Trey could barely contain his excitement. He jumped up and down and galloped around the car taking in the black leather interior and the modifications I had done. He came over to me scooped me up and spun me around. "Thank you, Thank you, Thank you." He said and pulled me so tight against him to kiss me so passionately I could feel his happiness through his pants. "You're the best." My cousin Hector got out of the driver's seat and handed the keys to Trey. He'd done all the modifications for me. Everyone on the street gaped at the extravagance of the present. Trey took the keys and got in the car rubbing his hands over the steering wheel, checking out the stereo system. Then he got back out and walked around it slowly in admiration.

"I love you so much." He said kissing me again "You are the best thing in my life."

"And you better not forget it," I teased.

"Man, wait til we get home," he said lowly to me.

"We can go now." I suggested "If you ready. You ok to drive?"

"Nah you better drive." He said honestly handing me the keys. I'd been drinking nothing but water for the last hour and didn't have even the slightest buzz. I couldn't have a hangover if I'm going to be singing at church the next day. "Let me go say goodbye to folks. The music had started again and people were moving back inside. Once we left, the venue was allowed to open to party goers off the street.

We drove to Mission Beach instead of home to let him get a feel for the car. The stereo was bumping music the whole way. Once we pulled up at the boardwalk, Trey wanted to get out and sit at the shore and so we did. We sat on the shore watching the waves roll in and out. My head was leaned back resting on his shoulders, his arms hung down the length of mine and our fingers locked.

"You are the most amazing and kind, and loving woman I have ever met," he told me.

"Well you are the most amazing and considerate man I've ever met."

"I like that you see me that way," he smiled.

"How else would I see you?"

"I don't know." He said "Women see me as someone to have sex with, somebody they look good next to, never really had an interest in me beyond the surface and I've never actually wanted them to because that was easier for me. But with you, I don't know... It's different. From the day we met, you've somehow seen me as more. I could see in your eyes that day that it wasn't sex you were interested in, you wanted beyond that. Being around you is different. It's warm, and I can't help but be happy when you're around."

"Being around you makes me happy."

"I see that, I've seen how you light up when I come around. Nobody has ever looked at me the way you look at me. I've never been needed like this before and I've never felt like I needed anyone before. I've never been scared to lose anyone, except for my grandma. Until I met and got to know you."

The immensity of his words started to scare me, what was he getting at? What was he saying? I felt like he was warming up to drop some bad news.

He paused before for a few minutes and we sat in silence rocking side to side as the cool early summer breeze blew across our faces. It was relaxing and peaceful. Trey broke the silence first.

"I was molested by my mom's husband when I was a kid, my brother and sisters as well." He confessed. "I was 9 when it started and 11 when my grandma saved us. Me and my brother were too scared to tell, too embarrassed, Quentin said people would think we were gay if we told. We tried to keep him off Keisha, but he beat the s--t out of us and my mom just... let him…. Didn't even try to help us, not even when he forced Jen to f--k some nigga for money when she was 14. When she was 16. Jen ran away from home and when my mom didn't report her missing that's when my grandma knew something was up and called the police herself. CPS came and Keisha was the one brave enough to tell them what was happening, she was 8. When it ended and Quentin got arrested. Quentin swore up and down that we were lying, and my mom married him just so she didn't have to testify. He got some kind of deal, went on the sex offender registry for life in exchange for minimum jail time. My mom lost custody and rights to us and my grandma raised us. My mom was never allowed contact with us until we turned 18 but I've never forgiven her."

"Baby, I'm so sorry that happened," I said. My voice cracking.

"You're the only person I've ever told this to." He said unaffected.

"You are the first woman I've ever trusted, the one I feel safe with and I hope that you won't look at me different. I don't want you to think I'm weak or less of a man."

I turned and faced him " I hate that someone would do that to you, that your mom didn't protect you from it. I love you and I would never see you any differently than I always have. You are all man and anything but weak."

"Please don't tell anyone. It's not something I want people knowing."

"First of all, I would never tell anyone anything so private about you. Second of all you have nothing to be ashamed of, you were a child, you didn't do anything wrong. I hope you know that."

"I know but still."

"Ok, as long as you know."

We were silent, as we sat on the beach, just holding each other, I would have loved to have stayed there all night but It was cold and we were tired and I had church in a few hours.

I was almost late for church. I was so drained from the night before that if James hadn't called to wake me up and make sure I was coming I would have slept right through it. I dragged Trey out of bed with me though he was all for skipping just to sleep in some more. It took me a while to find something church appropriate in my wardrobe. Almost everything in my closet was tight, short and/ or low cut. I settled for a pair of fitted jeans, my four inch beige suede wrap around heels with silver studs scattered around the sides. I found a butterfly blouse with a gold and silver butterfly spray painted on the front. Everyone gaped in the parking lot as we drove up in Trey's Phantom. It took us a while to find a big enough parking space. My mom was upset at the gift I'd given Trey for his birthday and badgered me about the cost.

"You need to spend your money wisely or you're going to go broke."

"Mom, I'm good. Don't worry about it. I got a couple million more coming in from Lyrical Chaos, and the next two seasons at the clubhouse. I'm good."

"I guess, Naomi just be careful."

I spent the majority of the service in the pews with Trey, who was falling asleep all the time. I kept nudging him to get him to wake up. My Uncle Pastor made an announcement about the cameras around the church and assured every member of the congregation that they would be blurred and their face would not be shown on television. They were there because I was in the middle of filming my show. The congregation responded in a scattered chorus of "amen" when he said that these cameras here were a way of exposing a wider audience to the word and the power of God. The church had implemented a new way of welcoming the guests and saying hello to each other. It was cute. Everyone would go around and hug and greet each other while singing "The Jesus in Me." It was simple, catchy and repetitive. Trey shook hands with the men who welcomed him to the church and hugged the little girls who thought he was cute.

After everyone was back in their seats and the "A" selection was finished. Aisha looked at me and held out the microphone, a huge excited smile on her face. I looked at Trey who was finally awake and he smiled and nudged me forward and joined the applause as I made my way to the front of the church. I looked at James who was sitting in the pulpit between his father and Poppy, all three giving me a reassuring smile and an encouraging head nod. My heart was pounding and my throat was somehow dry in fear. That was not a good thing, how could I sing when my throat is dry? Aisha laughed at the expression on my face which I imagined was like a deer in headlights and handed me the microphone. She leaned in kissed me on my cheek and whispered in my ear to let God use me. I turned around and faced the congregation. All those faces staring at me, the cameras staring at me, What have I gotten myself into? At the showcase, I couldn't really see the eyes on me beyond the front row, but here I could see everyone in clear High Definition. I closed my eyes and listened for my cue. When it came I imagined I was at home singing to myself. No one was there except me and God no one else was listening. I opened my mouth and the sound that came out was absolute perfection.

As I sang, I felt something come around me from all sides and shoot straight to my heart. I recognized the feeling. It'd been a long time since I'd been touched by the Holy Spirit but it's something you never forget, something that once you experience it you cannot deny or even doubt that Christ is real. This time the spirit didn't just touch me it smacked me all the way to the ground. I was captured and without warning every ounce of anger and pain, everything I had put in a box and tried to drown in an ocean of alcohol,came to the surface inside my heart and was being pulled through me on a string.

I continued to sing. My voice stayed amazingly steady throughout the entire song. More than steady, my voice was more powerful and strong than it had ever been before. I hit the high's and the lows and the growls and the shouts like never before. When the song was ended most of the choir was caught up in the spirit as well as the entire congregation. I was on my knees at the altar my arms crossed over my chest, sobbing through the burning and twisting of my insides. The musicians continued to play the song on a loop.

"Let it go. " a voice said to my heart. "Let it go, you have to let it go. All the anger all the hate let it go and allow yourself to be healed." I uncrossed my arms and placed my hands on the ground in front of me. I cried harder as each hurt was ripped from me in quick succession. My military ex's betrayal and his marriage. Finding out I was pregnant and every hurtful act or comment Anthony said or did against me. I felt every modicum of pain being pulled from my soul. The image of myself with sad eyes looking on as Anthony flirted with another woman in my face. "Forgive him." The image of myself covered in blood the night I lost Tiana. "Forgive yourself." I sobbed harder. I hadn't even admitted out loud to anyone that I blamed myself for Tiana, more than I blamed Anthony. I hated myself for not walking away, for allowing Anthony to take me to that point. Everything I tried to ignore or shrug off like I was unaffected, all came out at once, a spiritual and emotional purge. The entire church was affected and on their knees or on their feet with their hands in the air crying in the spirit. When I was done crying and I got up off the floor my heart felt light and I hadn't even realized it had been heavy. I was empty of any sorrow. I was refreshed and renewed inside and I felt happy. After I fixed my make up, I took my seat next to Trey, who had also been moved by the spirit, and locked fingers.

"You did good. I'm proud of you," he kissed me on the cheek.

"Thank you," I smiled.

James sermon was based off Philippians chapter four verse thirteen: "I can do all things through Christ which strengthens me." It was his mother, my Aunt Judy's favorite scripture. My cousin was a powerful speaker, he broke his message down into a vernacular that was most common for people our age, people who act like they're our age and for the younger members who tried to act to grown. The message was essentially about letting go and letting God lead you and take control. I see now why he chose Lord I Surrender as the sermonic hymn. Afterward James led the altar call at the urging of his father. Looking over at my grandfather you could tell he was very happy that his dynasty was carrying on in his footsteps. He was proud of his grandson, we all were and I knew, despite James' protestations, this would not be his last time in the pulpit; same as I knew this wouldn't be my last time singing in church.

SAMANTHA SANCHEZ

TWENTY SIX

The going away party afterward was warm and also a little sad. I was happy for James' success but horrified at the prospect of him leaving me. He surprised everyone when he proposed to Jaycee. We all agreed that it was about time, but getting down on one knee in front of all of your friends and family? Talk about pressure. She said yes of course but still. At the end of the evening I shed a few more tears and hugged James for what seemed like forever. I didn't want to let him go.

"I'm gonna miss you," I pouted.

"Me too. I'll call you as much as I can, I'll be able to keep up wit you anyway since your butt is always in the tabloids. Quit fighting folks, man," we both laughed.

"I'm gonna have to come to B-More for our CQT and stay in your big ol' mansion."

"Word," he smirked. "You gotta let go of me first though." With one last squeeze I finally let go of the cousin I loved so much. He shook Trey's hand goodbye.

"Thanks for comin' man," James said.

"No problem. Congratulations and good luck, man."

"Thank you. Hey, take care of my cousin, man. Don't let her kill nobody," I rolled my eyes.

"I got her." Trey chuckled wrapping his arm around my neck. I gave James one last hug and kiss goodbye.

"Keep singing," he told me. "You got a great voice."

I was so completely drained when we got home. I fell asleep right away. I woke up at about three in the morning with Trey asleep next to me. I was rested and refreshed I didn't know what to do with myself. I got out of bed and went in search of my bible. I found it in the hall closet behind a gallon of Carlo Rossi. I didn't know the bible as well as I should, considering what kind of family I had. Most I knew about it was from movies and the Hannah Barbera cartoons I'd seen in children's church and a few random scriptures here and there.

I started from the beginning: Adam and Eve, Cain and Abel, Noah. When I got to the story of Abraham and Sarah. God had promised Abraham a son but his wife had doubt because she was ninety years old, way past the age of bearing children. So she concluded that God meant that Abraham's line wouldn't be through her so she handed over her maid Hagar and gave

Abraham permission to sleep with her. Now when Hagar got pregnant she started to forget her place and Sarah got upset and blamed Abraham for Hagar's attitude. Sarah allowed her husband to lay with Hagar and then blamed Abraham for the result of that action, the result being Hagar's attitude, when she should have just stepped back in the first place and let God work instead of trying to do the work herself. I realized that I did the same thing to Anthony.

Yes he disrespected me all the time, yes he played games with me but it was my fault as much as his because I let him. When I found out I was pregnant, I should have done everything I could to eliminate unnecessary stress from my life. I should have been strong enough to separate myself from stressful situations and Trust God to take care of me, even if that meant quitting the show and walking away from the money. I realized that every choice I made led to the loss of my baby. It wasn't random, like walking down the street and getting hit by a bus but it was a result of the choice I made that God gave me a choice. I could have walked away but I didn't, I exercised my free will and I suffered the consequences. I was warned by the doctors about my blood pressure but I didn't listen. I was warned by the doctors about my blood pressure, I was warned by the Altar Worker that day at church.

"Your child will be anointed and a powerful leader. I know that you are going through a lot and that you are hurting but if you let him, God can ease your suffering." She'd said. But I didn't listen, I didn't hear it and the result was losing my child. Then I had the audacity to place blame on everyone else for the choices I made just like Sarah. Yes Abraham had a part in it, he could have said no instead of sleeping with Hagar just like Anthony could have manned-up and said no to peer pressure, but Sarah put herself in the position of having to deal with her husband's baby mama just like I put myself in the position to deal with my weak willed baby daddy.

The realization hit me like a fist in the stomach and I found myself crying in the living room. I was the cause of all of my own suffering of the death of my child. My baby would be alive but I couldn't set my pride aside. I was too concerned about how I would look to the rest of the world. I didn't want people to laugh at me or see me as weak. I was too hungry for money. I put myself above my child and I lost her.

"Forgive yourself," the voice who spoke to my heart earlier at church spoke to me again. "I've already forgiven you it's time for you to forgive yourself. Let it go, release it all into My hands and free yourself and be healed. You will have another child and you will have learned to do better by your experience. You are going to be ok from this day on all you need to do is forgive yourself, love yourself and trust in Me to always keep you and never forsake you." In that moment, I surrendered my heart to God. I decided that I wanted to do better and be better. It was time to stop running from my pain and give it over. Learn from it accept it and move past it.

When I wasn't doing the rounds at promotional events or interviews for the third season of The Breakfast Club. I was going to bible study. I wanted to gain a better understanding of the word but I didn't want to make the commitment of being in the choir and joining the church. I chafed against the pressure of it. There was enough drama in my life right now without adding more. I was admired by the teens and tweens who attached themselves to me asking me questions about what they'd seen that week on the show. I would try and keep my answers as vague as possible. Their parents sometimes too would ask me about the rest of the cast if it were all really real or made up. I had lost the desire to party and get drunk all the time. I still enjoyed it but the need to drown or distract myself wasn't there anymore. I still went out regularly, I got paid ten grand just to show up at a club but it just felt off for some reason. I was bored with the scene. I would rather stay home and watch a movie or go out on proper dates with Trey.

Trey and I never spoke again about the abuse he endured as a child and I tried to get him to come to bible study with me sometimes or to church on the days I would choose to go but he wasn't into it. He respected my decision to "Try God" but he didn't think he needed to and I think that he thought it was something that I would get over after a while. He was serious about opening a tattoo shop and enrolled in business courses at City College while continuing to stack up his money. I was proud of him for it and I prayed that God would speak to his heart and that one day he'd be ready to listen. In the meantime, much to his dismay, I was passionately over having my house serve as a kick it spot for his friends; Trey talking about "blood this and blood that." Keisha had gone back to her grandmother's place, and I was over the constant smell of weed in my house and on my furniture. I was tired of being a crash pad for the ones who were too drunk or too blazed to go home. I wanted silence. I wanted my place that I was paying rent on for me and my man to myself. Asking nicely, wasn't doing any good. They were too comfortable to even be bothered, too high and drunk to comprehend my words. So I had to take action.

I'd been stuck on Buffy the Vampire Slayer for weeks, I had the collection on DVD and had been binge watching. Trey thought it was funny, accusing me of thinking I was Buffy because I was in fight training. He probably thought I wouldn't go as far as to collect Medieval weaponry, which made it way more fun when I loaded my newly arrived crossbow and took aim. I'd already told the crew that I wasn't going to actually shoot anybody I just wanted to scare them, so they wouldn't rush to disarm me.

"What the f--k?!" Kev shouted as I walked out the room holding my crossbow, finger on the trigger ready to fire.

"Everybody get the f--k out my house!" I said loudly.

Trey laughed in surprise while everyone else scrambled out of their seats on the couch falling over themselves.

"Babe, why you trippin?" he asked.

"I live in a house with five other people for eight months out of the year, ya'll niggas can find another kick it spot for a while," I answered.

"Does she know how to use that thing?" Dante asked Trey. Trey just shrugged doubled halfway over in laughter.

"Wanna find out?" I asked lowering the aim to his foot.

He jumped back. "Nah! That's alright!" he said.

"Yo, your girl is psycho!" Kev said rushing to the door behind Dante

"Hey, I'll see you later," Trey choked out.

Once the door was closed, I started laughing too.

"Baby, What?" Trey started trying to contain his laughter "Where did you get that?"

"Ebay," I smiled.

"You crazy."

"I know. Crazy works when you want niggas to get out of your house."

"No more Buffy for you," he said.

I rolled my eyes, as if he could stop me from watching what I wanted. I walked back in the bedroom hung the crossbow back up and laid down. I still didn't get any sleep because Trey followed me making sure I didn't.

I had slowly began to see a different side of Trey. We were usually pretty push and pull, inseparable and couldn't get enough of each other, now that I was taking time out of the party scene, I worried that he saw me as boring. He had been different in some ways ever since his grandmother died. At first I thought it was depression from grief he would go from being anxious and restless to sleeping all day and all night. I wouldn't go out to a club unless it was a paid appearance but Trey was eager to go with or without me and often he'd be pissed at me for not wanting to go. I just couldn't understand it. He'd never directed his irritation and aggression toward me before.

I was with my cousin Talia celebrating her 20th birthday. We were going to have a retro sleepover. Before I started the show she and I, along with Joanna would have a junk food night. Pizza and ice cream and a Sex and the City Marathon. She wasn't old enough to drink yet but I bought some tequila anyway. I wasn't going to get drunk but I wanted to make Margaritas. She'd be fine as long as she was with me. What's one year anyway. We had just settled in our pajamas when I got the call.

"Umm Naomi." Ruby said when she called me on the phone that night. "You need to get over here to the club and get your nigga. We at the spot where you threw his birthday party"

"Why? What's he doing?" I asked. "Is he hurt?"

"Nah he ain't hurt but you need to get down here like now. I'ma send you a picture."

The picture came through and all the air left out of my body and the fire inside me sparked again.

"Oh Hell No!"

"What is it?" Talia asked.

I showed her the picture of my man with another chick on his lap like she was his woman.

"Oh My God," Talia expressed. "What are you going to do?"

"Come on." I put on the tightest dress I could find in my closet that I could get away with wearing. My hair was flat but the roots needed to be touched up. I didn't have time to do all that so I brushed it back into a tight pony tail. I'd given Talia a pale gold strapless party dress complete with heels as a birthday gift. I told her to put it on because we were going out. I was so grateful for her fake ID.

"MiMi, I don't want to get into any fights or get arrested or anything." She said putting her lip gloss on.

"T, I got you. You know I'm not going to let anything happen to you. I'm not going to fight."

"Ok but promise you won't smash a bottle over his head and end up in jail."

"I didn't go to jail last time did I?" I asked putting the final touches on my simple makeup. My lips were coated in a red gloss and I just put liner and mascara on my eyes.

We pulled into the parking structure a block away from the club. I gave her the keys to my Audi and told her she was going to drive back because I was going to take his Phantom which was technically my car since it was still registered in my name. I walked hard and fast, pissed off. I would not tolerate disrespect again. Not from any man. I don't care how fine he is or how much I love him. I walked in the club and met up with Ruby she pointed up to the deck where Trey was sitting. I saw the girl in the picture dancing for him by the pool table. She had her booty all in his face, he had his hands sliding up and down on her thighs. I stared for a minute until Kev and Omar pointed me out. He Immediately moved his hands and pushed the girl away. He had the "Uh-oh, busted." look on his face. I turned my back to him, grabbed Talia's hand and took her to the basement level of the club. I knew Trey would follow. He'd be scared by the fact that I didn't take off on him immediately. I had a different tactic than that and he would want to see what I was up to. At first I just danced with Talia and Ruby until I saw him come down the stairs looking for me then I retreated further back in the room. I found a guy who was looking super thirsty and approached him.

"Hi. What's your name?" I asked in his ear.

"I'm Rob."

"My name is Lyric." I said "I need a favor, Rob, my nigga bein' triflin and I want to give him a little taste of his own medicine. you down?"

"What you tryin to do, Ma?" he asked.

"Dance with me?"

He took my hand and led the way to the dance floor. Thanks to Trey's tutelage I was more in control with my body now. I knew how to move, what to shake and when to grind. I was aware of Rob's hands on my hips making sure they didn't go any lower or try to creep higher than my waist. We moved over to the wall and he hitched my leg around his waist and started grinding. I didn't even see Trey come up to us.

"What the f--k are you doing?" he asked snatching me up hard by my upper arm.

"Ow! Let go!" he started dragging me away, Talia, Ruby and I protesting his manhandling of me.

"Hey, man, let her go," Rob said putting his hand on Trey's shoulder. In a flash Trey's fist connected with Rob's jaw and Robs fist connected with Trey's head. The next thing I know Rob's friends and Trey's friends were all fighting. I tried to stop them. I yelled for them to cut it out. I didn't want to be in the tabloids in the morning. I even tried to physically stop Trey and Rob but Trey just shoved me out of the way and I fell on my behind in the middle of the floor. Talia and Ruby rushed to my side to help me up. Club security carried everyone involved in the fight out of the club. They asked me if I was ok, if I was hurt if I needed medical care. I told them no and followed Trey out the club they took him and his entourage out the back and Robs out the front.

"What the hell?!" I asked storming after Trey as he turned the corner away from the club. He turned around and walked up on me.

"What the f--k you thinking you doin dancing like that with some nigga?"

"Oh so you can have your hands all up on some groupie b---h with her behind in your face but I can't dance with a nigga?"

"Ya'll might as well have been f---in!" he said.

"F--k you nigga, gimmie the car keys," I said trying to reach into his pocket.

"Nah man, get off me, that's my car," he said pullin' away.

"It's in my name, just like everything else, so it's my car. Gimmie the keys."

Out of nowhere he growled and pushed me into the nearest wall so hard my head bounced off it.

"What is your problem?" Ruby asked Trey "MiMi, are you ok?" I took my hand away and there was a little bit of blood on my hand.

"Oh my God!" Talia said. "We should get you to the hospital."

I couldn't move. He realized what he just did because all the frustration just passed right from his face and was replaced by horror, concern and remorse.

"Hey!" someone shouted and I looked over and saw two officers coming over.

"Babe, I..." he said coming closer I put my hands up telling him to stay away from me.

He came up anyway and slid his hands up the sides of my dress and tucked something into the seat of my underwear both in front and behind.

"Please," he whispered.

I pushed him away in protest. with the police approaching I was too scared to remove whatever he placed half-way inside me.

"Get off me," I insisted.

"Step away from her." The first officer said "Ma'am are you alright?"

Trey stepped away his hands in the air as the second officer patted him down. And pulled out the car keys.

"Ma'am do you know him?"

I nodded yes "He's my boyfriend."

"Did he hurt you?"

"He pushed her into the wall just now and threw her on the ground inside the club."

Talia announced. I loved her for looking out for me but I wish she hadn't have said anything.

"She's bleeding on the back of her head."

"Is this true?" he asked.

"Yes, but it was an accident. I'm a clutz in heels." I couldn't have this all over the entertainment news in the morning. Bystanders were watching with cell phones out, recording what was going on. I couldn't allow him to be arrested, I would be vilified on the streets. No matter what happens you don't involve the police.

"Do you want to press charges? We should get you some medical attention."

"No, I'm fine, I just want to go home, but he has the keys to my car."

"Man, that's my car." Trey argued trying to snatch the keys from the officer that held them. The officer dodged the lunge and accused Trey of trying to assault an officer. I cringed as they slammed him down over the hood for resisting arrest.

"Is that really necessary?!" I defended. "Please this is all just a misunderstanding, Just let me get him home."

"He's going to spend the night in the drunk tank, you can pick him up in the morning."

Trey cussed and fussed

"Babe, be quiet or you're going to make things worse." I said. My head was searing with pain and I wobbled a little and Ruby caught me.

"Miss, you should really get someone to check you out. I can't let you drive. Do you want me to call for assistance?"

"I'll drive her Ruby offered. I haven't been drinking at all." The officer handed the keys to Ruby and I watched as they pulled away, taking Trey with them. Bystanders passed by whispering, recognizing who Ruby and I were and asking if I was ok.

Once we got to the car, I made sure nobody was looking and pulled the 2 small baggies out of my underwear, I thought it was weed when he slid it in there but when I looked, I noticed shining crystallized powder.

"Holy s---," I said. "What is this?"

"That's crystal meth," Ruby said. "That explains a lot."

I opened the baggies and poured it out. I'd never seen crystal before I'd only heard of it. Why did Trey have Meth? I opened the glove compartment and inside were more baggies of crystal as well as a gun. I poured it all out and wiped down the gun and threw it in the sewer.

I apologized to Talia for the night and suggested that she go back to the dorm and that I would make it up to her. I promised her that I would go and get my head checked out and I would but not before I searched my entire apartment for more guns and drugs. Ruby knew and decided she was going to help, thinking I shouldn't be alone that night. She knew what I was dealing with even if I didn't and way more than I thought Talia could have comprehended and I wanted to shield her from it as much as I could. I didn't want the dramatics, especially if she told her mom and word spread through the family.

SAMANTHA SANCHEZ

I was fine when he was just selling a little bit of weed but not this mess and he knew I wouldn't be, that's why he didn't tell me but there will be no more drugs in my house, in my cars in my life, I don't play that and he was going to have to choose. It was going to be me or this. It's not like he needed the money anyway he's getting paid for being on Lyrical Chaos and for the tattoos he was doing. So I don't get why he needs to sell this stuff. Ruby and I went through my entire house and found small vials of cocaine, mini baggies with pills and baggies with crystal meth as well as wads of cash. I piled it in a shoebox on the kitchen counter. Where did he get all of this stuff? And when?

After about an hour and three dizzy spells later. Ruby insisted I go to the hospital and get my head checked out, We were there for five hours waiting to get a scan. The good news was I didn't have a brain injury or skull fracture but I did have a concussion and I needed a few stitches. When they asked how I got hurt Ruby backed up my story that I fell in my heels and banged my head into the wall. It was about 11 am when I got home. And Trey was waiting for me.

"Baby?" Trey asked coming out of the room.

"S--t" He said mouth agape at the sight of a bandage around my head. He sounded tired and remorseful.

"You going to be alright?" Ruby asked.

"Yea. I'm good."

"Ok." Trey didn't speak until she closed the door behind her.

"Baby, I'm so sorry, are you ok?" He was genuinely concerned as he walked toward me.

But I moved aside.

"Four stitches and a bruised arm." I announced letting the sweatshirt fall from my shoulder revealing a bruise in the shape of his fingers around my upper arm. He looked pained and I could tell he was sorry but I was still mad.

"Baby I am so sorry," he said reaching for me. "You know I would never hurt you. I don't know what came over me."

"Don't touch me." I warned. I walked over to the kitchen counter where his drugs were piled in the shoe box.

"I threw the gun and the drugs from the car in the sewer. And I found this stuff in the bedroom closet and under the mattress, in your shoe boxes, inside the game cases, and in the cookie jar. Did I forget anywhere?"

"Nah," he said.

"Do you do drugs or do you just sell them? Don't lie."

"Both sometimes."

"What were you on last night?"

"Crystal."

"Are you stupid?!"

"No, I just needed to escape reality a little bit,"

"Escape reality? Do you understand the reality of what would have happened if that shit had fallen out of my panties with the cops standing right there."

"I know. I'm sorry, I wasn't thinking."

"How long have you been doin this?"

"I been selling them for a while. I only started using again when grandma passed."

"You've been selling drugs this entire time?!"

"It's not that big a deal."

"It is that big of a deal! You threw me on the floor and then slammed me into a wall. I have stitches in my f---ing head!"

"I needed the money."

"You have a job!"

"It's not enough, I gotta pay 200 rent on the chair a week and then 30% of what I make in tats to the shop owner."

"You could have told me. I would have helped you."

"That's your money. I wasn't going to touch it."

"Are you cheating on me too?" I asked my heart breaking at the thought. Other women scared me more than the drugs.

"Hell no. I promise you. I wouldn't do that to you. Baby, no. I swear to God I'm not cheating on you." He walked to me and put his arms around my waist. "That girl you saw last night was just a hoe, she was just dancing it didn't mean anything, I'm not f---ing her." I didn't know what to do or what to think all I could do was laugh. This is ridiculous! I sat down on the stool at the counter.

"What's funny?" he asked.

"Nothing."

"Then why are you laughing?"

"Because I don't know what else to do!" I said loudly in a panic. I stood up to get away from him "I don't know what to think!"

"Baby, I'm doing this for me and you."

"How?"

"The money is going toward school, so I can set up a shop and take care of us."

"We have money."

" You have money."

"There are better ways to earn money, it's called a job."

"I've tried that. I can't get a decent job cuz of my record I can't even get financial aid for school cuz it was a felony."

"You have the show."

"Not until we done filming."

"I don't know what to think Trey."

"What you want me to do, I need money to keep up, I need money for school, I need money to get that shop."

"Money to keep up? keep up with what?"

"You know, the Joneses. You, your lifestyle. The red carpet award show events. You look good so I need to look good too."

"I don't...."

"Don't say you don't care about that stuff, you do. I seen the way you smile during you photo ops, I seen how good a mood it puts you in. I've seen you get more confident in your walk when you dress up and I love that you do. You've come a long way from the girl that used to hang back from a group because you were afraid you couldn't keep up. You ain't afraid to be seen anymore. I just want to be seen with you. I want everyone to know that we together that you mine."

"Yes I like it but it's not that important. You know I hate the show I only keep doing it because you told me to use it to my advantage."

"I know that's why I'm doin what I do, so you you can quit after next season and we can still maintain the lifestyle."

"I'm not ok with this, Trey."

"What do you want me to do, boo?"

"I want you to stop."

"I can't do that."

My stomach wrenched and bile rose in my throat. "Then I can't be with you anymore." I choked out.

"For real?" he asked getting upset.

"Yes. For real. I love you but I can't. Not if you're going to be doing this. I'm trying to get my life right with God and I can't just turn away and pretend you're not doing or selling drugs."

"Look I won't do them anymore, but I'm gonna keep selling. A couple months ago you'd have laughed and told me do what I do just to keep you out of it and don't get caught. You sing one song and suddenly you go all church on me? What happened to my ride or die chick? You poss to be holding me down."

"I would have *never* been ok with you selling anything other than weed. You know that that's why you kept it a secret. I'll support any legit hustle you take on. I'd ride for you even if you were a janitor, but not while you gettin high and throwing me against walls and pushing me on floors, I can't do it."

"I don't want to live off your money."

"Then get a real job."

"I told you I can't."

"Then get an honest hustle."

"A legit grind don't bring in as much money."

"What's more important to you? Money or me?"

He didn't answer. Which hurt just as much as him not choosing me. If it wasn't an easy choice than there's no point in answering.

"Wow ok," I said. "Then you can leave."

"Baby..." he said shocked. "Come on stop trippin." He grabbed my hand and tried to lead me back to the bed."

"No." I pulled my hand away "You always telling me how much you love me and you never want to lose me but you choose drugs over me?"

"Baby," he reached for me but I pulled away.

"Get your stuff and go. I don't want you here when I come home."

"Really?! It's that easy for you?"

"You put stitches in my motherf---in head! No, it's not easy! But I'm not with that bull----! You just chose drugs and money over me so apparently it's that easy for you ."

I grabbed my car keys and phone and went over to Ruby's house.

"What happened?" she asked. I didn't answer I just started sobbing and sobbing, This was the worst feeling imaginable. Worse than when I found out my ex was engaged. Worse than Anthony constantly throwing other women in my face. I always hated it when people say they thought they would die over a guy but now I understood it. I loved him with every ounce of my being and I really and honestly felt like my life was over and I didn't know how to continue on without him. I made such a big deal about him that now people who counted against us would be laughing at me.

SAMANTHA SANCHEZ

TWENTY SEVEN

As expected, by Monday morning, Saturday night's events were all over the news and internet. Pictures of Trey being handcuffed and driven away in the police car, pictures of me standing there talking to police. News of the break up hadn't spread yet but it would soon enough. I did my best to stay strong and not wear my heart on my sleeve. I didn't want to be depressed again but I hurt so much without him, more than I ever thought possible. I didn't hold it in this time. Ruby and Talia and Joanna came over and offered a shoulder to cry on and brought ice cream and alcohol and the four of us finished the sleepover that was interrupted by Trey.

Talia went with me to the network music awards show 3 weeks later and kept my spirits up. She wouldn't let me stay sad and I didn't want to give that impression, I wanted to have fun. I enjoyed Talia's excitement at while seeing big name stars. I posed with The BFC and when they asked about Trey I simply said that he couldn't make it. Only Ruby, knew for certain that we had broken up but DeVon suspected. By now I'd learned to smile when I was dying inside. Monroe and Heather were there together and I was surprised but pleased to see her and pregnant at that. Athena wasn't there, she wasn't contractually obligated to be there so she was spending the summer in Hawaii with her boyfriend she'd be back next week when we moved back to the clubhouse for Season 5. Anthony still wouldn't look at me and I realized he was still hurt about what I said.

"Hey, can I talk to you?" I asked him before he could walk away with his date. She was a short Mexican chick who looked White. "I promise I'll give him right back." I told her. She looked at me carefully up and down trying to asses what I was up to. If she was someone who was going to stick around, I'd make friends with her later but right now she was a non-issue.

"What's up?" He said casually. I took his hand and pulled him inside the theater away from the majority of the media.

"I just wanted to say that I'm sorry."

"About what?"

"About what I said in Mexico, and about how I've treated you since we lost Tiana. It wasn't fair and I'm sorry."

"Ok?" he asked confused. "What brought this on?"

"It's a long story but I had a revelation and I realize it's not all on you. I could have done things differently too. I forgive you for your part and I'm asking you to forgive me for being such a b---h. Can you?"

"I guess so," he smiled.

"Oh you guess so?" I laughed. "Ok I'll take that as a yes. You want to hug it out?" I asked, opening my arms slightly. He wrapped his arms around my back and embraced me. I pulled away when he squeezed me a little too tight. Not wanting him to get the wrong idea. A picture had been snapped anyway and I knew the headline tomorrow would hint at a reconciliation between us. I worried what Trey would think, scared that he would believe that I had moved on so quickly.

"So did you and the pretty boy really break up? That's what DeVon said."

"I'll let you get back to your date. Stop listening to everything DeVon says," I said avoiding the question. "I'm going to go find my cousin." I walked away and as I did, My phone chimed and I looked down and saw that I had a text message from Trey.

Hesitantly, I opened it. **You look beautiful.**

I wore a calf length with the slits up the sides, black halter couture dress. With purple blended eyeshadow and clear lip gloss and royal purple knee high punk rock looking four inch heeled boots. My hair was straightened and brushed all the way back.

I smiled and my heart leapt a little bit. He was watching the red carpet live and spotted me. He still loved me. I missed him so much.

Thank you, I responded.

I miss you, he said.

I didn't respond. It was too hard. I needed to stay strong. He wanted money more than he wanted me. On the bright side, at least I knew he wasn't with me for mine. At least I knew everyone was wrong about that. He texted again

I love you.

Not enough apparently. Nothing's changed. I responded and turned the ringer off on my phone.

You promised me you'd never leave me,
You didn't choose me.

I turned the ringer of my phone off and buried it in my purse. I didn't want to argue. Arguing would make me cry.

I found Talia taking a picture with Snoop Dogg. I'd never met him myself and was very calm when introducing myself. I literally bumped into NeYo, well he bumped into me, and after apologizing he said he'd heard me singing I Dreamed a Dream on the show and that I had a nice voice. If I ever decided to pursue something with him have my people get in touch and he'll help me out. I was ecstatic but I held it in and gave a polite thank

243   SAMANTHA SANCHEZ

you and smile. I had never actually thought of myself as a singer. I was an actress who could sing. but a singer point blank? Touring, singing on stage in front of thousands of people? The pressure of the music industry? I don't know if I could do that.

Season 5 started and the living situations remained the same as the third season: Ruby and I upstairs, DeVon and Anthony downstairs to the left and Monroe and Athena to the right. I had chosen to actively be friendly with Anthony even if the memory of how he treated me was still etched in me, I was trying to move on from it. I reminded myself to forgive him and myself everyday. The first week of school I'd gotten cast in a production of RENT which was one of my favorite shows. I was cast as MiMi and now had to learn all of the songs. I knew them anyway I just needed to perfect them. It'd been five weeks since Trey and I broke up. I hadn't talked to him in two. It wasn't easy getting over him, but I chose to channel my pain into my art. The character of MiMi had a lot of longing in her. Yes, she has her struggles with addiction but I felt like she longed to to be loved, that she was trying to fill that void in her with drugs the way I did with alcohol. Funnily, the boy from my Grandpa's church with the exaggerated eye roll and female attitude was cast as Angel. It was his first semester in musical theater and he decided that he would dive in head first and audition. I admired his confidence, I was still terrified but it was a graduation requirement that I get into a show.

I had my eyes closed. I was out back on the patio by the pool singing along to the "Without You" instrumental track. I didn't have a duet partner so I just sang both parts so I could learn my cues.

"You sound nice," Anthony said. I didn't expect him to be right there and startled at the sound of his voice.

"Sorry," he laughed.

"Thanks," I said levelling out. "You coming to the show right?"

"Do you want me to?" he asked.

I don't know why, it was so awkward for us to speak to each other without trading insults or being hostile.

"Yea, I want everyone to come."

"When is it?"

"First 2 weeks of November."

"Ok," he shrugged. "I'm gonna go get some pizza, you want to come?"

"Which pizza place you going to?"

"The one by campus."

"Yea ok. I am kinda hungry."

"And you love pizza," he remembered.

As we sat at the restaurant awkwardly, cameras in our faces and people staring to see what was going on. Anthony shocked me with a question.

"Do you think we'd still be together if we hadn't lost Tiana?"

That was the first time I'd heard him say her name. Even the mention of her brought back a flood of emotions. It'd been almost a year and a half since her death and often the hurt was still as fresh as if it were a week ago.

"No." I answered him truthfully "We would have just had to deal with each other for the next seventeen years instead of 2 more semesters."

"Damn, you say that like it's a bad thing."

"Damn, you act like you care," I laughed mocking him.

"So even if she hadn't died, you still would have left me for ol boy?"

"You f---ed another b---h in my bed," I reminded him growing irritated at the memory.

"So if I hadn't done that, would we still be together?"

"Probably not."

"Why not?"

"Because we were never really together. Why are we even talking about this?" I snapped.

"Because I've been thinking, and I wouldn't mind trying again, starting over, you know?"

He reached across the table and grabbed my hands in his.

"I miss you. And I want to show you that I can be a decent dude." He smiled laughing at his own confession. The look on my face, as I would see later when I watched the episode, was a mix of shock and doubt, suspicion, anger and amusement. I didn't pull my hands away immediately. I was flattered by the attention and I missed Trey so much that I was emotionally vulnerable, but the echoes of our history bounced in my head.

"Let go of my hands please," I said calmly.

"Why?" He smiled.

The pizza arrived and he had to let go anyway. A cheesy pepperoni distraction gave me a minute to come up with a response that wasn't cutting.

"So what do you think?" he asked.

I took a long breath in. "I think that I just got out of a relationship and I'm not over him. I think that you feel this way now but you'll be over it in a week."

"No I won't because I've been sitting on this for a year."

"What are you even talking about? A relationship or just sex?"

"Which one do you want?"

"Honestly, neither. I don't trust you enough for a relationship and not to be mean but sex with you isn't an appealing offer"

"Why don't you trust me?"

"Look, can we just talk about something else please? I already told you I'm not over Trey."

"I can help you get over him, just think about it k?"

"Whatever," I said just to shut him up.

Truth was, I was still very much in love with Trey, he's who I wanted but I did care about Anthony once upon a time as well. It wasn't completely because of the pregnancy, I don't know what it was or why but I did. No matter the circumstances, we created a child together and as much drama as our relationship had been, we would always be bonded because of it. Maybe I could love Anthony one day too, maybe I already did but I loved Trey more even if we weren't together at the moment, I hadn't given up on the possibility of us getting back together and I owed it to the next man I got into a relationship with, not to be in love with the guy before him.

"You're singing is much better now." Anthony said "I mean you always sounded nice but it's like wow now."

"That's what confidence and vocal coaching will do for you." I said grateful for the topic change and enjoying the praise. It was rare coming from him and I liked it.

"I don't want you to wild out on me, but I wrote a song. I want you to sing on it."

"A song about what? Why me?" I asked taking a bite of pizza.

"A song about Tiana."

I froze mid chew. My first reaction was "How dare he try to profit off of my baby?" My second thought was, at least he was bringing it to me first and I didn't have to hear about it later if he tried to release it. I opened my mouth to respond but he interrupted.

"Don't get mad. I know you think that you're the only one that hurts over her but you're not. I feel it too I just don't wear it like you do."

I couldn't yell at him for making a song about my baby girl, she was half his. It was just difficult for me to accept that he cared as much as he said he did. He took no interest when I was pregnant. Then again maybe he feels guilty about it and this is his way of making amends.

"Just listen to the song. Please?"

Anthony didn't want anyone to know about the song, not even DeVon. It was personal to him. So I kept it quiet and I met him at the studio on campus the next day after my last class so he could play me a rough version of what he had. He introduced me to a producer friend of his, Bona Fide, whom I'd actually known since elementary school but lost track of after 8th grade. His real name was Ferris and it was awkward because I'd always had a crush on him in elementary school. He was one of my mom's favorite students. And now here he was a decade later and producing a song that I'm supposed to sing on with my baby daddy about our daughter. I greeted him warmly with a hug. He'd gotten quite handsome over the years. He was a little taller than me, not a lot but just enough. He was chocolate toned, mixed with Black and Dominican,with full lips that looked like they felt really soft. His thick hair curled naturally along the top of his head and I could see the muscles pushing through the sleeves of his T-shirt.

"How do you two know each other?" Anthony asked.

"We went to elementary school together."

"Wow. Small world."

"How's your mom?" Ferris asked.

"She's good. She's gonna be so happy to know that I saw you."

"Take down my number, I'd like to see her again," he said. I gave him my phone so he could input his number.

"So you sing now?" he asked.

"She has a great voice." Anthony complemented reminding us that he was there and why we were there. I think he was a little jealous because neither Ferris nor myself could stop smiling.

"Alright. I can't wait to hear what you can do," Ferris said handing my phone back to me.

I chuckled "Well let me hear the song," I said pulling up a seat.

"I don't have a name for it yet." Anthony told me. Ferris started playing the recording and then excused himself to take a phone call.

As the music played, I sat there and I listened to his words, amazed not only by Anthony's talent but by the depths and sincerity of what he was saying.

He spoke about his fears about the prospect of being a father, how he mistreated me out of that fear but then it all changed when he found out he was "going to be a daddy to a princess."

Something inside him changed and he "fell in love for the first time."

He said that when he got the news that she was gone, he couldn't believe it. He wished that he could change the things he's done, wished that he could have held her, that he knew it was his fault and wished he could see her smile. He goes on to imagine what life would have been like if she'd gotten a chance to grow up. He said he wanted to give her everything, protect her, spoil her. He would have a pretty little girl just like her mom. He ended saying that he loved her and he always would.

I found myself wiping tears from my eyes, picturing what could have been. I could see the image he painted so clearly. It was like a memory instead of a dream I had felt the same way. I thought about life with her in it, every day. Apparently so did Anthony. He grieved her as much as I did. He knew that I blamed him but I didn't know that he blamed himself too.

Ferris had walked back in sometime in the middle of the song and handed me a tissue.

"Thanks." I laughed embarrassed that he was seeing me cry. "I think you should call it Tiana's Requiem."

"I like it." Anthony said "What do you think, Bone?" he asked Ferris.

"Hmm, requiem is like a song in honor of the dead, so it works," he said.

"You like the song?" Anthony asked.

"It's beautiful."

"It just needs vocals."

"You think you can come up with something?" Ferris asked.

"You want me to write lyrics?" I asked looking back and forth between the both of them.

"I don't know how to write music. I can sing a song that is taught to me but coming up with one on my own..."

"It's not that hard." Ferris said "Just say what you feel and sing it."

"But notes and scales and pitch and key..."

"Boo, you can do it." Anthony said reaching for my hands. I pulled away so he couldn't grab them. I saw a smirk go up in the corner of Ferris's mouth.

"I can help you. If you want." Ferris offered "It's really not that hard you probably know how to do it and just don't know that you do."

"Ugh Fine. Gimmie a couple of days and let's see what I can come up with."

"Ok cool," Anthony smiled.

"Email me the track?"

"Yea."

"Alright, I gotta get to rehearsal. I'll see you later." I told Anthony. He stood and scooped me into an awkward hug I didn't return the embrace, just patted him on the back to signal him to let go.

"It was nice seeing you again," I said to Ferris actually hugging him.

"You too. Hit me up if you need help," he said as I walked to the door

"I will," I responded making my way out.

I had pages and pages of thoughts about Tiana, poems and wishes. I had never tried to write music before. I stayed up all night listening to the track. I texted Ferris that I had come up with some stuff but I didn't think it was any good. He told me he could meet with me in a couple days to go over it if I wanted and I agreed.

It took a week because of scheduling conflicts between Ferris and I, but after going through the journals I kept during the time and the stuff that I thought of now, we were finally able to come up with something I liked and recorded it. I sang the intro accapella and then some vocal runs behind Anthony's verses in addition to my verses, a hook and a bridge. Anthony loved it. He was so excited that he spun me around as soon as I walked out of the recording booth.

"That was awesome, you were awesome! I told you she could sing," Anthony said to Ferris

"Yea, that she can," Ferris said in agreement. Anthony's excitement rubbed off on me and I squealed in laughter.

"This thing is going to be a hit."

Obviously everyone's manager would have to sit down and hash out all the details but I too believed this song was powerful and amazing.

The next day the BFC decided to have a bonfire. A belated celebration of our latest semester in school and a celebration of my getting cast in RENT, and Monroe's position as choreographer for the show. We all decided to drive there together in Monroe's SUV, A Cadillac Escalade. When we pulled up there were rose petals on the ground in a makeshift path.

"Go see where it leads." Athena said. "We'll get the stuff."

Curiosity got the best of me but was worried that this was a set up. Anthony had said that he would meet us later on, but now I was scared that his current absence and these rose petals were his way of once again trying to woo me. If it was, I was about to be deeply annoyed.

I was right about it being a setup, but I was wrong about it being Anthony. When the path ended I looked up and there was Trey at the edge of the shore standing in the center of the roses that wound in a circle under his feet. Trey, the waves crashing behind him. He wore jean shorts and white button up shirt. His hair was freshly cut and his dimples deepened when he saw me, his smile was as bright as the sun. I had to fight the urge to rush to him and bury my face in his chest and take it all back. I wanted to tell him it didn't matter, to do what he wanted as long as he just loved me and stayed with me.

"Dance with me." he asked holding his hand out.

"There's no music."

As if he'd predicted I said that, music started to play as if from the heavens but the rational explanation would be that he had it wired into the boardwalks sound system. Or the producers did. People watched from behind barriers as I took his hand and he held me and slowly moved me around to the melody of Nat King Cole's "Unforgettable."

"I miss you," he whispered in my ear. "You been ok?"

"Not really," I confessed.

"Me either."

"How's your head?"

"It's fine."

"You know I'm sorry right? I never wanted to hurt you. I hate myself for it."

"I know."

We danced in silence for a minute before I couldn't take it anymore.

"What is all this Trey?" I asked looking him in the eye "What are you doing?"

"I'm dancing with you."

"Why?"

"Because you're beautiful and I love you." He put the arm of the hand he was holding around his neck and pulled the hand I had on his shoulder up higher. He buried his head in the gap between my neck and shoulder and started softly kissing me.

"Don't do that." I said fighting my body's natural reply to his kisses.

"Why not?"

"You know why not."

"You like it," he teased.

"That's not the point."

"Alright," he laughed. We continued dancing and he would sing the lyrics in my ear and hum the words he didn't know. His voice vibrated through me and my heart raced in response.

"So I want you to know that I heard everything you said. I gave it up" he said after a while. "All of it. I'm done. If that's what it takes to be with you... I choose you. You are more important than money and I should have said that to you the first time you asked. I f---ed up and I've been kicking myself ever since." I started to cry hearing the things I've waited almost 2 months to hear but I was still scared that I wouldn't be enough.

"Baby, why are you crying?"

"I don't know." I said.

"You're so silly woman." he said wiping the tears away with his thumb

"I know."

"And you're smart, strong, you're always worrying about other people especially me without worrying about yourself. Not to mention you're sexy as hell wit a nice booty and some Tig ol biddies." He laughed "You're kinda psycho and a little scary sometimes but I like that because I am crazy in love with you."

"Had to mention the boobs," I said with a smirk.

"Yea, had to and you got gold between them thighs too."

"Wow," I laughed.

"There's my smile," he said. "Baby, you are everything to me. I thought I could live without you, I tried but it hurt too much to be away from you. I've never felt that before and it made me realize just how much I never want to be without you. I want to be a better man because of you."

"Really?"

"Boo you are more valuable than all the money and diamonds in the world. I love you, I respect you. I see you the real you. I see Naomi. Ever since the first day we met at church I felt that there was something about you, I just had to be near you. I see the magic in you. In your eyes, in your smile, in your touch, in your voice, in your heart,even when you going off on people. You give so much of yourself to me and I want to be the kind of man who deserves you and the kind of man you deserve."

The song ended and my eyes almost popped out of my sockets when Trey bent down on one knee and pulled out a ten carat diamond out of his pocket. No box, just the ring alone.

"Naomi Marie Reyes will you marry me?"

Special Thanks

Wow! I never thought I'd ever be brave enough to actually publish this book. I've always talked and dreamed about it but, in truth, I've always been scared. Now that this day is here, I'm so glad that I've taken this step. I've been encouraged by so many people in my life, without whom, this book would still be sitting in my bottom drawer.

Mama, you have been my biggest and most fiercest supporter. From the time I was 12 years old and was given a writing assignment for homework. You realized before I did that I had a gift and bought me my first composition book. You watched me sit on the edge of your bed for years scribbling down and scratching out ideas, ripping pages out and starting again. Thank you so much for listening to every idea that came through my head. Thank you for bragging about me to anyone who would listen.

Daddy, you challenged me to prove that I could and would accomplish my dream. Thank you for always supporting me while at the same time reminding me to be cautious and careful in life. Whether you know it or not, you challenged me. This is only the first step, just you watch.

Nanny, thank you so much for everything. You helped teach me how to read and write as a child. You have every college essay (thus far) and every newsletter that I wrote and put together. You've listened to almost every rant I've gone on about my doubts and frustrations and you were the first one to read and edit this book. I hope I've made you proud.

Suzy and Uncle Robert... Suzy you have believed in me and my writing even when I didn't believe in it myself. You pushed and lectured even when I didn't want to hear it. You've dreamed the big dreams with me and I'm glad that you are my auntie. Uncle Robert, I know that I've been a bit difficult and frustrating during this process but it worked out right? Thank you so much. I am forever grateful for all you've done to help me realize my dream.

Divalicious, you live EVERY drama with me, the drama yet to be told and the drama yet to be had. We haven't been face to face in FOREVER but it's always felt like you're right here by my side. You are THE definition of a sister. You're closer than blood to me and I honestly don't know where I would be emotionally right now if I hadn't had you in my life. You keep me silly. Thank you so much! I love you, sissy!

To my very special friend "Sitch", watching you pursue your passion and follow your dreams reignited my desire to do the same. You inspire and encourage me more than you know and for that I thank you. I pray that everything you want for yourself in life comes to you because you definitely have the talent and drive to succeed and more so you deserve it. I'm gonna match you one day just watch.

Tony, You are my cousin of substance, the one who understands the most. We're both so "interrupted" that only we can understand the depths of each other's emotions. We are each other's shoulders to cry on. You gave me a journal as a christmas present one year, and the following new year I started writing down every thought and feeling I had that entire year. Those feelings that have now been reiterated throughout this book and I love you so much.

Dash, Dorian, Laru, and the inspiration for "Athena", you guys came into my life and so much stuff happened. Both good and bad times, the outcome being this story. It started as a joke, a way to relax me and keep me from going off when "Anthony" was pissing me off. It started as a "what if..." exercise and ended as the fulfillment of a story God had given me almost 20 years ago. You guys were there when I was at my most "emo" and angry point in life and, in your own way, loved me through it. I wish I could have put it ALL in this book, but it's probably a good thing that I didn't. Thank you so much for being there.

To the inspiration for "Freakboy" wherever you are, you will always have a place in my heart. I pray that you are well and happy. Thank you for loving all of me, for everything I am and everything you know I could be. I love you back even if you are a jackass. LOL

To the rest of my family and friends, those who have inspired their own characters and those who have not. Thank you for all of your help and love and support. Thank you to those who challenged me to be better and live up to my potential. May God bless and keep you all.

23705118R00148

Made in the USA
San Bernardino, CA
30 January 2019